The Party
System
in America

THE PARTY SYSTEM IN AMERICA

WILLIAM GOODMAN

Professor Emeritus

Southern Illinois University

Edwardsville

Prentice-Hall Inc., Englewood Cliffs, N.J. 07632

Library of Congress Cataloging in Publication Data

GOODMAN, WILLIAM
The party system in America.

Includes bibliographical references and index.
1. Political parties—United States. I. Title.
JK2261.G68   329′.02   79–11615
ISBN 0–13–652677–2

Printed in the United States of America

10 9 8 7 6 5 4 3 2 1

Editorial/production supervision
    and interior design by Joyce Turner
Cover design by Wanda Lubelska
Manufacturing buyer: Harry P. Baisley

Prentice-Hall International, Inc., *London*
Prentice-Hall of Australia Pty. Limited, *Sydney*
Prentice-Hall of Canada, Ltd., *Toronto*
Prentice-Hall of India Private Limited, *New Delhi*
Prentice-Hall of Japan, Inc., *Tokyo*
Prentice-Hall of Southeast Asia Pte. Ltd., *Singapore*
Whitehall Books Limited, *Wellington, New Zealand*

CONTENTS

PREFACE

When writing a book on the political party system, it is always the best of times, it is always the worst of times. There seems to be so much to say but so much has already been said. To set out to break new trails is to find, instead, well-worn paths. The party system appears to be an anomaly, a frontier where the landmarks have been identified and the travel guides already prepared. The urge for commentary must be restrained while coping with the accumulating mass of data spread throughout the literature. Nor can one be sure how far afield to pursue the subject because of the indeterminate limits of party politics. As the challenges beckon, the burdens increase.

A peculiar difficulty in writing about the party system is how much to discuss in the present tense and how much in the past. It was not until the late nineteenth century, we are told, that political parties acquired a status "somewhere between quasi-respectability and wholehearted acceptance." * Now, after being analyzed and dissected, generalized and aggregated, evaluated and conceptualized, political parties still appear to be in an indeterminate state, somewhere between passive acceptance and active rejection. They are generally assumed to exist and widely assumed to be deficient. Interpretations waver between bulletins variously reporting signs of stability, and signs of barely fluttering life. Political parties command attention both from those rebuking them for their existence and from those sorrowing over their coming demise.

No matter what happens in the future, the party system has already had a distinctive life history, and this continuity is the theme that underlies the present book. There are some rewards in this treatment, for the perspectives of the past do not require an historical treatise and the prospects for the future do not require prophecy. The intention is not to improve prediction but to clarify the present and scan the future with the benefit of hindsight.

The party system was a structural and integrative invention mothered

* Austin Ranney and Willmoore Kendall, *Democracy and the American Party System* (New York: Harcourt, Brace and Company, 1956), p. 147.

by the necessity for mobilizing people in order to govern them. The party system was, therefore, an adaptation; and its continued existence has exemplified the reality of impermanence. Sometimes we need to be reminded that the more things seem to be the same, the more they may be changing.

This sense of gradual movement is lost when the rapidity of change makes today always appear to be out of touch with yesterday. Still, we arrive where we are from destinations reached in the past. There is no way to remove ourselves to a new order of living where we can begin solely from the present. We cannot make a clean break by stripping off the shackles of an unprogressive past in the invigorating light of the morning of a new beginning.

There are always differences in motives as there are in perspectives. A variety of motives underlay both the rise of parties and their decline. The long period of withdrawal from parties has been the result of side-effects of reactions and reforms as well as purposeful rejection. The one constant factor is that the justification of the party system lies in its value to those who cast votes rather than to those who seek votes. Whatever an elite may think about the party system, in the final analysis, it will be the public that decides its fate.

Through the years, it has been the governed that adapted the parties to conform with their own well-being, as they have conceived their well-being in the world in which they found themselves. Their value-judgments will continue to determine the course of the party system but, just as there are many perspectives and motives, there are also many value-judgments. The party system cannot be discussed independently of prior conclusions of what is possible and what is desirable. The best that can be hoped for is an effort to be objective within the limits of a set of value-judgments.

The author frankly admits a preference for party continuity because the alternatives appear to be dubious at best and catastrophic at worst. The parties have not died yet, so they can still be discussed in the present tense. They play, comparatively, a more restricted role, but the restrictions need not become mortal wounds. There is still a role which is a genuine service in democratic society. The question, really, is if we want parties. There is a choice.

W. G.

ACKNOWLEDGMENTS

Many people have been unknowing accomplices in the writing of this book. Only a few have been aware of what they were aiding and abetting. It is remarkable that both groups have been equally helpful and would have been even more helpful if only the author had known how to take better advantage of what was offered. It is not remarkable—in fact, it should go without saying—that neither group would necessarily approve of what has been produced as a result of their help. In these litiginous times, if the author did not hasten to assure the reader that the whole book, particularly its deficiencies and omissions, was no one else's responsibility but his, he may immediately be served with a court order. To make this disclaimer is really not to forestall such embarrassment, but ready acceptance of a long-standing and necessary practice.

It would be a serious oversight, however, to fail to express appreciation to Stan Wakefield and others at Prentice-Hall who first made possible and then smoothed the path for producing this book. At least in matters of editorial judgment and technical proficiency, the author is grateful to admit the responsibility of others.

The Party
System
in America

1

The Making of the Party System

The party system in America can neither be said to be one phenomenon nor to have always been exactly the same phenomena. It may seem to be timeless because no one remembers when there were no parties but, neither in the United States nor in any other country, have parties always been essential for holding elections much less for the conduct of government.

Still, we make associations based on what our culture has produced and passed on to us. One historian concluded that "The existence of a free government without a division into parties is an impossibility." [1] Although it is no secret that Americans enjoyed personal freedoms long before political parties existed, the statement is provocative by defining democratic government itself as government *with* political parties. A government *without* parties would, therefore, not be democratic. If parties really have become this important, can we preserve democracy if parties eventually pass away? To explore this question, we need to know more about the system of political parties in America and the evaluations involved in them. In fact, evaluations are both implicit and explicit in defining and identifying political parties as they emerged in America.

PARTIES AS A POLITICAL SYSTEM

It appears that human society cannot exist without people's objectives and ambitions coming into conflict. Consequently, it becomes necessary to find means for peacefully settling or, more likely, minimizing these conflicts. Societies develop processes for negotiating compromises and reaching accommodations between clashing groups and individuals. The name *politics* describes these processes; and when the processes form established patterns of relationships and procedures, we have a *political system*. On the one hand, there are people and their clashing interests; on the other, the institutional structure for dealing with them. It is not necessary to have political

---

[1] Edward Stanwood, *A History of the Presidency from 1788–1897* (Boston: Houghton Mifflin Company, 1898) p. 123.

parties to have a political system. A party system is simply one kind of political system, one kind of structure for dealing with conflicts.

The Party as Organization

Because of the complexity of politics, there are different ways of defining a political party. A definition can emphasize one or another element depending upon different perceptions or purposes. If a party is conceived as a *thing*, in the concrete sense, it is an organization. What distinguishes people in party organization is their objective to win elections for public offices.[2] Looking at the end result, government officials are elected to office identified as members of one or another political party.

The definition of a party as an organization for the purpose of winning elections does not include motivations because there can be numerous reasons why people want to win. The definition does assume that a party competes with one or more other parties in electing its candidates. With only one party, there is a political system but not a political party system. In a party system, parties create "a pattern of interaction" and must "take one another into account in their behavior in government and in election contests."[3]

The Party as a Name

For those who are not part of any party organization, the most concrete thing about a party may very well be its name. A party then becomes an instrument and a symbol for those who share attitudes associated with the party name.[4] Carried further, "the crucial defining element" of a party has been reduced to its name so that a party would exist even if only one candidate for public office accepts the party label.[5]

It is not possible to say what a political party is, once and for all, because the definition varies with the context in which parties are discussed. By any definition, however, a party system is distinctive from other political systems.

[2] Joseph LaPalombara and Myron Weiner, "The Origin and Development of Political Parties," in *Political Parties and Political Development*, eds., LaPalombara and Weiner (Princeton, N.J.: Princeton University Press, 1966) p. 6. Kenneth Janda, *A Conceptual Framework for the Comparative Analysis of Political Parties* (Beverly Hills, Calif.: Sage Publishers, 1970) pp. 83, 88. Maurice Duverger, *Political Parties*, 2nd ed., (New York: John Wiley & Sons, Inc., 1959) p. xxiii.

[3] William N. Chambers, "Party Development and the American Mainstream," in *The American Party Systems*, eds., Chambers and Walter Dean Burnham (New York: Oxford University Press, 1967) p. 6.

[4] Austin Ranney, "The Concept of 'Party,'" in *Political Research and Political Theory*, ed., Oliver Garceau (Cambridge, Mass.: Harvard University Press, 1968) pp. 147, 159–61.

[5] Leon D. Epstein, *Political Parties in Western Democracies* (New York: Frederick A. Praeger, 1967) p. 9.

THE EMERGENCE OF PARTIES

Political parties are associated with national development, and the United States has the distinction of having created the first political parties of the modern world. This beginning of party politics occurred in the "American arena" within twenty years of the United States coming into existence as a sovereign nation.[6]

The first American party took the name "Federalist" and the second party, "Republican," which is identified throughout this book as "Jeffersonian-Republican" to distinguish it from the Republican party which came into being in the 1850s. The period of competition between Federalists and Jeffersonian-Republicans, designated the first party system, came to an end during the second decade of the nineteenth century. Like America itself, the party system had to be discovered more than once.

The re-creation of parties began in the period of the 1820s–1830s, when the second party system of Democrats and Whigs was born. With this event, the party system was finally established—although the second party system proved to be of short duration. The Whig party splintered during the 1850s, and the Republican party came into being. The first forty years of competition between Democrats and Republicans is designated as the third party system. Later realignments in the 1890s and 1930s have been distinguished as giving rise, respectively, to the fourth and fifth party systems even though the major party names did not change (Table 1.1).

A series of names and dates tells nothing about the circumstances of the rise of parties. Table 1.1 may even leave the erroneous impression there was no political system before the 1790s. On the contrary, there was a continuity in American politics in the years before parties just as there has been during the course of the party system itself.

Political Systems Before Parties

Politics existed in America from the beginning of colonial history, as Americans became activated and divided according to what they saw as their interests. William Penn was once driven to write to the inhabitants of Pennsylvania, "For the love of God, me, and the poor country, be not so governmentish!"[7] John Adams, our second President, when looking back at the political record of his fellow-countrymen from the vantage point of 1812, had no doubt of what had occurred. Divisions "began with human nature," he wrote, and had "existed in America from its first plantation."

---

[6] Chambers, "Party Development and the American Mainstream," p. 4.

[7] Quoted in Bernard Bailyn, *The Origins of American Politics* (New York: Alfred A. Knopf, 1968) p. 65; italics in original.

TABLE 1.1   The American Party Systems.

Periods *	Major Parties	Minor (Third) Parties **
1. 1790s–1816	Federalists Jeffersonian-Republicans	
1817–1820s	Jeffersonian-Republicans and Factions (Various names used.)	
2. 1830s–1854	Democrats Whigs	Antimasonic Free-Soil
3. 1854–1894	Democrats Republicans	American Constitutional Union Populist
4. 1894–1930s	Democrats Republicans	Socialist Progressive
5. 1930s– ?	Democrats Republicans	American Independent

    * All dates are obviously approximate.
    ** Those receiving 5% or more of the total presidential vote in at least one election.

In every colony, "a court and country party have always contended."[8] Adams correctly described the continuity of political systems, but colonial divisions were not parties by any definition used now.

Types of Factions. "Factions" is the most widely used word for the groups of people who jointly sought political objectives in colonial America. At least four factional political systems or variations existing before 1776 have been identified, and some colonies even changed from one system to another. Probably the most common type was "chaotic factionalism," where groups formed for competition in one election and then dissolved when the election was over. There were also systems of more stable factions which were at least "semi-permanent" because they were based on more enduring interests. Then, there were instances of no factional competition: Either a dominant elite suppressed opposition or it forestalled opposition by providing an opportunity for all interests to be represented.[9]

Deferential Politics. Colonial political leadership was more uniform than the political systems. In each colony, those who were accorded deference because of their recognized status exercised leadership. They did not attain status because they were elected; they were elected because

    [8] *The Works of John Adams*, ed., Charles Francis Adams (Boston: Little, Brown and Company, 1865) X, 23.
    [9] Jack P. Greene, "Changing Interpretations of Early American Politics," in *The Reinterpretation of Early American History*, ed., Ray Allen Billington (San Marino, Calif.: The Huntington Library, 1966) pp. 176–77.

they already had status. The system was aristocratic in that governments were conducted by men who were considered to have the capacity and wisdom to govern, and who usually, but not always, were the social and economic elite. Deference was balanced off by responsibility. The elites were expected to use their talents to govern for the benefit of the public.[10] Elites apparently accepted deference in colonial politics without question, but there is no actual evidence that the governed accepted the system quite so wholeheartedly.[11]

Deferential politics was also a result of limited colonial political development. The electorate in each colony was too small and scattered for the development of organized politics although the electorate did progressively increase in size. For instance, it was difficult for many southerners to vote because elections were held at distant county seats. Life was generally rigorous, and it is understandable that many people lacked the incentive to make any special effort to vote for the few local officials who were elected. Elections, to a great extent, were isolated events, and there was a general lack of continuing political relationships between the public and its leaders.

The transition from a political system of preparty factions to a system of political parties may appear clear-cut and simple when examined in retrospect. Actually, the transition occurred by increments, not by an avalanche, by a blending of forms rather than by a sharply discernible break in continuity. There is no anniversary date for political parties as there is for the Declaration of Independence or for the signing of the Constitution. The changes that are clear to us were not necessarily so for people living then. Even for those who realized that changes were in the wind, the kinds of changes could have been as inscrutable as they were unnerving.

It is also impossible to agree on a date for the appearance of political parties because they were not consciously or purposely created. In the absence of precedents, leaders invented parties by trial and error. They were not constructing a theory, but a response to a challenge. They were slow to see the need for better organized politics but quickly saw the need for greater public support. They built purposefully in adapting means to ends, but they were unaware they were building what the future would not only approve but even equate with freedom itself.[12]

Tracing the course of these developments involves two questions:

[10] *Ibid.*, p. 173.

[11] John B. Kirby, "Early American Politics—The Search for Ideology: An Historiographical Analysis and Critique of the Concept of 'Deference,'" *The Journal of Politics*, 32 (November 1970) 808–38.

[12] Joseph Charles, *The Origins of the American Party System* (New York: Harper & Row, Publishers, Harper Torchbooks, 1961) p. 92. William N. Chambers, *Political Parties in a New Nation; The American Experience, 1776–1809* (New York: Oxford University Press, 1963) pp. 14, 49.

What circumstances were associated with the rise of parties and what was distinctive about them?

The Circumstances

Factional politics seems to have been an intimate part of elitism based on deference, but factionalism was also the result of competition within the elite itself. That the elite were divided rather than unified became increasingly important. As their conflicts placed leaders under more and more pressure in seeking support among voters, deference for leaders declined. Elections were obviously becoming too important and too complicated for preparty systems. Challenges and responses reflected new tides in thinking, in the way people lived, and in the horizons of their expectations.

Although a party system first appeared during the 1790s, it was not until the 1820s–1830s that a fully favorable environment existed. That the party system had a false start and had to reemerge suggests how difficult it was to create parties. Even if they were not entirely accidental, neither were they preordained. Parties were initially indebted to democracy, not the other way around. Not only did freedom precede parties, freedom came more spontaneously than parties.

Certain "preconditions" for the emergence of parties in twentieth-century multinational research can be applied to eighteenth- and nineteenth-century America. New social and economic structures created new kinds of political relationships. Society became more complex as new entrepreneurial and specialized professional groups appeared and gave rise to more group conflicts. The growth of technology, particularly making for easier communication and transportation, meant increased physical *and* social mobility. Society became more secularized, particularly in education and in urban living.[13] These preconditions were associated with the appearance of parties, first, along the Atlantic Coast and later, in new states. Fragmentary data in Michigan indicates that the sharpest party divisions occurred in the most populous counties and towns which were "the most socially and economically complex, and possessed the best-developed communication facilities."[14]

The preconditions for parties in America can thus be sketched upon the broad canvas of the Industrial Revolution, but the background for parties should not be made too expansive and grandiose. Some influences

[13] LaPalombara and Weiner, "The Origin and Development of Political Parties," pp. 3–4, 22. Duverger, *Political Parties*, pp. 425–26. L. Harmon Zeigler and G. Wayne Peak, *Interest Groups in American Society*, 2nd ed. (Englewood Cliffs, N.J.: Prentice-Hall, Inc., 1972) pp. 29–34.

[14] Ronald P. Formisano, *The Birth of Mass Political Parties: Michigan, 1827–1861* (Princeton, N.J.: Princeton University Press, 1971) p. 91.

were more important than others, and some were probably not important at all. Further, the circumstances in America were not duplicated in all other countries which developed a party system.

At whatever point parties have arisen, there were different kinds of tasks, or crises, to resolve. In the United States, in the 1790s, the tasks proved to be manageable. For one thing, Americans were already integrated in the sense that no groups were agitating for separation or protesting infringement of their cultural heritage, in the manner of the Quebec separatists in Canada. For another, there was consent for governmental authorities. The age of constitutionalism had been born. Each state government was founded upon its own constitution and by 1789, the Constitution of the United States was operating following the bitter dispute over its ratification. National integration and legitimacy of government helped to set the tone of the country; but the absence of extreme crises was not a precondition for parties. At least in some other countries, such as Italy and France, parties arose when there were such crises.[15]

A special precondition for parties in the United States was "a common political arena," created by the Constitution. The new government made possible a national focus of attention upon national problems, but it was the parties, not the Constitution itself, which became the focusing mechanism.[16]

The Distinctiveness of Parties

Political parties were significant enough without confusing what had been accomplished *before* them with what was accomplished *with* them. Some things which were not distinctive about parties help to clarify what was.

In preparty political systems, men sought office either through votes or appointments and jockeyed for advantages. The objective to win elections even led to relatively stable political relationships in the 1770s–1780s in the case of two opposing factions in Pennsylvania and the group in New York supporting the governorship of George Clinton.[17] Although the status of public officials was greatly altered with the demise of defer-

---

[15] LaPalombara and Weiner, "The Origin and Development of Political Parties," pp. 14–17. Chambers, "Party Development and the American Mainstream," pp. 17, 62–63. Seymour Martin Lipset, *The First New Nation* (New York: Doubleday & Co., Inc., Anchor Books, 1967) pp. 18–26.

[16] Chambers, *Political Parties in a New Nation*, pp. 122–26. Paul Goodman, "The First American Party System," in *The American Party Systems*, eds., William Nisbet Chambers and Walter Dean Burnham (New York: Oxford University Press, 1967) p. 63. Morton Grodzins, "Party and Government in the United States," in *Political Parties, U.S.A.*, ed., Robert A. Goldwin (Chicago: Rand McNally & Company, 1964) pp. 102–32.

[17] Harry Marlin Tinkcom, *The Republicans and Federalists in Pennsylvania 1790–1801* (Harrisburg, Pa.: Pennsylvania Historical and Museum Commission, 1950) pp. 3–4, 19–21. Alfred F. Young, *The Democratic Republicans of New York* (Chapel Hill, N.C.: The University of North Carolina Press, 1967) p. 575.

ential politics, strategies in election campaigns did not suddenly change when parties appeared. Candidates who believed in deferential politics had been courting voters for some time, and these candidates were forced by circumstances to honor democratic political methods in order to be elected.

Nor did a high voting turnout necessarily depend upon political parties. Restrictions upon voting were gradually removed and in some colonies, restrictions were not always enforced. Both the voting rate and the size of the electorate in the eighteenth and early nineteenth centuries were larger than either the laws of those years or some subsequent judgments would suggest. Electoral competition by itself, with or without parties, apparently stimulated relatively high turnout during the first quarter of the nineteenth century.[18]

What was distinctive about parties was their durability and their giving a new meaning to voting.

Durable Group Loyalties.   The first place to look for parties is in the government after the adoption of the Constitution, and the House of Representatives "provided more accurately than any other body the common arena for party development." [19] However, parties did not spring full-blown when the first Congress assembled. The process of party formation has been laboriously traced by analyzing every roll call vote in the House of Representatives between 1789 and 1801. Until the mid-1790s, the members voted as factions in dealing with the problems of establishing the nation. When the Federalist and Jeffersonian-Republican parties began emerging after the mid-1790s, policy voting became subordinate to electing party members to office.[20]

James Madison had pointed out this same distinction between parties and factions in *The Federalist. Factions*, Madison concluded, were inherent in human affairs, for they were groups of people with similar interests in pursuing public policies or, what would be called today, *interest groups.* Factions can be identified in legislative voting by the divisions on each vote, but the division on one vote will not be the same on every other vote. A factional division on one issue will disappear on another issue, and opponents on one vote will be voting in agreement on the next. To

[18] Chilton Williamson, *American Suffrage: From Property to Democracy, 1760–1860* (Princeton, N.J.: Princeton University Press, 1960) pp. 3–39. Charles S. Sydnor, *Gentlemen Freeholders* (Chapel Hill, N.C.: The University of North Carolina Press, 1952) pp. 21, 29–31, 36–37, 123. J.R. Pole, "Suffrage and Representation in Maryland from 1776 to 1810," in *Voters, Parties, and Elections,* eds., Joel H. Silbey and Samuel T. McSeveney (Lexington, Mass.: Xerox College Publishing, 1972) pp. 61–71. Richard P. McCormick, *The Second American Party System: Party Formation in the Jacksonian Era* (Chapel Hill, N.C.: The University of North Carolina Press, 1966) pp. 97–99.

[19] Rudolph M. Bell, *Party and Faction in American Politics* (Westport, Ct.: Greenwood Press, 1973) p. 10.

[20] *Ibid.,* pp. 5–6, 13–16, 67, 108, 153.

Madison, the difference between factions and parties was clear: "When men exercise their reason coolly and freely on a variety of distinct questions, they inevitably fall into different opinions on some of them. (These are factions.) When they are governed by a common passion, their opinions, if they are so to be called, will be the same." (These are parties.) [21]

What distinguished parties was what Madison objected to, that is, their durability. Parties, compared with factions, are continuous because of the development of a loyalty to the group itself ("passion") instead of loyalty to interests ("reason"). This invidious comparison need not be taken too seriously, for Madison posed an either-or situation. Either there are factions rationally voting their interests, or there are parties irrationally voting group loyalty. Why are interests rational but acting with a group for group reasons irrational? What is rational to one may be irrational to someone else. Who decides who is right?

Further, Madison's argument in *The Federalist*, in the 1780s, was written a decade before political parties arose and understandably Madison was unable to appreciate any advantages to be derived from them. When he dealt with the actual political situation of the 1790s, he played a major role in the formation of the Jeffersonian-Republican party. Madison in action disregarded his own antiparty views, displaying both passion and reason in helping to build a political party to oppose and reverse Federalist policies.

Unlike an ad hoc faction that ordinarily has little if any organization, a party is a permanent organization that supplies its own incentive for action. This is an understandable result of group association. Instead of condemning it, as Madison did in *The Federalist*, many others, over the years, have condemned parties for not being more unified in voting on public policies in legislatures. What Madison saw as an evil to be avoided has, in fact, been avoided much of the time because the party incentive has not supplanted all other incentives. The parties have become far better known for intraparty differences than for party solidarity. Parties replaced factions, but the word "faction" has lived on in the party system to designate a segment within a party. It seems that *a party is not one group but the sum of its factions*. In the United States, at least, Edmund Burke's classic definition of a party, as "a body of men, united, for promoting by their joint endeavors the national interest, upon some particular principles to which they are all agreed," is a better definition of a faction.[22]

[21] *The Federalist* (New York: The Modern Library, n.d.) Number 10, pp. 53–62, *passim* and Number 50, p. 334. Bell, *Party and Faction in American Politics*, p. 3.

[22] *The Works of the Right Honorable Edmund Burke* (Boston: Wells and Lilly, 1826) I, 425.

Permanent Organization.   Although party divisions first appeared in legislative voting, it was organization that made a party uniquely different from a faction. Leaders discovered in the course of events that it was easier to deal with political forces through a permanent organization that stabilized relationships and made them more predictable. Party organization became an institutional relationship independent of the particular people who were active in the organization at any one time. In its structure, the organization extended from the central to the local levels as a durable social formation maintained by continuous communications.[23] Parties thrived because they were relevant in fulfilling practical needs as well as imbuing leaders and followers with the emotions of party loyalty, those *psychological attachments* which are *one definition of a party.* Parties have succeeded to the extent their leaders encompassed a wide assortment of perceptions and responses. Parties became the end product of a sense of personal identification with an institution, a composite of traditions, beliefs, and symbols.

All of this development took time. The Democratic party was the first to be organized from the national to the local levels when it created the first permanent national committee in 1848. The Whig party never did create a permanent national committee, but the Republican party began with one when the party was organized in 1856. The components of a party system were put together in the 1830s and 1840s, when political identities and institutional forms became the same throughout the whole country.[24] But the definition of a party as a permanent organization extending from top to bottom did not apply fully to both major parties until the second half of the nineteenth century.

More Meaningful Voting.   To the extent preparty politics was a confusion of shifting alliances, the alternatives presented to voters were the personalities of candidates and the competitive advantages of factions. Leaders in the preparty political system were more likely to be concerned with momentary victories and did not have to think about the future of their factions as leaders of permanent parties have to do. Because factional alliances could be so undependable, their effects upon government were often unpredictable from the point of view of the voter.

As an example, in preparty Massachusetts, voters tended to vote for the better-known candidate simply because they lacked information and had to make their choices on the basis of personal knowledge. The armed conflict, known as Shays' Rebellion, can be linked to frustration that re-

[23] LaPalombara and Weiner, "The Origin and Development of Political Parties," p. 6. Chambers, "Party Development and the American Mainstream," p. 5. Chambers, *Political Parties in a New Nation,* p. 10. Janda, *A Conceptual Framework for the Comparative Analysis of Political Parties,* p. 88.

[24] McCormick, *The Second American Party System,* p. 342.

sulted from the "inability to obtain any leverage over the governmental institutions of a preparty period." [25]

To the extent that voters could make some connection between their voting and subsequent government action, parties proved to be better than factions.[26] As a value-judgment, parties were better because they were a means of making government more coherent and responsive. Even if they were not the best of all possible creations, they were at least a reasonable adaptation to a given set of circumstances.

The Kind of Party System. Every country's party system is distinctive, and the American party system developed some particularly characteristic features. In all of the discussion about American parties there has been general agreement about the kind of system we have had but widespread disagreement in evaluating it. Different people do not see the same values in the system even when they agree on what kind of system it has been. The party system, by being many things to many people, cannot possibly satisfy everyone. What the system has been will be summarized here in the characteristics of the two-party system and in the tensions in governing and representing which it produced.

MAJOR AND MINOR PARTIES

What the American party system became was not entirely what would have been predicted. The multitude of criss-crossing interests could have led to a larger number of political parties. Instead, the conflicts have been contained within the structure of a two-party system. Explanations for this result have been found in either institutional or noninstitutional influences or in both.[27]

Two-Party System: Institutional Explanation

Rules and customs governing the election process also affected the party system. Electing members of legislative bodies in *single-member districts* has been a frequently cited institutional reason for having just two major

[25] Van Beck Hall, *Politics Without Parties: Massachusetts, 1789–1791* (Pittsburgh: University of Pittsburgh Press, 1972) pp. 71–74., quotation p. 74.

[26] Chambers, *Political Parties in a New Nation*, p. 27.

[27] General discussions can be found in Donald V. Smiley, "The Two-Party System and One-Party Dominance in the Liberal Democratic State," in *Comparative Political Parties: Selected Readings*, ed., Andrew J. Milnor (New York: Thomas Y. Crowell Company, 1969) pp. 54–64. Kay Lawson, *Political Parties and Democracy in the United States* (New York: Charles Scribner's Sons, 1968) pp. 31–39. Allan P. Sindler, *Political Parties in the United States* (New York: St. Martin's Press, 1966) pp. 50–59. William Goodman, *The Two-Party System in the United States*. 3rd ed.. (Princeton, N.J.: D. Van Nostrand Co., Inc., 1964) pp. 30–39.

parties. It is thought that the use of single-member districts will encourage the formation of large political parties in order to increase their chances of electing one candidate. The tendency, therefore, will be toward two parties so that each has, approximately, an equal chance to win. The formation of additional parties, which would fragment the vote and complicate party strategies, would be self-defeating. This explanation assumes a highly pragmatic type of political thinking and a concern with winning elections to the exclusion of any other consideration.

Whatever the logic of these assumptions, the single-member district system by itself is not a sufficient explanation. Two-party countries such as the United States and Great Britain have single-member legislative districts along with a two-party system, but France also has single-member districts with a multiparty system. The difference between the two Anglo-Saxon countries and France has been accounted for by another legal provision. In the United States and Great Britain a *candidate needs only a plurality, not a majority,* of the vote to win. In France, on the contrary, if a candidate for the National Assembly does not receive a majority of the votes, a run-off election is held between the two highest candidates.

After analyzing 121 election results in twenty Western democracies between 1945 and 1965, Douglas Rae found a strong association between plurality election and the two-party system except in countries, like Canada, with strong local minority parties. The relative effects of plurality election and the single-member district, where they existed together, could not be distinguished.[28]

Maurice Duverger had previously concluded that plurality election favored the two-party system, and this association approached "most nearly perhaps to a true sociological law." With further refinement, however, this "law" became progressively less certain. Duverger noted that the tendency was to create two parties in individual districts, that is, to create local two-party systems. While plurality "works in the direction of bipartism; it does not necessarily and absolutely lead to it in spite of all obstacles."[29] In the United States, some of the evidence goes against Duverger. In many individual districts, one party is dominant and there is no effective two-party system, but Democrats and Republicans consistently compete on the national level.

A special explanation for the two-party system in America, therefore, is provided by the election of a president from a single district, the nation itself. Presidential elections are complicated by the requirements of the United States Constitution and state laws in determining *how electoral votes* are to be cast. Superficially, the electoral college presents a problem

[28] Douglas W. Rae, *The Political Consequences of Electoral Laws* (New Haven, Ct.: Yale University Press, 1967) pp. 94–96.

[29] Duverger, *Political Parties,* pp. 217, 223 quotation p. 228.

for the plurality explanation because the Constitution requires a candidate to receive a majority of all the electoral votes cast in order to be elected. Actually, the way the system works, there is no problem because the individual states merely require that the political party which receives more votes than any other party, that is, the plurality, will win all of a state's electoral votes. The constitutional requirement of a majority of the electoral votes to be elected takes no account of the popular vote, and sixteen presidents since 1824 have been elected with less than half of the total popular vote.

There are no legal requirements that candidates for Congress and state legislatures must receive a majority to be elected. Winning candidates normally receive a majority because only two candidates are running. In these elections, it can be argued that the two-party system explains why most winning candidates receive a majority, rather than using legal provisions as an explanation for the two-party system.

The logic connecting both plurality elections and single-member districts with the two-party system is the assumption that parties only run candidates for office in order to win. If a majority is required, with provision for a run-off election, more parties will be encouraged to enter the race because the more candidates, the less likely any one of them will receive a majority. Even those parties eliminated by the first election may still have influence in the run-off election by supporting one of the two remaining candidates. If there is no provision for a run-off and the highest candidate always wins, only candidates of large parties have a chance.

Institutional explanations can be intriguing but they appear to put the cart before the horse. That legal requirements should inadvertently create a substantive characteristic like the two-party system is a strain on credulity. For instance, in colonial America, single-member, plurality elections did not necessarily create two factions, although where there was genuine competition, it was usually between just two factions.

It has been argued that the electoral-college system of the Constitution is necessary to maintain the two-party system, but no one ever contended that the Framers of the Constitution wanted a two-party system. Most of them opposed parties outright. If the constitutional provisions relating to presidential elections are read without political parties in mind, it can easily be concluded that the Framers anticipated state interests would become factions on the national level, and certainly not just two factions. The connection between the electoral college and two major parties was not seen until long after the Constitution was written, when parties had already taken form. It is state laws requiring plurality election of electors on a general ticket that not only magnifies presidential victories but manufactures them; however, state laws have never been said to be the cause of the two-party system.

Obviously, a whole battery of state and federal laws facilitate a system limited to two parties because the people who made the laws were members of those parties. An excellent illustration is the *Federal Elections Campaign Act of 1974* which insures each major party its equal share of presidential campaign funds, but other parties qualify for funds only if they received a specified percentage of the national popular vote at the previous election. The institutional influence has been intentional, not accidental, and the intentions would have been thwarted if there had been a public outcry against the laws. At the very least, the public has acquiesced in the encouragement of two parties, suggesting that the noninstitutional explanation may be more promising.

Two-Party System: Noninstitutional Explanation

A political system is expected to reflect the people who are governed by it. The two-party system has, therefore, been explained by the values of Americans, their consensus, and their political pragmatism. These characteristics are not confined to Americans alone but have sometimes been related to the nation's British inheritance.

Anglo-Saxon political systems have had a tendency toward the two-party system in various parts of the world. Confining political conflict to just two choices has even been traced to the Norman Conquest of England and to the clash of Catholics and Protestants at the end of the sixteenth century over the relative power of bishops and the Crown. These examples may have led to the expectation that society would be organized into two groups and, thus, serve "as a condition for the two-party system." [30]

Of course, the two-party system is not necessarily peculiar to English-speaking countries. If it were, there would be nothing further to explain, except how America happens to retain such a distinctive British institution when so many ethnic strains have intermingled among us. If nonAnglo-Saxons have accepted the premises of the two-party system, there must be something besides cultural inheritance involved. The non-institutional explanation in America must be something pervasive enough to include all of us.

Being limited to two major parties creates the illusion that politics is an either-or choice. Dualism becomes a fact in the structure of voting even though conflicts are many-sided. It may also be a source of satisfaction to see conflicts simplistically, as being only two-sided. Aversion to seeing more than two sides may betray an intolerance of both fragmentation and complexities. There is no way of knowing how accurate these indications

[30] Roy F. Nichols, *The Invention of the American Political Parties* (New York: The Macmillan Co., 1967) pp. 7-8, 10-11, quotation p. 11.

are, nor can we say that all people who prefer unity and simplicity have a fondness for two parties.

Consensus. Two large political parties are an expression of a loosely woven political fabric that presumably is held together by mutual opinions and values. To proceed along this line soon brings us to consensus, a frequent explanation for American society as a whole. It means a low intensity of disagreement or a wide agreement on many questions. If there has been a national consensus, the two-party system must be a product of it. If there has not been consensus, why did we not develop a multi-party system?

According to one interpretation of the American historical record, political divisions have been overemphasized. Instead there has been a "common climate" of opinion in favor of the capitalistic system. Americans have persistently adhered to "the rights of property, the philosophy of economic individualism, the value of competition." When property rights have been challenged, as in the periods of Jefferson and Jackson, the fight was not between property and no property, but between different kinds of property.[31] Another interpretation is that American politics has revealed an ability to change systems while maintaining continuity. Most of the time, conflicts revolve around the application of the belief system rather than conflicts over the belief system itself.[32] A third view is that tensions have arisen because American consensus consists of a belief in both equality and in achievement. The two beliefs have been continuous but often in conflict with each other.[33] Consensus can be equated with continuity and with stability of beliefs but certainly not with tranquility.

There is a point of diminishing returns in pursuing the concept of consensus. Intense political conflicts in America have been mediated by major parties which have been basically nonideological. Political tensions have remained low compared with some other countries which have a multiparty system. In the midst of controversies, the American acceptance of how the game should be played can very well reflect consensus, but the two-party system, as a practical matter, remains the same whether it results from consensus or from something else.[34]

The American party system has been an exercise in politics as the

[31] Richard Hofstadter, *The American Political Tradition and the Men Who Made It* (New York: Random House, Vintage Books, 1948) pp. vii–ix, quotation p. viii.

[32] William L. Shade, *Social Change and the Electoral Process* (Gainesville, Fl.: University of Florida Press, 1973) pp. 14–15.

[33] Lipset, *First New Nation*, pp. 115 ff.

[34] John Higham, "The Cult of Consensus," in *The American Political Experience: What Is the Key?* ed., Edward Handler (Lexington, Mass.: D. C. Heath and Company, 1968) pp. 40–48. Howard A. Scarrow, "The Function of Political Parties: A Critique of the Literature and the Approach," *The Journal of Politics*, 29 (November 1967) 788–89. John C. Wahlke, Heinz Eulau, William Buchanan, and LeRoy C. Ferguson, *The Legislative System* (New York: John Wiley & Sons, Inc., 1962) p. 152.

art of the possible, and this pragmatism itself may be evidence of a sort of consensus. Those who aspired to decision-making power in government have concentrated upon personal relationships and have dealt endlessly with details in securing agreements. If this type of political thinking has been characteristic of American party leaders, it could hardly have been alien to the American public. It has to be presumed that leaders learned what voters were likely to punish and reward. There had to be a convertibility between what was offered and what was accepted. If Americans wanted a flexible system within which to seek open-ended objectives, the two-party system certainly has filled the bill.

Consensus and Party Competition.   In one respect, it is remarkable that anything connected with the party system should be attributed to consensus. Not only did it take years for parties to be accepted, but it also did not instantly occur to Americans that political competition was consistent with liberty. Thomas Jefferson "apparently believed that public opinion would cause a change of administration policies on vital points without there first being a change of the officers of the Administration." [35] Had Jefferson been correct, neither parties nor competition would have been necessary. John Taylor, Jefferson's contemporary, believed that only one party could be devoted to a country's interests.[36] By implication, there should be one democratic party without competition.

It took some time to accept the idea of competition between parties in America. The popular acceptance of competition has remained stronger in rhetoric than in voting behavior. Perhaps the actual preference for a one-party system over the years in so much of the country is better evidence of consensus than our expressions of belief in a two-party system.

Minor Parties in a Two-Party System

If consensus helps to account for two major parties, then a lack of consensus must account for the existence of minor, or third, parties. Every four years since 1872, there have been more than two presidential candidates. The largest number of minor-party candidates was twenty-five, in 1976. Inasmuch as the importance of these parties is not measured by their membership but by the size of the vote they receive, they are generally disregarded. The total popular vote cast for *all* minor party candidates in any one presidential election is sometimes less than 1 percent and usually no more than 2 to 3 percent. In only ten presidential elections since 1832, have candidates other than those of major parties received the electoral votes of at least one state.

[35] Charles, *The Origins of the American Party System*, p. 85.
[36] Nobel E. Cunningham, Jr., *The Jeffersonian Republicans: The Formation of Party Organization, 1789–1801* (Chapel Hill, N.C.: The University of North Carolina Press, 1957) p. 75.

The varying number of other parties does not seem to have disturbed consensus. Their weakness in presidential elections is partly accounted for by the electoral-college system which gives an advantage to a candidate who has supporters concentrated *within* states instead of *distributed across* the country. There has consistently been some dissent from the major parties. Since 1840, the two major parties won all of the electoral votes in 25 of 35 elections but won all of the popular votes only in 1864 and 1868.

Minor party candidates have done best when political tensions were unusually high. Nine candidates in eight presidential elections have received 5 percent or more of the popular vote and three of the nine were former presidents of the United States (Table 1.2). Yet discontent by itself is not always a reliable guide to minor-party voting. In 1932, when the effects of the Great Depression were at a high point, there were nine minor parties whose combined popular vote was only 2.9 percent. In 1892, when discontent was not comparable to that in 1932, three minor parties received 11.0 percent of the vote of which the Populists alone received 8.5 percent.

That discontent is only expressed occasionally through minor parties makes it appear there has been an insistence upon having a two-party system. Americans are committed to a two-party structure more strongly than to balanced competition between the two major parties all of the time.

TABLE 1.2   Minor Parties Receiving over 5 Percent of Total Vote
Cast in Presidential Elections, since 1832.

Party	Candidate	Year	Percentage
Progressive	Theodore Roosevelt *	1912	27.4
American	Fillmore *	1856	21.1
Progressive	LaFollette	1924	16.6
American Independent	Wallace	1968	13.5
Constitutional Union	Bell	1860	12.6
Free-Soil	Van Buren *	1848	10.1
Populist	Weaver	1892	8.5
Antimasonic	Wirt	1832	8.0
Socialist	Debs	1912	6.0

Note: Percentages taken from Svend Petersen, *A Statistical History of the American Presidential Elections* (New York: Frederick Ungar Publishing Company, 1968).

* Former presidents of the United States.

GOVERNING AND REPRESENTING

Americans have had a choice between two parties uniquely designed to govern because both were organized as instruments for governing and were representative of their coalitions of voters. It is impossible for a party to govern without being representative, and without the power to govern, officially there is no one to represent. Having the ability to win an election is one thing. Having the experience and expertise to carry on the government after winning is another.[37] Governing and representing are, thus, two parts of the whole, and each has its own separate requirements. Through its organization, each party developed the ability to govern and, through its coalition, became representative.

In theory, public officials represent all constituents; as party leaders, they think in terms of the constituents who elected them. As a general rule, they would like to broaden their coalition but do not want to alienate the supporters they already have. A party is limited, therefore, in its representative role because of the inherent limitations upon the number of supporters a party can have.

The Size of Coalitions

If one party's leaders were able to include everyone in their coalition, there would be no parties. As strenuously as the two major parties have fought each other, each has had a vested interest in the other's existence. When the Federalist party died early in the nineteenth century, the Jeffersonian-Republican party also began to die. As a coalition becomes unwieldy in size, it begins to disintegrate because of internal divisions and factional secessions.

As William Riker pointed out in his discussion of the "size principle," since the end of the Federalist party, "in *every* instance in which an American party has approached becoming a coalition of the whole, the leaders of the party have in some way decreased its size."[38] The problems a party encounters if its size is too great are illustrated in legislative bodies when one party has an overwhelming numerical advantage. Thomas P. O'Neill, while Speaker of the House of Representatives, made the point clearly: "People with maverick ideas conform to party loyalty when they're needed. If they're not needed they'll slide on you. I learned when

---

[37] James Sterling Young, *The Washington Community 1800–1828* (New York: Columbia University Press, 1966) pp. 108–9.

[38] William H. Riker, *The Theory of Political Coalitions* (New Haven, Ct.: Yale University Press, 1962) pp. 54–66, quotation p. 65; italics in the original.

I was Speaker of the Massachusetts House that it's easier to maintain discipline when the margins are closer.[39]

That a party is more cohesive if its legislative majority is relatively small does not mean that a party seeks to elect fewer members any more than a party abhors a landslide because it makes the party coalition unwieldy. Party leaders are seldom plagued with the problem of having too many supporters. Their problem is to build and maintain a coalition large enough to win. Then, when they govern, they are preoccupied with such questions as: Which interests should be accommodated? Which pressures are irresistible? To whom should the party be responsive at any given time? The range and number of issues competing for attention are usually too vast for equal treatment, and leaders have tried to filter out issues so that they can deal with a limited number of conflicts.[40]

Innovation and the Party System

Coalition politics and the art of governing became joined in the grand strategy of reconciling and accommodating in order to win. This is the characteristic role of party leaders. Taking initiatives risks loss of support. Lord Bryce observed that the "fewer have become their (parties') principles, the more perfect has become their organization. The less of nature the more of art; the less spontaneity the more mechanism." [41]

On occasion, parties have been innovative. They contributed to a sense of legitimacy and integration during the first party system and became the means for mass mobilization and participation during the second party system. They exerted an independent influence in the North during the Civil War in contrast with the South where there were no parties.[42] Most of the time, however, changes in the party system have followed from changes either in the social structure or in constitutional practices rather than being instigated by the parties themselves.[43] That parties have generally been undeveloping institutions has meant that they were stable

[39] Quoted in Vera Glaser, "White House 'Godfather,' " *St. Louis Globe-Democrat*, March 13, 1977, p. 11B.

[40] E. E. Schattachneider, *The Semi-Sovereign People* (New York: Holt, Rinehart and Winston, 1960) pp. 62–68, 82, 109–11.

[41] James Bryce, *The American Commonwealth* (New York: Commonwealth Publishing Company, 1908) I, 3.

[42] Chambers, "Party Development and the American Mainstream," pp. 19–24, 63. Eric L. McKitrick, "Party Politics and the Union and Confederate War Efforts," in *The American Party Sytems*, eds. William Nisbet Chambers and Walter Dean Burnham (New York: Oxford University Press, 1967) pp. 117–51.

[43] Morton Grodzins, "Political Parties and the Crisis of Sucession in the United States: The Case of 1800," in *Political Parties and Political Development*, eds. Joseph LaPalombara and Myron Weiner (Princeton, N.J.: Princeton University Press, 1966) pp. 303, 321, 323, 324.

even when the society was not and this failure to develop has had some beneficial consequences.[44]

Changes in the party system have appeared to come slowly, even imperceptibly, but the process of evolution did not suddenly arrest itself and come to a stop at any one particular point. Certain features of the system, such as party organization, have remained remarkably constant. Popular reactions to the system have certainly not been constant. What seems unchanging is that once the party system was established, there was an "organized struggle for power within the narrow limits of basic agreement." The "battles though exciting, would never be dangerous" because what had been created was "a mechanism designed as nearly as possible to solve the problem of perpetual political motion." [45]

The kind of party system America has had can be summarized in the ways leaders of two major parties have met the problems of governing and representing. In order to understand what the party system has been and what it is becoming, the next two chapters will explore its foundations in party organization and in coalition building.

[44] Theodore J. Lowi, "Party, Policy, and Constitution in America," in *The American Party Systems,* eds., William Nisbet Chambers and Walter Dean Burnham (New York: Oxford University Press, 1967) pp. 274–76.

[45] Nichols, *The Invention of the American Political Parties,* p. 381.

SECTION ONE

THE FOUNDATIONS

A party system is a reflection in many respects of the time and circumstances of its origins. The American party system did not arise in a state of nature where it could make a record on a clean slate. Long before, a locally oriented way of life had been created by people who lived remote from one another over an area of great geographical distances. Their ways of thinking, their hopes, and their fears were translated into governmental institutions.

The Framers of the Constitution did their work against this same cultural and political background which repudiated centralization of power in favor of autonomy in local settings—the grass-roots, as they were to be called. The Framers had no practical alternative but to provide for a federal system of government in which powers were divided or shared between the states and the central government. They went even further and institutionalized the separation of legislative, executive, and judicial branches and reinforced this separation of powers with a scheme of checks and balances. Thus each branch could restrain the others. Within this constitutional structure, the representatives of different interests were forced to accommodate themselves to one another because of interacting pressures of different constituencies which would select the members of the three branches. This carefully constructed mechanism was designed to insure that everyone, majorities as well as minorities, would be checked.[1]

Structure reveals intention, but structure cannot insure success in transferring intention into practice. The Framers' efforts succeeded because separation of powers and checks and balances proved to be an accurate reflection of American preferences. For example, when the capital was established in Washington, D.C., government officials

---

[1] James Madison, *The Federalist*, Numbers 10 and 51 (New York: The Modern Library, Random House, n.d.). James MacGregor Burns, *The Deadlock of Democracy* (Englewood Cliffs, N.J.: Prentice-Hall, Inc., 1963) pp. 18–23. Madison's concept for controlling power should not be interpreted as a desire to discourage popular control of government. See George W. Carey, "Separation of Powers and the Madisonian Model: A Reply to the Critics," *The American Political Science Review*, 72 (March 1978) 151–64.

chose to group themselves, both in their living and working arrangements, as members of the three separate branches. This sense of identification with constitutional roles, rather than with the partisan roles that would bridge the three branches, reflected mistrust of power among the officials themselves and, intentionally or not, reinforced the small constituent parties back home.[2] This *compatibility of structure and attitudes has been continuous.* As soon as "the building of majorities for programmatic goals," has appeared in one of the branches, its power "was almost like clockwork checked by one of the other two." Whenever personal power appeared to be threatening, "almost immediately the Madisonian system reacted like white corpuscles rushing to an open wound."[3]

This was the setting for the party system. These were the forces which guided party leaders as they built party organizations and party coalitions.

[2] James Sterling Young, *The Washington Community 1800–1828* (New York: Columbia University Press, 1966) pp. 78–82.

[3] Charles R. Adrian and Charles Press, *American Politics Reappraised* (New York: McGraw-Hill Book Company, 1974) p. 152.

2

Parties as Organizations

What the United States Constitution provided, as well as what it reflected, marked out the original limits of the "common political arena." Although parties became the instruments for focusing political attention, they had to conform to federal and state constitutional procedures for electing officials. Fragmentation in government became fragmentation in the election process. Separation of powers became separation in the election of executives and legislators. The large number of officials elected at varying periods with overlapping terms of office created a crowded and confused election calendar. The bewildering series of nominations, campaigns, and voting days for one or another group of candidates emphasized local interests even in state and national elections.[1]

American party organization thus became *fragmented* in adjusting to the federal system of government, to the demands for local autonomy, and to competing groups wanting direct representation of their interests. Along the way, each party became divided between its party in the government and its party organization outside of the government. These are the pieces of the large picture of party organization to be examined in the present chapter.

CREATION OF ORGANIZATION

Nineteenth-century parties have been distinguished from twentieth-century parties in the way they came into existence. The former grew out of *legislative groups* and *independent local electoral committees,* but the latter came from a *central authority* which was independent of legislators and

[1] David B. Truman, "Federalism and the Party System," in *Federalism Mature and Emergent*, ed., Arthur Macmahon (New York: Doubleday and Company, Inc., 1955) pp. 130–32. Richard P. McCormick, *The Second American Party System: Party Formation in the Jacksonian Era* (Chapel Hill, N.C.: The University of North Carolina Press, 1966) pp. 344–45.

which itself created local organizations.[2] The significance of this distinction was to affect the whole history of the American party system. Each party's organization grew out of the need to nominate candidates for public office, and the action was taken locally. What was needed was a nominating method that would establish beyond question who the official party candidates were. This would prevent upstarts or malcontents from using the party's name without authorization. The problem came down to who had the authority to speak in the name of the party.

Conventions and Committees

The adoption of representative conventions solved the problem. It was a practice already in use by religious denominations. Although there were rudimentary beginnings during the first party system, it was not until the 1830s that party conventions began being held in counties, districts, and states, wherever public officials were elected. The delegates to the conventions became legitimate party representatives through their election by party members at the grass-roots. Although party conventions were unwieldy, they were especially valuable in whipping up party spirit while giving the appearance of popular participation. They often resembled religious revival meetings and imbued both delegates and rank-and-file party members with the desire to concentrate their energies in electing the "regular" party candidates who were nominated.[3]

Being large, raucous, and of momentary duration, conventions were ill-suited for deliberative purposes. Consequently, the campaign committees, appointed at conventions, eventually became permanent and were authorized to call the next convention. It was the committees which became the seats of *organizational power* because they developed an independent existence of their own. The term "party organization" came to mean this series of committees on the various geographical levels and their leaders, in time, were designated "bosses."

When the nomination function was taken away from conventions, with the adoption of the direct primary in the 1900s, conventions lost much of their importance. They have survived as representative party bodies to adopt resolutions, ratify decisions of party committees, and in some states, to choose national convention delegates, candidates for presidential elector, and the state's members on national committees.

[2] Maurice Duverger, *Political Parties*, 2nd ed. (New York: John Wiley & Sons, Inc., 1959) pp. xxiv-xxxvii.

[3] McCormick, *The Second American Party System*, pp. 95, 347, 349. James Staton Chase, "Jacksonian Democracy and the Rise of the Nominating Convention," *Mid-America*, 45 (October 1963) 230–34. Robert D. Marcus, *Grand Old Party: Political Structure in the Gilded Age 1880–1896* (New York: Oxford University Press, 1971) pp. 260–61.

Division Within Party Organization

At the outset there was no need to make a distinction between the party in government and outside of the government, for each arose from common origins. Many public office holders and candidates for office were committee members and convention delegates. Chairmen and other leaders of the committees were in close association with their party members in government offices. The first real break occurred in making presidential nominations, and it may or may not be significant that the change came during the 1820s, when there were only warring factions of the Jeffersonian-Republican party competing with one another.

During the first quarter of the nineteenth century, the Jeffersonian-Republicans in Congress met together in a *Congressional Caucus* to nominate presidential candidates. The Caucus established the right of national officials to act for the party on a national matter. The Federalists held a Congressional Caucus in 1796 but thereafter relied upon understandings among Federalist leaders. Even Jeffersonian-Republicans never fully accepted the Caucus. Some of them questioned the propriety of their designating who should become president and refused to attend caucuses. The Caucus was contrary to the spirit of the Constitution, or at least of the intention of the Framers, who had concluded that the selection of presidents by Congress would violate separation of powers. It was really a subterfuge to note that the Caucus acted in a party capacity, not in an official congressional capacity. Besides, the point was irrelevant because the real objections to the Caucus were political rather than constitutional.

By 1824, many leaders of the fragmented party sought the presidency, but the Caucus could nominate only one candidate, William Crawford. The other candidates, Andrew Jackson, Henry Clay, and John Quincy Adams, had their names put forward by their state legislatures, by popular mass meetings, or simply by their supporters in a state running a slate of presidential electors. The Caucus was doomed when it was frontally assaulted with the argument that the people should have something to say about who would be President instead of centralizing the decision in the far-off national capital.

Something of the same process had occurred in those states where a party's legislative caucus nominated candidates for governor. The legislative caucus had gradually evolved into the state convention. The national convention, on the contrary, appeared all at once in the early 1830s and completed the chain of the convention system, (Table 2.1). Although members of Congress could be elected delegates to national conventions, by the 1840s state and local leaders had become dominant in presidential nominations.

The significance of these developments was that committees and conventions assumed control of nominations and insured the separation in

TABLE 2.1　Methods of Nomination and the Evolution of Political Party Organization.

	Local	State	National
		Government Levels	
Preparty	Caucus or Self-announcement	None	None
Transition	Mass Meetings	Legislative Caucus	Private understandings among leaders
Party	County Conventions and County Committees	State Conventions and State Committees	Congressional Caucus; succeeded, finally, by National Conventions and National Committees

each party between those in government and those outside. The results of this separation had momentous results for the parties and for American government.

PARTY ORGANIZATION IN THE GOVERNMENT

It could be expected that government officials of the same party would develop a close association among themselves for party purposes as well as maintain a close link to their party organization. This expectation fails to take account of the immense variety of patterns. The federal government is different from the states, and no two states are exactly the same. The most important fact that affects party in the government is separation of powers, so we begin with party organization in legislatures and then their relationships with executives.

The Party in Congress

There is simplicity in the federal legislative structure, compared with the states, for there is only one Congress to describe. As in state legislatures, however, congressional party organization is purely for internal purposes.

It is unrelated to the party committee structure outside of the government and is separate from the executive branch.

Each party in each house meets in *caucus* to conduct party business, and at the beginning of a new Congress every two years, it chooses the *party's floor leader, assistant leader (whip), a policy committee,* and approves assignments of its members to the *standing committees.* The majority party caucus approves the chairmen and decides the party ratio of members on each standing committee. These decisions are normally routine or the result of private negotiations although the potential of party power does exist.

In the 1970s, the House Democratic Caucus asserted this power. It expressed dissatisfaction with some committee chairmen by removing them and selecting their successors. It also voted itself the authority to approve or disapprove the appointment of any subcommittee chairmen who had either been censured by the House or convicted of a felony in a court of law.

Congress is a study in contradictions. Although candidates run under party names, they do not vote as party members when they are elected. Parties do not have real meaning in terms of what generally happens in Congress, and voters do not expect a distinctive set of policies to result from one party as opposed to the other.[4] Simultaneously, Congress is a cockpit of opposing parties and an institution which transcends parties. The members reveal an "extraordinary looseness in party performance and at the same time the passionate attachment to party labels."[5] Party disloyalty outside of Congress is usually ignored, for example, on the infrequent occasions when members have failed to support their party's presidential candidate. However, when two Democrats in the House supported Republican Barry Goldwater for President in 1964, they were stripped of their seniority.

Discipline. Members have made congressional life as agreeable and as comfortable as possible by developing devices for their own protection. Perhaps the best example is the custom of *seniority.* Longevity in office entitles members to better committee assignments, allows them to move up in committee rankings, and insures them preferences in such matters as office assignments. Longer tenure also gives members more opportunities to ingratiate themselves with voters through services to constituents.

The more important members become in Congress, the more powerful they can become in their own state or district. If they are popular with the voters, their party organization at home has neither the incentive nor the courage to oppose them. The party in Congress does not threaten

[4] Donald Stokes and Warren Miller, "Party Government and the Saliency of Congress," *Public Opinion Quarterly,* 26 (Winter 1962) 531–46.

[5] Clarence A. Berdahl, "Some Notes on Party Membership in Congress," *The American Political Science Review,* 43 (1949) 732.

their reelection and the worst the senatorial or congressional campaign committees can do is refuse to contribute money to an incumbent's campaign. Franklin Roosevelt showed, by his failure in 1938 to purge individual Democrats he considered disloyal to his program, that even a President cannot rely upon his personal popularity to discipline his own party.[6]

Discipline by either house of Congress, as distinct from party discipline, is unusual but can be effectively used if the justification is so clear that the leaders have a will to act. Senator Joseph McCarthy was censured in 1954 because he had antagonized his colleagues by violating the Senate's norms of decorum and civility. Rarely have the institutional mores been enforced as vigorously as they were in 1970, when the House stripped Adam Clayton Powell of his seniority and committee chairmanship, and subjected him to deductions from his salary to make up misspent funds.

Instances of illegal or unethical conduct by members have generally been handled by waiting for the member to retire, resign, or be defeated for reelection. Now, however, growing public awareness and intolerance of misconduct are making it more difficult to evade issues of congressional ethics. Between 1976 and 1978, the House reprimanded one member for financial misconduct and three other members in connection with the South Korean influence-buying investigation.

Party Voting in Congress. Members are expected to vote with their own party on whatever is considered a *party* matter such as election of the *Speaker of the House* and *standing-committee assignments*. When it comes to voting on bills, however, the situation is different, and the party machinery operates on a basis of persuasion and influence. The whip and his assistants keep in touch with individual members to carry messages from the leaders and to report back the members' sentiments and what the vote count is likely to be.

The extent of party voting, overall, is limited by the relatively large number of noncontroversial votes where a majority in both parties agree. Otherwise, party voting is measured by the percentage of Republicans versus the percentage of Democrats on recorded roll calls. The percentages selected depend upon how rigorous a standard one wishes to set. The minimum standard of 51 percent of Republicans opposed to 51 percent of Democrats, used by *Congressional Quarterly* to develop its party unity score, results in a total score for each house that is usually under 50 percent of the total roll calls.[7] Generalizing for congressional voting as a whole, it appears that:

1. The unity in each party in either house varies from one Congress to another just as the overall score in one house may be higher or lower than in the other.

[6] Charles M. Price and Joseph Boskin, "The Roosevelt 'Purge': A Reappraisal," *The Journal of Politics*, 28 (August 1966) 660–70.

[7] See annual volumes of *Congressional Quarterly Almanac*.

2. The majority party, particularly with its own President, tends to be more unified because of the focus of the President's program.

3. The minority party tends to fragment because of the difficulty of developing a program, and is therefore likely to react as individuals to the proposals of the majority.

4. Party voting depends to a great extent upon the issues; the most consistent difference between Democrats and Republicans appears on the role of the government in the economic and social life of the country.

5. There is always an opposition vote but those making up the opposition vary from issue to issue; there is no institutionalized minority or opposition.

6. A great deal of voting is a response by issue-oriented factions or blocs which seem to thrive precisely because the parties are not ideologically distinct. An ideological faction may be bipartisan, as the Conservative Coalition, or made up of just one party, as the Democratic Study Group which formed its own suborganization within the party.[8]

7. The factional nature of the two major parties has led to a separation between southern and northern Democrats and eastern and midwestern Republicans, although the extent of the bipartisan alliance of these factions varies over time.

8. Despite the appearance of accidental combinations of groups and individuals, there is an order or rationale in the voting records even though it is not always possible to be sure of the source of cohesion, whether it be party, constituents, lobbyists, colleagues, the White House, or the members' own staff. Therefore, it is easy to overemphasize both cohesiveness and lack of cohesiveness.[9]

The Party in State Legislatures

Generally speaking, members of state legislatures operate under greater restrictions than members of Congress. There is relatively greater turnover in the states so seniority becomes more important. Legislative leaders generally have considerable freedom to set the agenda, manage floor procedures, appoint committee chairmen, reward dependable colleagues with committee assignments, dispense patronage, and grant personal favors.

[8] Kenneth Kofmehl, "The Institutionalization of a Voting Bloc," *The Western Political Quarterly*, 17 (June 1964) 256–72.

[9] See, in general: David B. Truman, *The Congressional Party: A Case Study* (New York: John Wiley & Sons, Inc., 1959) pp. 93, 192. W. Wayne Shannon, *Party, Constituency and Congressional Voting* (Baton Rouge, La.: Louisiana State University Press, 1968) pp. 172–79. Aage R. Clausen, "State Party Influence on Congressional Policy Decision," *Midwest Journal of Political Science*, 16 (February 1972) 77–101. Gerald Marwell, "Party, Region and the Dimensions of Conflict in the House of Representatives, 1949–1954," *The American Political Science Review*, 61 (June 1967) 380–99. Charles O. Jones, "The Minority Party and Policy-Making in the House of Representatives," *The American Political Science Review*, 62 (June 1968) 481–93. William H. Riker and Donald Niemi, "The Stability of Coalitions on Roll Calls in the House of Representatives," *The American Political Science Review*, 56 (March 1962) 58–65. Raymond E. Wolfinger and Joan Heifetz, "Safe Seats, Seniority, and Power in Congress," *The American Political Science Review*, 59 (June 1965) 337–49. John W. Kingdon, "Models of Legislative Voting," *The Journal of Politics* 39 (August 1977) 592.

Most state legislators pursue a career outside of the legislature and are more dependent upon their leaders for help in passing bills or in servicing constituents. The element of time is usually more crucial, especially in states where the length of sessions is limited and members must work against a deadline.

The fact that state legislators are more dependent than members of Congress does not necessarily mean that legislative party organization is strong in the states. It is the role of parties rather than the role of legislative leaders which distinguishes one state legislature from another. Legislative divisions in one-party states tend to be ad hoc factions. In some two-party states, the legislature is under highly centralized party control.

Legislative party discipline, it seems, should be greater in urban, industrial states, where the parties represent different social and economic groups. If each party is a coalition of people of similar interests, each party's legislators will already be motivated to follow the leaders and vote together on public-policy questions. This is the situation in Pennsylvania, where the parties are competitive, have a clearly discernible difference in their socioeconomic-status base, and are strong in the legislature. In both California and Washington, however, the parties are competitive but are not representative of different social classes. In Washington the parties are organized, but party voting is limited while in California, the legislators resist party control.[10]

Traditional attitudes reflecting different political state cultures have an effect upon the role of party even when the parties are competitive. In New York and Connecticut, party discipline is accepted and expected. The relationship between the party in the legislature and the party organization outside is so close that a disloyal legislator can incur the wrath of both groups of leaders. The individual legislator is likely to need party support to be elected and unlike a member of Congress, cannot expect to win votes by attacking the legislature as an institution.

In other states, where the attitude toward parties is less receptive, party authority must be exercised with greater care because the show of party discipline may be resented as an intrusion upon the legitimate independence and integrity of the legislators.

Separation of Powers

The *federal* and *state governments* differ in the degree to which they adhere to *separation of powers*. Governors often have a voice in the selection

---

[10] Thomas R. Dye, "State Legislative Politics," in *Politics in the American States: A Comparative Analysis*, 2nd ed., eds., Herbert Jacob and Kenneth N. Vines (Boston: Little, Brown and Company, 1971) pp. 193–206. Hugh L. LeBlanc, "Voting in State Senates: Party and Constituency Influences," *Midwest Journal of Political Science*, 13 (February 1969) 33–57.

of presiding officers, floor leaders, and standing-committee chairmen. The President is not expected to become involved in these internal legislative decisions. When Franklin Roosevelt openly took sides in a fight among Senate Democrats over a new floor leader, his candidate was elected but at the expense of much ill will within his party.

Whatever the extent of party government in state legislatures, the governor is likely to exert a direct influence. In one-party states the dominant party usually organizes and controls the legislature through the faction allied with the governor. Governors, in turn, use their powers of office to bargain with individual legislators who want support for their bills, patronage for supporters, and state money spent in their districts. Governors in two-party states have the same kinds of powers but are more likely to work through the legislative leaders of their own party. Further, when parties are competitive, the governor is the party leader in the state, and the governor's program and views are well reported by the media. A legislator who opposes his own party's governor incurs the enmity of both the governor and the party leaders.

In the *federal* government, separation of powers prevents unification of the government itself and likewise overshadows political parties. The party winning a presidential election is not really incorporated into the organization of the executive branch, and the party in Congress remains distinct. The President maintains *liaison* with Congress through subordinates and lobbies in the same manner as interest groups do. He consults with congressional party leaders on his appointments, his strategies, and his substantive programs, but consultation is not exclusively a party matter. Leaders of both congressional parties attend many of the conferences, for the recognition of status cannot be subordinated to party affiliation. Presidents have often been dependent upon votes of the opposition party and have made special overtures to its leaders, as Carter won the support of Howard Baker, Senate Republican leader, for the Panama Canal Treaty in 1978.

There was a sharp swing of the pendulum in *presidential-congressional* relations during the 1970s. After years of being accused of acting like a "rubber-stamp" in deferring to presidential proposals and initiatives, Congress became assertive in combatting the "Imperial Presidency." As an aftermath of the Vietnam war, in particular, and a generally negative reaction to the Presidency after Watergate, Congress restricted the President's freedom of action and constitutional prerogatives in making foreign policy. Congress also became less agreeable to presidential proposals on domestic policies.

One means increasingly being used to maintain controls over the President and the bureaucracy is the use of the congressional "veto power," whereby specific decisions cannot go into effect unless approved by Congress or unless neither house disapproves within a given period of time.

Even Jimmy Carter began protesting against what he considered infringements upon presidential powers by his own Democratic majority in Congress.

This resurgence of *legislative power* has not been accompanied by greater congressional unity. At one and the same time, there has been a reaction within Congress against both presidential and congressional leadership and a weakening of respect for congressional traditions. A large part of this change is due to a new generation of members. At the beginning of the new Congress in 1979, more than one-half of the senators had served no more than six years and about one-half of House members had been elected since 1974. Seniority is no longer a means for keeping freshmen members in line or insuring the powers of committee chairmen. Members not only are more independent as individuals but are also organizing into caucuses for specific groups and constituent interests, such as the Black Caucus, Hispanic Caucus, Suburban Caucus, Steel Caucus, Congresswomen's Caucus, and so on.

If these trends toward ever greater fragmentation continue, the constitutional role of Congress, which has long overshadowed the partisan role, will itself be undermined and will further accentuate separation of powers. With the weakening of congressional party organization and discipline, political parties will cease to be a bridge between the Capitol and the White House. Special-interest voting may eventually lead to a Congress of purely *temporary factions* as described by James Madison in *The Federalist*.

Separation of powers in the federal government has not only divided the parties between the two branches but has also led to a different relationship of the President and Congress with their party organizations outside of the government.

The President and Party Organization

Making presidential nominations in national conventions brought presidential candidates under the control of the party committees in the states and made candidates largely independent of their party in Congress. In effect, there grew up a presidential and congressional faction within both parties. Now, the *presidential primary* has had the effect of separating presidential nominees from their party organization in the states.

Individual members of Congress may be important factors within their own state delegations at a national convention, but the party in Congress has no influence as such. Members pay public tribute to their presidential nominee without having any real responsibility for his nomination and sometimes little enthusiasm for him. They are directly concerned only if the presidential nominee can have an effect on their own reelection. They are more likely to see the nominee, not so much as the titular head of their party, but as someone to deal with if he is elected.

Once a presidential candidate is nominated, he becomes the official leader of his party and exercises the prerogative of designating the *chairman of his party's national committee*. The party organization outside of the government comes into the orbit of its presidential nominee during the campaign and remains there if he is elected. The national party chairman becomes a defender and a spokesman for the President; for example, in 1978, John C. White, Chairman of the Democratic National Committee, publicly warned Democratic members of Congress to stop attacking Carter if they expected political considerations from the White House.

Presidential control over the national committee was established in the nineteenth century and led House Republicans to create their own congressional campaign committee in 1866, when they broke with President Andrew Johnson. Later, the House Democrats followed suit with a Democratic congressional campaign committee. When senators began being directly elected, each party in the Senate created its own senatorial campaign committee.

The result is that each party has three committees on the national level, each with a different clientele and without formal liaison or coordination. The congressional and senatorial committees raise money for the campaigns of individual candidates in their party. They provide research services such as information on the voting records of the other party's candidates. In addition, they give aid in organizing campaigns and in the uses of publicity. Each national committee transfers some money to its congressional and senatorial committees and there are various informal efforts at cooperation.

For well over a century, national conventions preferred presidential nominees with a background in state and local politics. The Congressional Caucus, in contrast, had previously instituted a sort of apprentice system by choosing nominees with experience in the federal government. From 1840 to 1976, not counting incumbent presidents and military heroes who were nominated, presidential candidates have been evenly divided: Eighteen had national political experience, and eighteen had been principally or exclusively active in state politics. Since World War II, presidential primaries, and the new opportunities for media exposure have favored nationally known candidates with the result that members of Congress and vice presidents have become serious contenders. Since 1960, five candidates, excluding incumbents, have had a national political background, and only one, Carter, had a state background.

Congress and Party Organization

Members of Congress at one time were dependent upon their party organizations back home, particularly senators when they were elected by state legislatures. Now senators have their personal organizations and may have only a weak link to their party's state committee, which is normally most involved in gubernatorial elections. Before the adoption of the direct primary, each party held a convention in each congressional district to nominate candidates for the House of Representatives. This organization has largely disappeared.

Members of the House are elected from artificial districts that are not part of any governmental structure, except where a district is composed of one or more whole counties. They are not part of the usual party structure, except where convention delegates or members of state committees are chosen from congressional districts. Members of the House became autonomous by being isolated from their party committees. They have reported little communication from state party leaders, and local party leaders have reported less communication with them than with city, county, and state officials. Only in the Northeast was the local party organization found to be in close touch with House members or active in their election campaigns.[11]

The separation of members in each house from their *party organization* and from the *President* logically followed from the desire for independence. If each party had integrated its public officials and its committee structure, the result would have been to bring outsiders into government councils. In addition, if the President had maintained close connection with the party leaders in the states, he would have had additional leverage on his party colleagues in Congress. As it is, members of the President's congressional party are shielded both from the President and from the organization outside of the government. Congressional leaders whose party did not elect its President are at an even greater advantage because they are, in fact, the party's spokesmen on public questions. Why should members of Congress permit their party colleagues who have no official responsibility to tell them how to vote?

Vain attempts have been made to bring representatives of the party organization and the congressional party together in an official body. In 1972, the Democratic floor leaders and one additional Democrat from each house were added to the Democratic national committee, but four Democratic members of Congress on the national committee of approximately 290 members are not likely to have much impact upon either the committee or the congressional party.

The official efforts of the party outside of the government to influence public policy have been confined to the platforms adopted at national conventions, but members of Congress are members, frequently chairmen, of platform committees. It is interesting that members of Con-

---

[11] Charles L. Clapp, *The Congressman: His Work as He Sees It* (Washington, D.C.: The Brookings Institution, 1963) p. 354. Avery Leiserson, "National Party Organization and Congressional Districts," *The Western Political Quarterly*, 16 (September 1963) 637, 639, 643–45.

gress have been far more prominent in convention policy decisions than in making nominations. No matter who writes a platform, neither party can repudiate its members in Congress or its President, the people who make the party's record because they are on the firing line.

Party organization and party in government have been separated in policy-making but have been linked in the distribution of patronage.

Patronage

Appointing friends and supporters to public offices was one of the advantages of winning an election long before there were political parties. *Patronage* was quickly adopted by party leaders and became one of the principal means for developing party spirit. Through the control of appointments, government employment was used to maintain the party.[12] A victorious party became, among other things, an employment agency with a system of applications, referrals, and clearances.

A local public official was supposed to make appointments which were agreeable with his party's local leaders who, in turn, demanded that they be consulted on appointments all the way up to the state capital. Patronage was a powerful reinforcement of local control within the states, but the process did not stop there. Federal appointments were also brought under state and local control. If, to begin with, there had been national parties, as distinct from parties within the states, the constitutional appointive power of presidents could have been used to bolster centralization, but presidents had to accept the fact that the weight of the parties lay at the fringes of the system, not at its center.

It is easy to overlook separation of powers in the awarding of patronage. Nearly all of the attention has been given to appointments within the executive branch. In both the federal and state governments, *legislative patronage* is handled within each legislative body. The Congress now has created a tremendous number of positions, for example, those serving each house as clerks, sergeants-at-arms, and door keepers; the staffs of the Senate and House Office buildings; and the staffs of the standing committees. Even more likely to be overlooked in both federal and state governments is *judicial patronage*. Judges appoint masters and administrators in addition to the regular court personnel—if they are not chosen directly by the voters. In the federal government, the President appoints the judges subject to senatorial concurrence, so this patronage becomes part of the rewards within the province of the President. The

---

[12] See, for example, Carl E. Prince, "Patronage and a Party Machine: New Jersey Democratic-Republican Activists, 1801–1816," *William and Mary Quarterly*, 21 (October 1964) 571–78.

prominence of patronage within the executive branch has placed the President at the nerve center of the party organization and made him a direct participant in patronage controversies.

In the awarding of *executive patronage*, Congress is in a position both to be pressured and to exert pressure. Local influence can more easily be applied to members of Congress because of their grass-roots contacts. To make sure it could exert pressure, Congress has required senatorial approval of presidential nominations, and senators insured their coordinate status with the President through the device of "senatorial courtesy". If a senator objected to a presidential nominee who would serve in the senator's state, the Senate could extend to the senator the courtesy of refusing to approve the nominee. Consequently, a senator expects to be consulted on patronage in his own state when the senator and the President are of the same party.

Although the House has no official part in the appointive process, members of the President's party expect consideration on patronage in their own districts, if necessary, through the support of the senators from their state. Members of both houses can join together on their own initiative or under pressure from back home to insure appropriate appointments to positions within their states such as federal district judges and United States district attorneys. Restrictions on the President do not end there, however. Appointments to cabinet posts, the military and diplomatic services, and the hosts of other federal positions here and abroad, also involve senatorial influence because of the requirements for senatorial confirmation.

It is not surprising that government executives, responsible for administrative performance, became more concerned with their long-run record in office than with the short-run appeasement of their parties. Even President U.S. Grant, who was closely associated with "spoilsmen" in the Republican party, condemned patronage as "the bane of the Presidential office" and asserted that the President "is necessarily a civil service reformer because he wants peace of mind." [13] Presidential independence from party patronage in the federal government has become well established in the twentieth century. In the administrations from Truman to Kennedy, political considerations were found to be less important than an appointee's experience and qualifications, except in those positions considered less consequential. [14]

Perhaps no feature of the party system has attracted more attention than patronage. The difficulty in assessing its value from the party point

---

[13] Quoted in Leonard D. White, *The Republican Era, 1869–1901* (New York: The Macmillan Company, 1958) p. 286.

[14] Dean E. Mann, "The Selection of Federal Political Executives," *The American Political Science Review*, 58 (March 1964) 81–99.

of view is being sure how much we actually know about its effects. Most investigations have been limited in scope, and the authors are wary of generalizing beyond their specific data.[15]

A serious question can be raised about the effectiveness of patronage in enforcing party discipline. Investigations of the party system in the nineteenth century, when patronage was at its height, make it appear that patronage certainly did not have a centralizing tendency, but was part and parcel of party decentralization. At best, patronage appeased the various party factions. At worst, the squabbling over patronage created more dissension than any other single party activity. Between the best and the worst, it is at least fair to say that patronage can create more problems than it solves.

Those who want appointments jealously compete with one another and often are dissatisfied with the positions they receive.[16] An adage extracted from the wisdom of patronage-givers is that to make an appointment is to create one ingrate and nine enemies. In many cases, patronage no doubt helped to strengthen the position of leaders, but to what extent and how often we cannot say for sure. Judging from twentieth-century experience of presidents and governors, patronage has not always been effective in helping them to secure control over their parties.[17]

Actually, it is a mistake to assume that the only purpose of patronage was to unify a party, when unity itself has not been a primary purpose of parties. This misconception may have helped to increase the unpopularity of patronage, making it appear to be haphazard if not irrational. Patronage can benefit the party as a trade-off for money and support during a campaign. It may give continuity to day-by-day activities of the organization without necessarily increasing unity. In countless cases, patronage does not serve a *party* purpose.

A county chairman can demonstrate that he is the leader if all appointments have to be cleared through him. This aggrandizement of a leader may tend to discipline a party in a particular county; but the leader is likely to be more self-motivated than party-motivated, for the giver of patronage is rewarded as much or more than the recipient. Patronage may satisfy local expectations which have no particular relationship to building party strength. Finally, after a party has come into office, its leaders have

---

[15] For example, Daryl R. Fair, "Party Strength and Political Patronage," *Southwestern Social Science Quarterly*, 45 (December 1964) 264–71.

[16] Frank J. Sorauf, "Patronage and Party," *Midwest Journal of Political Science*, 3 (May 1959) 115–26.

[17] For example, the experiences recounted in Harlan Hahn, "President Taft and the Discipline of Patronage," *The Journal of Politics*, 28 (May 1966) 368–90. Cornelius R. Cotter and Bernard C. Hennessy, *Politics Without Power: The National Party Committees* (New York: Atherton Press, 1964) pp. 138–48. Daniel Patrick Moynihan and James Q. Wilson, "Patronage in New York State, 1955–1959," *The American Political Science Review*, 58 (June 1964) 286–301.

sometimes decided to be compassionate and not remove all of the other party's appointees.[18]

To recognize that patronage can serve various purposes is not likely to make it more popular with the public but does make for a better understanding of the motives and interrelationships within party organizations. Patronage has been one of the constant sources for the pulling and hauling among members of the committees on the various geographical levels, but this source of party disunity may ultimately be removed by the Supreme Court. It has already said that political removals violate freedom of speech and may yet decide that hiring solely on political grounds violates the Constitution.

There are, of course, other sources of disunity to be seen as we turn our attention to the members of committees which make up the party organization outside of the government.

THE PARTY COMMITTEES

The structure of American political parties is familiar—even if not well understood. Because organizational charts are usually shown as a hierarchy of levels of authority and responsibility, party organization is visualized as a pyramid (Figure 2.1).

It is true that party organization reaches from one national committee down through fifty state committees, to county committees, to

FIGURE 2.1   Major Party Organization by Geographical Levels.

[18] W. Robert Gump, "The Functions of Patronage in American Party Politics: An Empirical Reappraisal," *Midwest Journal of Political Science*, 15 (February 1971) 87–107. Joseph P. Tucker, "The Administration of a State Patronage System: The Democratic Party in Illinois," *The Western Political Quarterly*, 22 (March 1969) 79–84.

precinct leaders or committees. There is probably not a committee for one or both parties in every county and in many precincts, no organization at all. To think of this structure as a pyramid is misleading if it is interpreted as creating a real hierarchy. On the contrary, each level from the county up, is a self-contained unit for some decision-making. Committee members want collegial relationships, not those of superior and subordinate. The internal, horizontal, or vertical connections of the committees are not adaptable to an organizational chart.

There is a constant interchange among members and a considerable amount of formal intraparty organization. In some states, county chairmen have an association, and there are regional associations of state committee members. State chairmen of both parties have a national association and regional organizations. County chairmen may be ex-officio members of state committees. All Republican state chairmen are members of the Republican national committee. The man and woman holding the highest Democratic state committee positions are ex-officio members of the Democratic national committee.[19]

Cadre Parties

Parties which arose in the nineteenth century were likely to be cadre parties as distinct from the mass parties of the twentieth century.[20]

Except for some minor parties, *mass party organization* is unfamiliar in the United States. Mass parties are found throughout Western Europe where they are generally based on a membership held together by ideological ties of social class and occupation or religious affiliation. They are mainly supported by members' dues and do not rely upon specialists to raise campaign money or to organize voters. Instead, they maintain cohesiveness through political education and indoctrination of their members as well as through social and recreational activities.

American major parties are classic examples of *cadre parties*. There are no formal requirements for joining them. Anyone who claims to be a member of one of the parties is a member. Both parties are loosely-knit and are led by a relatively few people. They achieve their status by virtue of their prestige, skill, or fortunes and know how to organize campaigns, handle voters, and raise money. Cadres seem to have been indigenous in American politics. Even in early nineteenth-century New

---

[19] For general discussions of national and state party committees, see Cotter and Hennessy, *Politics Without Power*. Robert J. Huckshorn, *Party Leadership in the States* (Amherst, Mass.: University of Massachusetts Press, 1976).

[20] Duverger, *Political Parties*, pp. 61–67. William Nisbet Chambers, *Political Parties in a New Nation: The American Experience, 1776–1809* (New York: Oxford University Press, 1963) pp. 51, 106–7, 125–26, 163–65.

York, when there were factions rather than parties, specialists appeared possessing "status, know-how, and money." [21]

It is easier to describe *what a cadre party* is than to identify *who are the cadre* in the United States. Properly speaking, the cadre does not include everyone among the thousands of people who are the members of party committees. At least, at the county and precinct levels, many of these people are not specialists, and some of them actually do little or no party work. Every member of a party committee is not equal to every other member in activity and influence because of the wide variety in their motivations and role perceptions. A large proportion of committee members on the local level accept membership because of entreaty or pressures. Even those who are active do not necessarily see their job as getting out the vote on election day or doing year-round party work. Some are more concerned with promoting welfare or discussing issues. Some committee chairmen do not accept responsibility for candidate recruitment, money raising, or organizing campaigns.[22]

The specialists of cadre parties include those committee members who have a personal stake in and responsibility for management—often no more than the chairmen and members of executive committees. Specialists also include public officeholders, candidates for public office, and fund-raisers. Many of these are not members of any party committees but may be powerful through their influence upon the committees or upon candidates. It is not always possible to know exactly who are the cadre in either party on any level at any one time. When the discussion is confined to the members of the committees, as it is here, it is more useful to speak of the leaders as distinguished from the rank-and-file, granting a substantial difference in the activity and influence even among leaders.

Inclusive and Exclusive

Leaders of party committees are *inclusive* in seeking public support for their party in winning elections but *exclusive* in maintaining their power to run party affairs. These two motives can come into conflict because of the factional nature of each party.

If the existing leaders of a party committee are beaten by a rival faction in the nomination of the party's candidates for public office and if these candidates subsequently win the general election, the rival faction may elect its own favorites to the committee leadership positions. If a

[21] Alvin Kass, *Politics in New York State, 1800–1830* (Syracuse, N.Y.: Syracuse University Press, 1965) p. 26.

[22] There is now a tremendous amount of literature on this subject. A good general source is Hugh A. Bone, *Political Party Management* (Morristown, N.J.: General Learning Press, 1973). Also Huckshorn, *Party Leadership in the States*, pp. 14–18, 23–32, 100–7.

party's committee members are convinced they would lose their positions or power by their own party's election victory, they may prefer to lose the election to the other party, an exhibition of what has been called "parasitic professionalism." [23]

Carrying intraparty competition to this extent is a serious modification of the definition of a party as existing for the purpose of winning elections but, by definition, *a party* is also a *permanent organization*. The party committee structure creates motives of its own, separate from the original purposes of the organization itself. When a party is too weak to win elections, the motive of exclusiveness may become the only incentive for maintaining the organization. The motivation for the existence of Republican committees in the states of the Democratic Solid South was the opportunity committee members had to receive federal appointments from a Republican President. These Republicans really had nothing else to do except fight to hold their power on the committees. Parasitic professionalism can easily be overemphasized, and it should not be blamed for the lack of party competition in general.[24]

The theme of the party system has been inclusiveness as both candidates and leaders of party committees reached out for voter support. Thomas Jefferson was an early exponent of inclusiveness when he remarked in his first inaugural address, "We have called by different names brethren of the same principle. We are all Republicans, we are all Federalists." Of course, Jefferson did not open his party to the Federalists so they could take over Republican committee positions.

Effectiveness of Party Organizations

One of the most publicized and presumably, widely accepted myths is that party organizations have been extremely efficient and that their leaders have possessed ingenious and shrewd political minds. The mystery is how leaders, who may be frustrated by the inherent limitations on their authority and their own expendability, are able to spend so much time devising clever strategies. Another mystery is how the hesitant and halting party organizations described in some empirical studies can become such smoothly operating machines during an election campaign.

Chairmen, vice-chairmen, and other influential committee members are themselves a varied group. Some are able, some mediocre, and all of them are enmeshed in day-to-day problems. The most skillful among them may excel in the so-called "nuts and bolts" operations of the organization, or in raising money, or in projecting an image of a happy party. Whatever

[23] John D. May, *Sources of Competitive Disequilibrium between Competing Political Parties* (Morristown, N.J.: General Learning Press, 1973) pp. 8–10.

[24] As in Walter Karp, *Indispensable Enemies* (Baltimore, Md.: Penguin Books, Inc., 1973) pp. 11–20.

their particular abilities, they find their potential effectiveness limited because they must spend so much time keeping internal peace and getting their colleagues to pull together. The loss of an election leads to recriminations and finger-pointing in deciding who was to blame. Victory leads to self-congratulations and insistence upon sharing the rewards.

Just as patronage did not always conform to expectations, party officials can be criticized for ineffectiveness because they are not doing what it is assumed they should be doing. *Party organization* may be misleading because of what it is and what it is not. It can vary in the intensity of feelings from a hotbed of human activity to supine inertia. It can be tightly self-centered or a tenuous relationship among men and women answering to the same party name. A party committee on any geographical level exists because there is enough equilibrium to maintain identity and to support some objectives. The structure is not bound together by hoops of steel but preserved by invisible cords of social relationships, mutual interests, and habitual reactions. Just as there are variations in party involvement, there are also differences in attitudes toward the institutional commitment. Party organizations, although permanent, are more akin to voluntary associations which "are not rationally organized in terms of the relationship between structure and function." [25]

Political organization, at least in the twentieth century, has been much too important to leave to the party committees and the resulting organizational free-for-all has clearly limited the effectiveness of the committees. The American genius for adding organization upon organization seems to have reached its highest expression in the competition to supplement, influence, or circumvent party organizations. It is not entirely the committee structure within the parties themselves that fragments the political structure, but the proliferation of these other groups as well.

There are the auxiliary or extraparty units such as *ward clubs* formed by the regular organization to appeal to special clienteles. On the national level, the National Federation of Republican Women, the College Republican National Committee, and the Young Democratic Clubs are housed in their respective national committees' headquarters in Washington, D.C. Auxiliary organizations are normally supportive of the regular party although the Young Republicans and Young Democrats have occasionally been at odds with their respective national committees.

There is a lengthy list of organizations formed independently of the committees, usually for the purpose of injecting some ideological point of view into a party or sponsoring particular candidates. Many of these groups are small and basically ineffective although they all aspire to be taken seriously. There are a dozen or more of them attempting to direct

---

[25] Allan Kornberg, Joel Smith, Mary-Jane Clarke, "Participation in Local Party Organizations in the United States and Canada," *American Journal of Political Science*, 17 (February 1973) 47.

the Republican party in opposite ideological directions, for example, the Ripon Society and the United Republicans of America. Americans for Democratic Action has proved to be an enduring attempt to hold liberals together within the Democratic party.

The competing formations in California, the Republican Assembly begun in 1934, and the Democratic Council organized in 1953, were unusual. Both were ideologically oriented and had the advantage of operating outside of the laws applying to the official party committees. The Assembly and the Council were forums for discussion of issues and centers for social activities in the suburbs. They endorsed candidates in local and state primaries, carried on their own campaigns, and raised their own money. They declined because of loss of membership and their failure to nominate some of the candidates they endorsed. It is a matter of interpretation, to some extent, whether they simply outlived their usefulness or were finally unable to compete successfully with the regular party organizations.[26]

Finally, the multitude of political interests and pressures long ago led candidates to create ad hoc campaign organizations, with a nonpartisan aura, to appeal for votes outside of their parties.

A Changing Organization?

The decentralized and pragmatic characteristics of American political parties are not unalterable just because they are traditional. It has largely gone unnoticed that both Republican and Democratic state committees throughout the country have gradually been centralized and bureaucratized. Nearly one-third of state chairmen are paid a salary while half of these receive a full-time salary and consider their party position as their occupation. Two-thirds of the chairmen employ a full-time executive director and, in some states, there is a full-time staff serving the committee.[27] This trend in organization can change the character of the committee system by giving a continuity to its leadership and its general operations. Other trends portend a different kind of change.

Following World War II a new breed of committee members appeared who became identified as "amateurs" because their incentive was to emphasize *issues*, as distinguished from the "professionals" who were inclined to subordinate issues in the interest of *party harmony*. The names "amateur" and "professional," whether in suburban, city, or rural committees, do not refer to differences in individual effectiveness or skill, but

---

[26] John R. Owens, Edmund Costantini, and Louis F. Weschler, *California Politics and Parties* (London: The Macmillan Company, Collier-Macmillan Limited, 1970) pp. 201–18.

[27] Huckshorn, *Party Leadership in the States*, pp. 34–36, 54–57. Charles E. Schutz, "Bureaucratic Party Organization Through Professional Political Staffing," *Midwest Journal of Political Science*, 8 (May 1964) 127–42.

to different incentives for doing party work. Even this distinction was found in some investigations to be clearer when people first entered the organizations. The institutional influence, in time, made it more difficult to identify pure types.[28] The insurgency which arose within the Democratic party in the late 1960s carried the role of amateurs to a new peak of intensity. These insurgents really need a new designation and a very descriptive one is "activists-purists."

The Democratic party set out upon a course of sweeping reform after its 1968 national convention was torn by bitter factional confrontations. New rules to satisfy the activists-purists were adopted by the national committee for the 1972 *delegate-selection process* and were enforced upon state party leaders and state delegations at the 1972 convention. This exercise of authority came as a shock to many people, particularly to the professionals, but was subsequently sustained by the Supreme Court. The justices held that a party, through its national convention, can enforce its own regulations even to the extent of nullifying state laws; specifically, delegates elected in a state's presidential primary can be unseated in favor of other delegates acceptable to the national convention.[29] This decision was of considerable significance in clearing the way for party centralization irrespective of ideological orientations.

In 1974, the Democrats held a *Charter Conference*, the first of their regular quadrennial midterm conventions, and adopted the first formal constitution of a major party.[30] Three factions were distinguished among the delegates: the caucus groups (activists-purists) who maintained their separate identity from the party, women and blacks for example; the professionals; and the reformers. Both the caucus groups and the reformers attempted to bind the party to ideological positions. However, the reformers differed from the caucus groups and were akin to the professionals in their demonstration of party loyalty.[31]

---

[28] See, for example, James Q. Wilson, *The Amateur Democrats* (Chicago: University of Chicago Press, 1962). Peter R. Gluck, "Research Note: Incentives and the Maintenance of Political Styles in Different Locales," *The Western Political Quarterly*, 25 (December 1972) 753–60. Dennis S. Ippolito and Lewis Bowman, "Goals and Activities of Party Officials in a Suburban Community," *The Western Political Quarterly*, 22 (September 1969) 572–80. M. Margaret Conway and Frank B. Feigert, "Motivation, Incentive Systems, and the Political Party Organization," *The American Political Science Review*, 62 (December 1968) 1159–73. Dennis S. Ippolito, "Motivational Reorientation and Change among Party Activists," *The Journal of Politics*, 31 (November 1969) 1098–1101.

[29] *Cousins v. Wigota*, 419 U.S. 477 (1975). Austin Ranney, "Changing the Rules of the Nominating Game," in *Choosing the President*, ed., James David Barber (Englewood Cliffs, N.J.: Prentice-Hall, Inc., 1974) pp. 83–84. On the 1972 Democratic convention, seen Denis G. Sullivan, Jeffrey L. Pressman, Benjamin I. Page, and John J. Lyons, *The Politics of Representation: The Democratic Convention 1972* (New York: St. Martin's Press, 1974).

[30] Denis G. Sullivan, Jeffrey L. Pressman, and F. Christopher Arterton, *Explorations in Convention Decision Making: The Democratic Party in the 1970s* (San Francisco: W. H. Freeman and Company, 1976)

[31] *Ibid.*, pp. 58–59.

The appearance of such highly issue-oriented members within the party cadre has the potential for deepening factional divisions in the Democratic party, particularly in attempts to centralize the party on the national level and force the state parties into line. Although the intensity of the intraparty struggle moderated after 1974, the Democrats had begun a process, if continued, of making themselves more nearly a mass party than a cadre party.

Parties as organizations have been complemented by parties as coalitions. This representative function, which completes the foundations of the party system, will be taken up in the next chapter.

3

Parties as Coalitions

Because American political parties have been too heterogeneous to be united on issues, they have usually been most unified when competing with each other for public offices. Pragmatic concerns with winning elections have caused party leaders to reach out for new voting support while trying to hold onto their regular followers. Inevitably, there has been a certain amount of "overlapping" in the two parties' bidding for the votes of the same people. This creates an illusion that the whole body politic is "up for grabs" in every election.

On the contrary, while each party has attempted to win elections by expanding its coalition to include a majority of the voters, it expands by trying to draw in groups closest to the coalition, not those farthest away. The strategies for accomplishing this result have been adapted to the times. In the nineteenth century, each party was trying to mobilize its coalition as fully as possible. In the twentieth century, so many voters are ambivalent about the parties that they have to reach further beyond their coalitions in order to persuade a majority.

The creation of a party called for groups of people who chose to be members, and their choice, once made, was not easily changed. Historically, the opposition only penetrated a party coalition during periods of unusual unrest. There would have been no such party loyalty if leaders had attracted followers at random. Obviously, there was something distinctive about each party's coalition; something different in the parties' orientations, in their understanding of the nation and the world. By the building of such coalitions, the parties became representative.

COALITIONS AS COMMUNITIES OF INTEREST

Party competition both divides people and unites them. Yet, by becoming national and eventually continental, parties were able to transcend their own coalitions while continuing to represent them. James Madison was impressively correct when he foresaw the large republic as exerting a moderating force upon factions. He did not foresee that geographical size would have the same moderating effect upon parties, and that every major party coalition would hold together for all elections, local, state, and national.

Diversities Within Coalitions

What is particularly striking in the American party system is the seeming contradiction of building two coalitions which are at once distinctive from each other and at the same time composed of diverse and even conflicting groups. The contradiction can be explained only by the necessity for winning a majority in a two-party system. A majority is formed when groups join forces with one another for one common purpose. A party transforms these groups into a coalition of one partisan community without threatening the existence of the groups themselves. In a society composed of a heterogeneous population, a party's coalition is neither socially nor ideologically homogeneous, but made up of "diverse elements functionally related to each other for the purpose of winning elections." [1] A coalition pulls together to win elections although many within the coalition have different reasons for winning. A party is a *community of interest* only in the electoral sense, but the force of this community has been surprisingly strong. It becomes progressively easier to maintain a coalition as people have experience in dealing with one another and develop mutual understandings. Camaraderie and a shared sense of interdependence make for an institutional "pull" that can smooth over difficulties and even surmount crises.

Following the realignment of the 1890s, the Democratic party became a coalition of northern urban and rural interests joined with the Solid South. The urban and southern factions became increasingly strange bedfellows, especially with the rise of a new nativism following World War I. The Ku Klux Klan had revived during the War and expanded from its southern base to many northern and western states in an attack upon Catholics and foreigners. At their national convention in 1924, perhaps the most bitter in party history, the pressures from the Democrats' incompatible cultures could no longer be dealt with in the traditional party fashion of give-and-take through private discussions. The northern urban faction, supporting New York Governor, Alfred E. Smith, who was himself a Catholic, clashed violently with the southern faction whose spokesman, William J. Bryan, argued against the party's condemning the Klan in its platform.

Yet, the party did not break up in 1924. Eight years later, with the unifying stimulus of depression, all factions eagerly joined together to reap the benefits of a landslide.

[1] Paul Kleppner, *The Cross of Culture* (New York: The Free Press, 1970) pp. 93–94.

Distinctiveness of Coalitions

Parties have not existed just because factional leaders were amenable to compromise and developed the habit of dealing with one another. Each party also needed a *distant community of political interest* to provide the basis for working together. On some occasions, it may have seemed there was nothing distinctive about the parties beyond a combative urge and the sheer will to win. These motivations were also true of factions and by themselves did not foster permanent organization and a stable coalition. In order to identify what has been distinctive about coalitions, it is necessary to identify the coalitions themselves and on this point there have been disagreements.

One source of the disagreements has been the *incomplete mobilization of coalitions*. No matter how closely a group has been associated with a party, some members of that group have remained outside of the party coalition. Whatever the community of interest, some people who seemingly should have been part of the community, in fact, were not.

Another source of disagreement has been the confusion created by parties appearing, simultaneously, to be polarized and to be all things to all people when they were neither. Actually, political leaders have approached their communities of interest in terms of practical every-day affairs by emphasizing the advantages in voting for one party over the other. They most frequently stressed economic advantages that they characteristically magnified through simplification and distortion in order to make a point. In political discourse, therefore, political leaders often have presented economic issues as struggles between rich and poor, special interests and public interests, one economic group or class, as opposed to another.

Some historians have reinforced the relation of *economics and politics*, but they have generally been more analytical than the political leaders. Exemplified by Frederick Jackson Turner and Charles A. Beard, those historians who have stressed the dependence of politics upon economics have been called the school of "economic determinists." They have given attention to such documentary sources as party literature, private letters, speeches, and writings which often stressed economic party differences. Specific presidential elections have lent themselves to economic analysis where election returns could be related to some predominant economic group or activity in counties or states.

The parties' distinctive economic communities of interest, reinforced by partisan and media reiteration, has apparently become the most widely-accepted interpretation.[2] Making allowance for the incomplete mobiliza-

[2] For a short summary and illustrations, see Joel H. Silbey, *Political Ideology and Voting Behavior in the Age of Jackson* (Englewood Cliffs, N.J.: Prentice-Hall, Inc., 1973) pp. 2–4, 18–46.

tion of coalitions, the rule seemed to be: You most likely vote according to where you are in the distribution of property or wealth. Who you are, politically, can be determined by identifying objectively who you are economically.

A reaction against *economic determinism* began in the 1940s and 1950s, when the social sciences were developing the methodologies which have come to characterize them as behavioral sciences. For want of a better name, those who reject economic determinism can be called the school of "behavioralist historians." They do not deny the importance of economics but in the words of Lee Benson, a pioneer *behavioralist*, economic determinism "is logically fallacious because, in formal terms, it tries to discover the relationships between two variables (economic class and political affiliation) without considering the possible influence of other variables." [3]

The behavioralists realize that most individuals of bygone days cannot be singled out and put under a microscope, but the individual can be examined as a member of identifiable groups. With aggregate data, "one does not even see individual voters through a glass darkly; rather, to shift the metaphor, one creates a screen of information about aggregates and reaches through to individuals by inference." [4] Behavioralists assume that individuals perceived how politics affected them as members of ethnic, religious, occupational, and other kinds of groups. Even though cross pressures would have been exerted upon individuals, their sense of shared values gave meaning to their world of politics, and partisanship became one means of response to that world. By the recognition of multiple influences, it is possible to appreciate the individual voter who has largely been ignored except as a member of a class or a section. [5]

In this conception of party coalitions, an individual votes consistently with his perceptions and beliefs as a member of the community with which he identifies. Politically, the individual subjectively determines who he is.

What the behavioralists require is comprehensive data. They contend that systematic investigation of voting behavior, relating *demographic data* to voting returns over extended periods of time, provides a more reliable guide than either political speeches or opinions expressed in letters, editorials, or other documents by political elites. [6] The smaller the geographical unit investigated, the less likelihood of overlooking crucial factors, for demographic characteristics can be expected to be regularly distributed

[3] Lee Benson, *The Concept of Jacksonian Democracy: New York as a Test Case* (Princeton, N.J.: Princeton University Press, 1961) p. 141.

[4] Ronald P. Formisano, *The Birth of Mass Political Parties: Michigan 1827–1861* (Princeton, N.J.: Princeton University Press, 1971) p. 9.

[5] Richard P. McCormick, "Suffrage Classes and Party Alignments: A Study in Voter Behavior," in *Political Ideology and Voting Behavior in the Age of Jackson*, ed., Joel H. Silbey (Englewood Cliffs, N.J.: Prentice-Hall Inc., 1973) p. 118.

[6] Lee Benson, "Research Problems in American Historiography," *Ibid.*, p. 91.

throughout a small unit. Still, deviant voting (evidence of the incomplete mobilization of a coalition) will occur within even the smallest unit, such as a precinct. These deviations defy explanation because they cannot be explained with existing knowledge.[7]

It should not be forgotten, in dealing with what appears to be deviant voting, that the party system established a two-party tradition in voting. People acquired a party affiliation by family inheritance or otherwise and voted for their party's candidates *because* of their *affiliation*. This influence is real even though it cannot be pinpointed in election returns. It follows that voting party loyalty, which is separate and apart from other group loyalties, may appear to be deviant but in the context of the party system, really is not deviant at all.

If for whatever reason, behavioralists find unexplainable voting, so must economic determinists when they simply scan election figures. If the difference in the totals for each party is small, something must be wrong with the voting or with the economic classes. How can close party votes be interpreted as a class vote unless the classes are about equal in size? As a Whig asked after the election of 1844, "Are there 22,000 *aristocratic* voters in New York (City)? Wonderful country,—wonderful city,—where more than half of the population constitute *aristocracy*!" [8]

The illogical assumption that the rich and the poor naturally vote for different parties was shown in the effect a larger electorate had upon election returns. In New York in the 1820s and in North Carolina in the 1840s. changes in the states' laws increased the number of voters by enfranchising the relatively poor. Comparing the party distribution of the vote before and after, neither party in either state particularly benefited from a larger electorate. The new, poorer voters apparently divided about the same as the more affluent voters divided previously.[9]

Conflicting interpretations prove again that the American party system does not readily lend itself to easy generalizations. In many instances the lack of comprehensive data limits behavioralists. They may be guilty at times of trying to squeeze too much out of the available information, but they appear to have done a superior job of seeking out relevant data and then ordering and analyzing them. The bulk of the data strongly warns us that the coalitions have been a composite of numerous influences which converged into a generalized party difference. Within these limitations, the behavioralists found that, from the 1830s to the 1890s, the parties represented two different ethnocultural communities of interest which

[7] Silbey, *Ibid.*, pp. 180–83.

[8] Quoted Benson, *The Concept of Jacksonian Democracy*, p. 143; italics in the original.

[9] McCormick, "Suffrage Classes and Party Alignments," pp. 117–27. Also Alvin Kass, *Politics in New York State 1800–1830* (Syracuse, N.Y.: Syracuse University Press, 1965) Chapter 6 and pp. 165–69.

were expressions of the ways people thought and reacted to a wide range of public and private affairs.[10]

COALITIONS OF THE NINETEENTH CENTURY

Cultural distinctions in America were inherent in the *diversities* among people who migrated to this part of the New World, and their mobility insured the spread of their influences throughout the continental United States. Settlers carried a mixture of subcultures as they moved relentlessly westward from the seventeenth through the nineteenth centuries, a period which has been called the "rural-land frontier." These migrations "left residues of population in various places to become the equivalent of geological strata." Evidence of the residues of distinctive cultures in politics has continually been detected, even among delegates in eight state constitutional conventions during the 1960s and 1970s.[11]

One prominent cultural difference is *religion*. That people differed in politics as they did in religion may seem a commonplace observation. That politics and religion, therefore, tended to create the same allies should not be surprising. Alexis De Tocqueville made the point that "Every religion is to be found in juxtaposition to a political opinion which is connected with it by affinity." The human being, if permitted, "will regulate the temporal and spiritual institutions of society upon one uniform prin-

[10] The following discussion is based on: Benson, *The Concept of Jacksonian Democracy*. Formisano, *The Birth of Mass Political Parties*. Michael Fitzgibbon Holt, Forging a Majority: *The Formation of the Republican Party in Pittsburgh, 1848–1860* (New Haven, Ct.: Yale University Press, 1969). Thomas B. Alexander, Peggy Duckworth Elmore, Frank M. Lowrey, and Mary Jane Pickens Skinner, "The Basis of Alabama's Antebellum Two-Party System," in *Voters, Parties, and Elections: Quantitative Essays in the History of American Popular Voting Behavior*, eds., Joel H. Silbey and Samuel T. McSeveney (Lexington, Mass.: Xerox College Publishing, 1972) 99–120. Richard J. Jensen, *The Winning of the Midwest: Social and Political Conflict, 1888–96* (Chicago: The University of Chicago Press, 1971) pp. 63–69; and Jensen, "The Religious and Occupational Roots of Party Identification: Illinois and Indiana in the 1870s," in *Voters, Parties, and Elections: Quantitative Essays in the History of American Popular Voting Behavior*, eds., Joel H. Silbey and Samuel T. McSeveney (Lexington, Mass.: Xerox College Publishing, 1972) pp. 167–83. Kleppner, *The Cross of Culture*.

[11] Daniel J. Elazar, *American Federalism: A View from the States*, 2nd ed., (New York: Thomas Y. Crowell Company, 1972) p. 103, in general, pp. 103–14. Ira Sharkansky, "The Utility of Elazar's Political Culture," *Polity*, 2 (Fall 1969) 66–83. Samuel C. Patterson, "The Political Culture of the American States," *The Journal of Politics*, 30 (February 1968) 187–209. Sean Kelleher, Jay S. Goodman, and Elmer E. Cornwell, Jr., "Political Attitudes of Activists in the American States: Some Comparative Data," *The Western Political Quarterly*, 26 (March 1973) 162–69. Alan D. Monroe, "The Cultural Basis of American Politics: Testing Elazar's Theory," Paper delivered at Southern Political Science Association, Atlanta, Georgia, November 10, 1978. Conversely, it has been contended that Elazar's data either were time-bound or applied to elites, not to mass ideologies. Timothy D. Schilty and R. Lee Rainey, "The Geographic Distribution of Elazar's Political Subcultures Among the Mass Population: A Research Note," *The Western Political Quarterly*, 31 (September 1978) 410–15.

ciple" in order "to harmonize the state in which he lives upon earth with the state which he believes to await him in heaven." [12]

Ethnocultural Divisions

Two distinct religious traditions underlay the ethnocultural coalitions of the nineteenth century. One tradition, the *pietists*, arose from the religious revivals of the eighteenth century and carried on an intense struggle with the *liturgicals*.[13]

In religious doctrine, the pietists stressed the need to be saved in order to avoid damnation. They emphasized, not the church, but the individual in personal conversion to Christ and in continuous proof of conversion through pure behavior. In the secular realm, pietists believed government should remove obstacles to a pure society by such positive legislation as Sunday blue laws, prohibition, and abolition of slavery. Pietists associated immigrants, especially Roman Catholics, with corrupt politics, the decay of the cities, and evil in society in general. By the 1850s, this anti-immigrant strain became a full-fledged nativist movement to restrict immigration, place curbs upon aliens, and destroy parochial schools.

The liturgicals did not spring from the revival movement. Their religious doctrine stressed salvation through adherence to church beliefs, rituals, and hierarchy. The church itself, they believed, should take care of morality and salvation, and government should not interfere in these activities. Liturgicals feared that government would impose standards of morality upon them by law and even the non-Catholics among them were likely to oppose the nativist movement.

During the second and third party systems, pietists generally were Whigs and Republicans; liturgicals, generally Democrats. To varying extents, animosities between natives and immigrants were related to the political parties, but these divisions were neither exact nor consistent. The sharpest cleavages were found among immigrants. Native Catholics apparently voted more heavily Whig than new Catholic arrivals. Pietistic and liturgical Protestant immigrants were more likely to divide along the same lines as native Protestants, except when the Whig appeal to nativists drove immigrant pietists into the Democratic party.

This cultural distinction between pietists and liturgicals was seemingly contradicted when wealth and economic status were considered. Where it has been possible to identify individuals composing the economic elite, Whigs outnumbered Democrats, sometimes by as much as two-to-one,

---

[12] Alexis de Tocqueville, *Democracy in America* (New York: The Colonial Press, 1900) I, 304.

[13] "Liturgical" is Jensen's term and is used here. Kleppner uses the term "ritualistic."

although Republican and Democratic percentages among the elite were much closer during the 1850s. However, cultural differences between the parties' leaders proved to be much greater than economic differences. In Pittsburgh and selected areas in Michigan, leaders differed more clearly in their religion than in the value of their property.[14]

In New York, the parties differed as a whole in their *moral attitudes* and ways of life. Translated into governmental policies, New York Whigs wanted to use government to stimulate business development and create an industrialized society. New York Democrats believed that government should regulate as little as possible and leave people alone. The same kind of division was found in Michigan. Democrats supported the separation of law and morality while Whigs leaned toward authoritarian positions of community norms and paternalistic government to promote economic development. Democrats cared less about religion, were more tolerant, pragmatic, and secular. Laissez-faire proved to be as important a source of party conflict in religion and morals as in economics.

In the realignment of the 1850s, cultural hostility intensified to the point of moral crisis.[15] The new coalitions reflected both continuity and change. The Republicans, by opposing the expansion of slavery and attacking the aristocratic institutions of the South, managed to blend the pietistic, moralistic Protestant culture of the Whigs with popular egalitarianism. In stressing abstract rights instead of the economic appeals of the Whigs, the Republicans also lost some of the native-born Whig elite to the Democrats and blurred the class lines which had existed between Democratic and Whig leaders.

The outcome of the Civil War shifted the zone of political conflict to problems which had been submerged by the questions relating to slavery. In the block of states extending from Iowa to Ohio, the post-Civil War vote cut across occupational groups and social classes; both parties had support from immigrants and natives in urban and rural areas. The pietist-Republican and liturgical-Democratic controversy over the role of government in ordering individuals' lives continued to underlie the coalitions. *Party differences* were found in such long-standing issues as *prohibition, parochial schools,* and *Sunday blue laws.* The basis for both the cultural and political divisions was theology rather than language, customs, or national heritage.

[14] Frank Otto Getell, "Money and Party in Jacksonian America: A Quantitative Look at New York City's Men of Quality," *Political Science Quarterly,* 82 (June 1967) 232–52. Robert Rich, " 'A Wilderness of Whigs,' The Wealthy Men of Boston," *Journal of Social History,* 5 (July 1971) 263–76. Alexandra McCoy, "Political Affiliation of American Economic Elite," in *Political Ideology and Voting Behavior in the Age of Jackson,* ed., Joel H. Silbey (Englewood Cliffs, N.J.: Prentice-Hall, Inc., 1973) pp. 142–53. Holt, *Forging a Majority,* pp. 323–26, 349–54.

[15] For an insight into this realignment process, see Mark L. Berger, *The Revolution in the New York Party Systems 1840–1860* (Port Washington, N.Y.: Kennikat Press, 1973).

The National and Local Party

The identification of nineteenth-century party coalitions as ethnocultural communities of interest clarifies the representative role of parties but complicates the analysis. Dealing with these divisions involves more variables than dealing with economic divisions. To identify people according to their economic status is potentially all-inclusive because everyone is presumed to have some kind of economic status. But, everyone did not fall into one of the cultural divisions. Part of the electorate chose a party for some other reason, such as social class, although they could have accepted one or the other cultural position on the role of government. In twentieth-century research, it was found that the strength of group influence can be so great that those involved in community patterns of social relationships need not identify with the community in order to vote like the community.[16] This same situation could have existed in the nineteenth century as well.

The differences between the two parties' ethnocultural coalitions were real on the local level, but how were these differences translated on the national level? What was the relationship between the votes cast by people as cultural partisans and the official position of the parties conveyed in platforms and campaign pronouncements?

One answer can be found in the observation that "the usual ground for coalitions in American presidential politics is not a common policy, but a common enemy."[17] Once committed to a party, a person does not have to agree with all positions the party takes or even with any of its official positions if the other party is the enemy. The composition of a party coalition can vary from election to election as the identification of the enemy varies. In Pittsburgh, in the 1850s, Whigs were able to maintain their majority when economic classes divided along ethnic and religious lines in response to national issues like Free-Soil. The Democrats made gains under reverse circumstances, when people could be drawn away from national issues and did not vote their ethnic and religious differences.[18]

The enemy can also appear in different guises to different people. In the 1850s, a prominent national figure could have been an abolitionist, and an obscure person, unknown outside of his own town, could have been adamant about keeping slaves out of the territories. Both of these people could have voted for the Republican party on the slavery question for virtually opposite reasons: One wanted the slaves to be free; the other wanted them kept in the slave states.

Another answer can be found in the subtle connection between na-

---

[16] Robert D. Putnam, "Political Attitudes and the Local Community," *The American Political Science Review*, 50 (September 1966) 652.

[17] Robert D. Marcus, *Grand Old Party: Political Structure in the Gilded Age 1880–1896* (New York: Oxford University Press, 1971) p. 67.

[18] Holt, *Forging a Majority*, pp. 82, 306–7.

tional and local perspectives within a party. National party platforms between 1844 and 1880 stressed the powers and sphere of activity to be exercised by the federal government relative to states, local governments, or individuals.[19] It is questionable if the cultural partisans in their local settings were much concerned with any abstract question of the location of power in the federal system. When pietists advocated more or stronger government action, they wanted the powers exercised by whichever government could effectively achieve the desired ends; the liturgicals objected to the powers being exercised by any government.

In their platforms, editorials, and campaign oratory, throughout the nineteenth century, the Democrats officially favored lower tariffs while both Whigs and Republicans officially favored higher tariffs. Nevertheless, it is difficult to "prove" that local voting was a rational or calculated response to the economics of the tariff issue. No relation between voting and tariff policy was found in New York sheep-growing counties in the 1840s. Many farmers were not solely dependent upon sheep; and those who were dependent may not have voted Whig because in these counties the Democrats also favored tariff protection. A relationship was found in those New York manufacturing towns with "tariff-oriented industries," but it is quite possible that some employees voted Democratic to oppose their bosses and that some employers themselves were not Whigs.[20]

If voters had seen the tariff solely as an economic issue, it seems that immigrant workers during a depression would logically have voted for the party which claimed to protect American workers from foreign competition. In case of lay-offs, immigrant employees would likely have been the first to lose their jobs. Workers, however, may have perceived the tariff as an appeal to nativist biases rather than an economic issue. If so, native-born workers were more likely to vote Whig or Republican and immigrants to vote Democratic.[21]

Nineteenth-century voters who looked at public questions through the prisms of their various cultures did not respond to issues out of impersonal concern for the public interest as expounded by an issue-oriented national elite. That political leaders may be concerned with issues which much of the electorate tends to ignore has been pinpointed since the development of survey research in the twentieth century. In 1952, the national political air was filled with oratory attacking and defending the Truman Administration on such issues as corruption and communism. Yet, in the Survey Research Center sample of that year, only 24 percent of respondents specifically mentioned Democratic corruption and only 3 percent men-

---

[19] Benjamin Ginsberg, "Critical Elections and the Substance of Party Conflict: 1844–1968," *Midwest Journal of Political Science*, 16 (November 1972) 603–25.

[20] Benson, *The Concept of Jacksonian Democracy*, pp. 158–59, 161–62.

[21] Holt, *Forging a Majority*, p. 83.

tioned communism.[22] Even for these respondents there is no way of knowing how these issues influenced their votes.

Finally, the need for party unity and the need to pursue public policies cannot always be reconciled. In the period from 1890 to 1920, national issues of trusts and tariffs obscured ethnic and religious differences, the issues upon which local party loyalties depended. If these local issues had, instead, obscured national issues, any party action on the national level would have been far more difficult.[23] That party leaders, reinforced by their party press, used national issues as the *subject* of their appeals but adopted a *style* of presentation reflecting their understanding of their supporters' local concerns merely proved the need to relate issues to the people.

The duality of national and local parties is inconsistent only if it is assumed that national and local perspectives should always be the same. But duality is consistent with the decentralization of the party system as a whole. It would, indeed, be remarkable if parties at one and the same time were decentralized in organization and centralized by national policy positions. In order to govern and to be representative, each party had to respond to local pressures, but some policies were national and had to be treated in national terms. In order to carry out their representative roles, nationally, the parties were forced at times to keep the connection between the national and local issues somewhat nebulous.

COALITIONS OF THE TWENTIETH CENTURY

As the "rural-land frontier" of the nineteenth century gave way to the "urban-industrial frontier" of the twentieth, the party system reflected a curious combination of continuity and change. Realignment in the 1890s intensified sectional party divisions that had begun with the breakdown of national parties in the 1850s but did not basically disturb the ethnocultural character of the political party coalitions. This division, in fact, was intensified by the waves of nonAnglo-Saxon and Catholic immigrants who contributed to the growing separation of native stock from foreign stock and, as previously noted, led to a new *nativism* in the 1920s.[24]

[22] Angus Campbell, Gerald Gurin, and Warren E. Miller, *The Voter Decides* (Evanston, Ill.: Row, Peterson and Company, 1954) pp. 51–52.

[23] Samuel P. Hays, "Political Parties and the Community-Society Continuum," in *The American Party Systems: Stages of Political Development*, eds., William Nisbet Chambers and Walter Dean Burnham (New York: Oxford University Press, 1967) p. 161. Marcus, *Grand Old Party*, pp. 6–8.

[24] Jensen, *The Winning of the Midwest*, Chapters 6–8, 10. Kleppner, *Cross of Culture*, pp. 298–349 *passim*, 361, 368. V. O. Key, Jr., "A Theory of Critical Elections," *The Journal of Politics*, 17 (February 1955) 3–18. Elazar, *American Federalism*, p. 113. David Burner, *The Politics of Provincialism* (New York: Alfred A. Knopf, 1968) pp. 4, 79–94.

A more significant development during the 1920s became the aspirations of large-city ethnic groups to move out of the tenements and make a place for themselves in America. Their drive for self-improvement created what has been called an "urban frontier" culminating in the "political revolt of the cities" in 1928. In that year, the Democratic presidential candidate, Alfred E. Smith, lost to Republican Herbert Hoover, but received a very large ethnic-Catholic vote. Soon thereafter, in the realignment of the 1930s, there was an historic shift in party dominance as both sectional and ethnocultural forces were combined in the Democratic coalition.[25]

Class Distinctions

The rise of the New Deal in the 1930s emphasized social classes in politics and made it appear that economic determinism had finally taken a firm hold. However, political rhetoric emphasizing economic differences proved to be different from class politics based on class consciousness.

Ideally, at least, for a class system to exist, there must be both class consciousness and objective criteria for determining classes. The United States has satisfied neither requirement. Our national experience, beginning with the absence of feudal forms of social organization and continuing through the frontier psychology and the Protestant Ethic, has not been conducive even to a belief in classes.[26] A class is often confused with a categoric group, which is a "collection of individuals who have some characteristic in common," but these shared characteristics are not the same thing as having a sense of group consciousness and a pattern of group interaction.[27] Class requires a system of social strata where those on the same stratum identify with one another.

Most definitions of class are used for purposes of analysis, but people in general cannot be expected to identify with classes defined in this way. Various definitions undoubtedly capture differences in economic interests, but they are not class differences nor are they the only basis for opinions and behavior. For a *class response* to be meaningful politically, it must be in terms of *subjective* class, that is, the class people place themselves in. Of course, subjective class may be different from *objective* class, the one a person is assigned according to some classification system created for the purposes of research.

To illustrate how real this problem is, a Gallup poll in 1964 found,

[25] Samuel Lubell, *The Future of American Politics* (New York: Harper and Brothers, 1952) Chapters 3, 4. Burner, *The Politics of Provincialism*, pp. 228–43, 252. John M. Allswang, *A House for All Peoples* (Lexington, Ky.: The University Press of Kentucky, 1971) pp. 38–40, 54–56, 182–90, 232.

[26] Leonard Reissman, *Class in American Society* (Glencoe, Ill.: The Free Press, 1959) pp. 11–26, 204–5.

[27] David B. Truman, *The Governmental Process: Political Interests and Public Opinion* (New York: Alfred A. Knopf, 1951) pp. 23–24.

first, that more than one-fourth of the sample with incomes $10,000 and above, as well as three out of ten professional and business respondents, identified with the working class. Second, the poll discovered that more than one-fifth with incomes under $3,000 and over one-third of those in blue-collar occupations identified with the middle class.[28]

It appears that the main reason for the failure of socialist parties in the United States has been the low-level of American class consciousness, along with the pervading middle-class orientation among working people in general and labor-union members in particular. The best showing of a Socialist party candidate was Eugene Debs' 6 percent of the total presidential vote in 1912. (See Table 1.2, in Chapter 1.)

If ever there was a time when forces of radicalism should have been strong, it was during the Great Depression of the 1930s. Instead, it appears that a large number of the unemployed withdrew from community life rather than turning to radicalism. There is no way of knowing if they continued to support the political and economic systems but if they rejected them, they failed to act. Instead of becoming radical, the unemployed continued to accept the American belief in individualism and optimistically looked to the future. From such evidence, the premise of low-level class consciousness can be accepted even though there has not been much direct measurement of class consciousness itself.[29]

The *measurement of class voting*, therefore, is greatly complicated by the ambiguousness of the class concept itself.

Class Voting

In order for there to be a class vote, classes must first, be distinguished and second, voting by each class must be distinctive.

The problem is to find names for classes which have subjective meaning to people and which, at the same time, can be objectively defined. Subjectively, people fit themselves into the categories offered them in surveys. For example, when the choices are among "lower, middle, and upper classes," the bulk of respondents have been likely to choose "middle". When "working" is offered as a fourth choice, the bulk divides between "working" and "middle." These two categories appeared to come closest to satisfying the requirements of class. Working class and middle class are differentiated objectively according to occupations, approximating the distinction between

[28] Lloyd A. Free and Hadley Cantril, *The Political Beliefs of Americans* (New York: Simon and Schuster, 1968) pp. 17–18. Lester W. Millbrath and M. L. Goel, *Political Participation: How and Why Do People Get Involved in Politics?* 2nd ed. (Chicago: Rand McNally College Publishing Company, 1977) p. 91.

[29] Sidney Verba and Kay Lehman Schlozman, "Unemployment, Class Consciousness, and Radical Politics: What Didn't Happen in the Thirties," *The Journal of Politics*, 29 (May 1977) 291–323.

blue-collar and white-collar respectively. The two terms have been found to be generally acceptable to the public.

Before 1936, data on class voting were generally unsatisfactory because of the lack of systematic investigations for the entire country linking voting to occupational differences. Through 1932, the *Literary Digest's* record of accurately forecasting national percentages in presidential elections indicated that class voting was not distinctly different, for the *Digest* polled people primarily in the middle and upper economic strata. In 1932, the New Deal did not create what was to become known as the *New Deal class coalition*. Franklin Roosevelt promised better economic conditions for the nation, not for any one class, and his support came from both working-class and middle-class voters.

Because of the limitations in linking individuals to election returns, there had always been, what Daniel Boorstin called, a "mystery of the majority." [30] Beginning in 1936, this "mystery" began to be penetrated as polling became a separate and independent means for identifying party coalitions. Questioning a sample of respondents made the individual "the important unit of information and unit of inference" and "the datum and focus of inquiry." [31] The results of polling still did not tell how any given individual voted, but demographic identification of individuals revealed the nation-wide voting preferences of occupational groups.

In 1936, Roosevelt lost much of his middle-class support and, from then on, was increasingly dependent upon those who identified with the working class. The highest class polarization, however, occurred in 1948, when Truman was the Democratic candidate. In that year, the proportion of working class voting Democratic was 40 percent greater than the proportion of middle class voting Democratic. Otherwise, between 1936 and 1960, this proportion varied from 15 to 25 percent.[32] In 1952, both self-identified working class and middle class saw *class* interests, as distinct from other interests, linked to the Democrats. Nevertheless, in 1956, for the first time since the 1930s, a majority of the working class reported a preference for Eisenhower, the Republican candidate.[33]

What may be difficult to understand is that people do not necessarily divide according to economic differences when it sometimes appears that everyone thinks they do.

[30] Daniel J. Boorstin, "The End of Our Two-Party World," in *American Politics and Its Interpreters*, eds., Louis Reichman and Barry Wishart (Dubuque, Iowa: William C. Brown Company, 1971) pp. 126–33, quotation, p. 126.

[31] Kenneth Prewitt and Norman Nie, "Review Article: Election Studies of the S.R.C.," *British Journal of Political Science* (October 1971) p. 481.

[32] Robert R. Alford, *Party and Society* (Chicago: Rand McNally and Company, 1963) Chapter 8; Alford, "The Role of Social Class in American Voting Behavior," *The Western Political Quarterly*, 17 (March 1963) 182–87.

[33] Heinz Eulau, *Class and Party in the Eisenhower Years* (Glencoe, Ill.: The Free Press, 1972) pp. 2, 45, 103, 105, 130; and Eulau, "Identification with Class and Political Perspective," *The Journal of Politics*, 18 (May 1956) 245.

There are two generalizations about class voting that are difficult to reconcile, the role of *middle class consciousness*, and the strength of *class consciousness*. Middle-class consciousness is a unifying thread linking all groups and has thereby retarded political behavior along class lines. The middle class is a class in the sense of a "desire to identify with others" and "a consciousness in which class is the organizing focus," but it is too monolithic to be either a social class or a predictor of voting.[34]

However, the complexities of American society do not create an ideal class system but neither do they make America a classless society. Class consciousness is not necessarily as weak as respondents' answers to survey questions indicate. The extreme differences between upper and lower strata are likely to lead to a class consciousness which would be expressed as a class difference in voting. When dealing with less polarized strata, voting may, from time to time, reflect economic differences.[35] Even though there may be little actual economic differences among people, subjective class can be important. When either white-collar or blue-collar identified with the working class, they were more receptive to federal government welfare and regulations than when they identified with the middle class.[36]

What is uncertain is the extent of politically meaningful class consciousness. What is certain is that class is only one factor to be considered in voting. Because of the number of political influences, "the importance of a single factor for voting behavior is almost meaningless, unless the relationship is examined in various other subgroups of the population." [37] The subgroups which have frequently been examined are religious and ethnic groups.

Religion and Ethnicity

Religious and ethnic differences are somewhat easier to define than class differences. The principal religious groups are Protestant, Catholic, and Jewish. The principal complication in identification arises with Jews. They are not simply a religion but an ethnocultural group of many nationality backgrounds and consequently, can be classified in either religious or ethnic categories. The word "ethnic" means, first of all, foreign stock. Those born outside of the United States of non-American parents and those born in the United States if one or both parents were born abroad are defined by the Census Bureau as foreign stock. Obviously, ethnic is generally more broadly defined. The most common, if not universal, quality attributed to an ethnic group is a distinctive culture, resulting from racial, religious, linguistic, and

---

[34] Alford, *Party and Society*, p. 289.

[35] Reissman, *Class in American Society*, pp. 275–90.

[36] V. O. Key, Jr., *Public Opinion and American Democracy* (New York: Alfred A. Knopf, 1963) pp. 143–44.

[37] Eulau, *Class and Party*, p. 135.

other traditions irrespective of when their forebears arrived in the United States.

Politically, in the case of religious divisions, there seems to be far more fascination with a "Catholic vote" than with a "Protestant vote" because Catholics, being one denomination, are portrayed as a cohesive religious minority and as more church-oriented than Protestants.[38] In 1956, the Kennedys circulated a document arguing there was a Catholic vote and that a Catholic candidate on the national ticket would bring Catholics back to the Democratic party, but the accuracy of the document was severely attacked.[39] John F. Kennedy's nomination in 1960 did bring Catholics back to the party. Catholics favored the Democrats by 56 percent in 1952, 51 percent in 1956, but by 78 percent in 1960. Between 1934 and 1964, Catholics had voted from 20 to 24 percent more Democratic than Protestants, but in 1960, Catholics voted 48 percent more Democratic than Protestants.[40]

Although Jews swung to the Democrats later than some other groups in the New Deal coalition, their commitment to the party has been impressive. If Jews are considered a religion, they represent the most unified religious vote in the country. If they are considered an ethnic group, they are second only to blacks in their support of the Democratic party. Jews have been Democrats regardless of class differences as measured by levels of education or by affluence. Like blacks, who have voted Democratic irrespective of black candidates, Jews have voted Democratic without regard to Jewish candidates.[41]

Ethnic voting, in the nineteenth century, was generally associated with domestic policies; in the twentieth century, it has been associated with foreign policies. German, Italian, and Irish communities voted heavily Democratic in 1916, in part, because President Wilson had kept us out of World War I; but the same groups voted heavily Republican in 1920 in the aftermath of the War and particularly in opposition to the Treaty of Versailles. Some Germans deserted the Democrats again in the war years of 1940 and

[38] Wesley and Beverly Allinsmith, "Religious Affiliation and Politico-Economic Attitudes: A Study of Eight Major U.S. Religious Groups," *Public Opinion Quarterly*, 12 (Fall 1948) 377–89. Seymour Martin Lipset, *Revolution and Counterrevolution* (New York: Basic Books, Inc., 1968) pp. 276–78. John H. Fenton, *The Catholic Vote* (New Orleans: Hauser Press, 1960) pp. 17–20, 56.

[39] "Can 'Catholic Vote' Swing an Election?" *U.S. News & World Report*, August 10, 1956, pp. 41–46 and "More About 'Catholic Vote' in U.S. Elections," August 17, 1956, pp. 42–46, 132–35. Aaron B. Wildavsky, "The Intelligent Citizen's Guide to the Abuses of Statistics," University of California, Berkeley, Reprint, 1964, Number 94720.

[40] Philip E. Converse, Angus Campbell, Warren E. Miller, and Donald E. Stokes, "Stability and Change in 1960: A Reinstating Election," *The American Political Science Review*, 55 (June 1961) 272–78; and Converse, "Religion and Politics: The 1960 Election," in *Elections and the Political Order*, eds., Angus Campbell, Philip E. Converse, Warren E. Miller, and Donald E. Stokes (New York: John Wiley & Sons, 1966) pp. 104–6. Andrew R. Baggaley, "Religious Influence on Wisconsin Voting, 1928–1960," *The American Political Science Review*, 56 (March 1962) 70.

[41] Lawrence H. Fuchs, *The Political Behavior of American Jews* (Glencoe, Ill.: The Free Press, 1956) pp. 76–81. Nathaniel Weyl, *The Jew in American Politics* (New Rochelle, N.Y.: Arlington House, 1968) pp. 159–78.

1944 but swung back to the Democrats in 1948, when Truman emphasized both domestic affairs and the dangers of the Soviet Union. Jews followed an opposite pattern, strongly supporting Roosevelt in 1940 and 1944 but casting a smaller vote for Truman and giving some support to Henry A. Wallace, the Progressive party candidate in 1948.[42]

Ethnic politics, by hindering assimilation, has had the effect of weakening class politics; but, in the absence of issues specifically relevant to ethnic groups, ethnic politics should have declined. It was kept alive in some states by party leaders and ethnic candidates who benefited from an ethnic vote. What seemed to be a sudden revival of ethnic consciousness in national voting occurred somewhat accidentally. The Civil Rights Revolution of the 1960s, with its emphasis upon ethnic identity at a time when the status of workers was being downgraded, made it more prestigious to be seen as a member of an ethnic group.[43] The reassertion of ethnic voting power in the 1960s and 1970s would not have been possible unless there had been a considerable amount of "integration-with-out-assimilation" among those immigrants and their families who had adopted American culture but continued their social relationships within their own ethnic groups.[44]

COALITIONS AND THE NATIONAL VOTE

Each major party was an integrative mechanism in the nineteenth century because its coalition was composed of voters whose motives and responses were played out within their own localities. The significance of this connection between the national party and its local vote was constantly manifested and even directly affected presidential campaign strategy. In 1884, James G. Blaine, the Republican candidate, turned to the tariff issue as a neutral position to offset his unfavorable image among pietistic Republican voters.[45] Using a national issue to distract attention from local issues seems incredible now.

[42] Burner, *The Politics of Provincialism,* p. 22. Lubell, *The Future of American Politics,* pp. 132, 134, 141–47. Allswang, *A House for All Peoples,* p. 40. Howard W. Allen, "Isolation and German-Americans," *Journal of the Illinois State Historical Society,* 57 (Summer 1964) 143–49. Fuchs, *The Political Behavior of American Jews,* p. 80. Weyl, *The Jew in American Politics,* p. 161. Mark R. Levy and Michael S. Kramer, *The Ethnic Factor* (New York: Simon and Schuster, 1973) pp. 226, 247.

[43] Nathan Glazer and Daniel Patrick Moynihan, *Beyond the Melting Pot,* 2nd ed., (Cambridge, Mass.: The M.I.T. Press, 1970) pp. xxxiv–v.

[44] Levy and Kramer, *The Ethnic Factor.* Michael Novak, *The Rise of the Unmeltable Ethnics* (New York: Macmillan Co., 1972). Michael Parenti, "Ethnic Politics and the Persistence of Ethnic Identification," *The American Political Science Review,* 61 (September 1962) 717–19, 721–22. John C. Leggett, *Class, Race, and Labor: Working-Class Consciousness in Detroit* (New York: Oxford University Press, 1968) p. 129.

[45] Marcus, *Grand Old Party,* p. 9.

It is probably not coincidence that parties in the twentieth century have been losing their integrative role and that voters are reported as seeing national, rather than local, differences between the parties.[46] Voters are responding more to instantaneous *mass media communication* which gives the appearance that elections turn on national issues. Apparently, national concerns are not as conducive to party unity as local cultural concerns. Yet, the transformation from local to national issues may be somewhat illusory. People may not evaluate issues in terms of their national impact so much as from a parochial or group impact. The difference is that, whatever the impact, it is no longer confined to local communities but travels along a network of both public and private communication systems. The transition from local to large-group responses has changed the ability of the parties to form cohesive coalitions.

This transition can be seen quite clearly in the 1930s. The Democratic party, while seeming to base its coalition on class appeals, actually brought about what has been called "the final triumph of pluralism." Franklin Roosevelt perfected the strategy, used by McKinley in the 1890s, of giving to every major group what it wanted.[47] Although the New Deal became comparable to a pietistic doctrine of social evangelicalism and secular righteousness harnessed to big government, its policies seemed to reduce group polarization. Reactions of pietists and liturgicals could no longer be measured in absolutes but only in degrees, if they could be distinguished at all. Former liturgical groups, like Catholics, switched sides and became supporters of an activist, regulatory government.[48]

One logical result of the new group politics may have been the break in the continuity of presidential coalition voting in 1952, when neither social characteristics nor party identification could account for the increased Republican vote in every major demographic group.[49] Since 1952, Democrats have received relatively more support from the poor, blacks, union members, Catholics, Southerners, and central-city residents; the Republicans have received relatively more support from each of the reverse groups. Except for blacks, however, these have been loose coalitions because loyal-

[46] James Q. Wilson, *Negro Politics* (Glencoe, Ill.: The Free Press, 1960) pp. 37, 117. Richard J. Heuwinkel and Charles W. Wiggins, "Party Competition and Party Leadership Attributes," *American Journal of Political Science*, 17 (February 1973) 169. Lester G. Seligman, Michael R. King, Chong Lim Kim, and Roland E. Smith, *Patterns of Recruitment: A State Chooses Its Lawmakers* (Chicago: Rand McNally College Publishing Company, 1974) pp. 196–97. Thomas A. Flinn and Frederick M. Wirt, "Local Party Leaders: Groups of Like Minded Men," *Midwest Journal of Political Science*, 9 (February 1965) 94.

[47] Jensen, *The Winning of the Midwest*, p. 308.

[48] Richard L. Rubin, *Party Dynamics: The Democratic Coalition and the Politics of Change* (New York: Oxford University Press, 1976) pp. 38–41.

[49] Campbell and others, *The Voter Decides*, p. 75. Donald E. Stokes, Angus Campbell, and Warren E. Miller, "Components of Electoral Decision," *The American Political Science Review*, 52 (June 1958) 367–76.

ties were neither total nor constant.[50] Depending upon the responses within a complex society, an election can emphasize an occupational vote, an income vote, an ethnic vote, a religious vote, or a party vote.

This lack of continuity in coalitions also appears to have freed the party system from the fixed animosities which characterized the ethnocultural coalitions. But, as one kind of conflict has become muted, another has intensified. Ethnic intransigence has been replaced by the intransigence of the activists–purists. A description of the McGovern Democratic faction in 1972 can also be applied to the Goldwater Republican faction in 1964: It was "ideological, moralistic, and evangelistic," refused compromise, and was anti-coalitionist. It "embraced a fundamentally religious notion of purity, suitable more to a third-party movement than to the standard-bearers of a coalition party." [51]

The foundations of the party system have been two organized and representative parties capable of governing. In the next Section, we will look at some of the ways these foundations were undermined.

[50] Robert Axelrod, "Where the Votes Come From: An Analysis of Electoral Coalitions, 1952–1968," *The American Political Science Review*, 66 (March, 1972) 11–20, and "Communications," *Ibid.*, 68 (June, 1974) 717–20.

[51] Seymour Martin Lipset and Earl Raub, "The Election and the National Mood," *Commentary* 55 (January, 1973) 43–50. Also Lanny J. Davis, *The Emerging Democratic Majority* (New York: Stein and Day, 1974) pp. 18–19, 70–71, 162–63. Nelson W. Polsby and Aaron Wildavsky, *Presidential Elections: Strategies of American Electoral Politics*, 4th ed. (New York: Charles Scribner's Sons, 1976) p. 37.

SECTION TWO

THE CHALLENGES

The continuity of the party system gave it the appearance of a perpetual-motion machine, but the foundations of organization and coalitions could not be perpetual in the sense of being static. Eventually, changes of great magnitude occurred that challenged the foundations themselves.

The electorate responded less enthusiastically to parties and became less concerned with public affairs. Reformers demanded substantial changes in political processes. Weakening individual attachments to parties and pressing demands for reforms were contradictory to the extent that the first was a rejection of involvement and the second was a demand for greater involvement. If one of them had occurred without the other, the effects upon the party system would have been less extreme. By occurring together, they seemed to magnify the result as though one had intensified the effects of the other.

In Chapters 4 and 5, the challenges of popular withdrawal from parties and the effects of reforms will be taken up. By themselves, they would have been enough but they were also accompanied by a revolution in communications. The results of these changes, the subject of Chapter 6, were a far more serious challenge to the party system.

4

Symptoms of Withdrawal from Parties

Robert Burns, the Scottish poet, wished we had the power to see ourselves as others see us. A more modest wish is to discover how we see ourselves. The party system gives Americans an opportunity for this kind of introspection. What it reveals, among other things, is a frustration in coping with the void between what we have and what we expect. Americans have appeared to demand political systems in theory whose characteristics they do not entirely approve of in practice. They invented the party system but never were able to incorporate parties fully into the American concept of representative government.

Although democracy assumes the competence of the people to direct public affairs, the doctrine does not simultaneously provide the means for the public to govern itself. *Competence* to direct public affairs depends upon a link between the people and the government for translating expressions of a popular will into actual government policies. In a political party system, the parties become this kind of link.[1]

Of course, they are not the only link. Americans have wanted channels of formal representative institutions but have resisted the confinements of the party system by insisting upon being represented in other ways as well. As a result, the interplay of private interests restricts the linkage function of parties in the determination of public policies. A well articulated American antiparty tradition foreshadowed and reinforced these tendencies.

THE ANTIPARTY TRADITION

There may have been something in the American heritage that both encouraged the proliferation of political organizations and still made them suspect. In both Britain and the United States, beliefs in the values of dissent and opposition finally overcame suspicions of political parties, but

[1] E. E. Schattschneider, *Party Government* (New York: Rinehart & Company, Inc., 1942) pp. 9–16.

the British proved to be more receptive to parties and better prepared to accept "the hard facts of political life." [2]

Parties may have been more difficult to accept on this side of the Atlantic Ocean because Americans made liberty into an ideology of consensus and then gave the ideology a unique property. Louis Hartz advanced the thesis that the uniqueness of America has been its way of thinking, apart from such environmental influences as abundant land. Americans forsook the European class societies of feudal origin and became middle class without having to develop, in the European sense, a middle-class consciousness. The American way of thinking produced a peculiar kind of "liberal society" where self-evident principles appeared to be voluntarily and universally accepted even though many people, in fact, did not accept them. By making the principles absolute, they cast a radiating glow of consensus about the political system.[3] Perhaps a reason for the long periods of dominance by one political party in American history may have been the party's ability to appear as the more acceptable embodiment of the common creed.

In the early years of American nationhood, all was not a happy consensus about self-evident principles. Not only did clashing interests lead to divisions, but their very existence became a source of controversy. Those who opposed discords per se have been described as a "type of mind which could not accept strife as a permanent condition of civic existence, or was unable to conceive of a lasting regime of ordered conflict." [4] They believed that political contention threatened the cohesiveness of the new society, but they also had a separate concern. Political divisions were equated with majority rule which, in turn, was equated with tyranny because a majority can be as oppressive as any other form of dictatorial rule. To predicate government policies upon the wishes of a momentary majority was denounced as a threat to good government and to the true consensual values of the society as a whole.[5]

Although the party system first appeared in America, its most renowned leaders did not fall over one another to pay tribute to the new invention. Attacks upon *parties* in the eighteenth and nineteenth centuries were really a continuation of the attacks upon *factions*. Because the two were not differentiated for a number of years, people were not always aware they were criticizing two different systems. George Washington

[2] Carolina Robbins, " 'Discordant Parties,' A Study of the Acceptance of Party by Englishmen," *Political Science Quarterly*, 73 (December 1958) 505–29.

[3] Louis Hartz, *The Liberal Tradition in America* (New York: Harcourt, Brace and World, Inc., 1955) pp. 3–66, *passim*.

[4] Richard Hofstadter, *The Idea of a Party System* (Berkeley, Calif.: University of California Press, 1969) p. 18.

[5] One of the best expressions of this philosophy was John C. Calhoun, *A Disquisition on Government* (New York: Political Science Classics, 1947), originally published in 1853.

summed up years of anguish in his Farewell Address when he pointed out that "combinations and associations" were "destructive" because they both served "to organize faction" and "to put in the place of the delegated will of the Nation, the will of a party." John Quincy Adams echoed the philosophy of his own father as well as Washington, when he declared in his inaugural address in 1825, that "this baneful weed of party strife" had been "uprooted." [6]

It was impossible, of course, to create American unity by proclaiming the end of political divisions. The oratory of a new group of leaders gradually drowned out the strident attacks upon parties by relating parties to individual aspirations. The popular acceptance of parties was a tribute, among other influences, to excellent public relations. By constant reiteration, the Jeffersonian-Republicans and their successors drummed home the message that parties were necessary for democratic achievement because, in no other way, could the elite of deferential politics be confronted and contained. In addition to establishing effective political democracy, it was argued that the party system made possible the realization of America's highest expectations. Prosperity and national advancement would make America an example for the entire world.

At the same time, there was no way to obscure the fact that parties were actually private organizations run by individuals, not by the people as a whole. Parties represented management and strategy through organization, the manipulation of many by a few. Despite the contributions parties could claim on behalf of the governed, there was persistent—though increasingly muted—dislike for organized appeals to voters and for party recruitment of candidates, who became the only choices presented to the people in a general election.

Nevertheless, accent upon the positive features of parties and the unquestioned public acceptance of them proved so persuasive that by the middle of the nineteenth century, writers and commentators began to tolerate parties as a necessary part of the price to be paid for freedom. Consequently, they ceased stigmatizing them as enemies of good government. By the late nineteenth century, parties were finally welcomed as the means for achieving democracy. In this long process, "party was metamorphosed from an abomination to a necessary evil to a positive good." [7]

It is a melancholy irony that parties became philosophically legitimate at approximately the point when *withdrawal symptoms* from parties

---

[6] Inaugural Addresses of the Presidents of the United States from George Washington to Harry S. Truman, 82d Cong., 2d Sess., House Document No. 540, 1952, p. 45.

[7] David Hackett Fischer, *The Revolution of American Conservatism: The Federalist Party in the Era of Jeffersonian Democracy* (New York: Harper & Row, Publishers, 1965) p. 193. Austin Ranney and Willmoore Kendall, *Democracy and the American Party System* (New York: Harcourt, Brace and Company, 1956) pp. 121–47.

became evident. Some commentators on democracy had caught up with the people just as they were responding to the changes in their lives brought on by the industrial system.

THE FLIGHT TO THE FUTURE

Perhaps it has become impossible to appreciate the changes which were in progress at the turn of the twentieth century. Previously, freedom had been inseparable from great amounts of land and self-reliant individuals. This style of living had required most Americans to have a practical competence to do a great variety of things and to succeed in various occupations. The spirit of equality in an environment of opportunity favored the jack-of-all-trades, not the specialist. The grid system of rectangular squares, which had been adopted in laying out the territories west of the Alleghenies, was itself "designed to promote equality and independence." This national landscape fostered a private life where people could be self-sufficient and did not have to conform to any prescribed religious or social requirements. It was a way of life "which to many of us represents old-fashioned, traditional America." [8]

It was this private life in "island communities" which gradually gave way to an *urban-industrial society*, where greater value was to be placed upon impersonal rules in a regulated and hierarchical order.[9]

The new thinking was characterized by a growing optimism in the ability of people to improve their lives through greater efficiency. The location of authority and influence more and more corresponded to the centralized corporate form of organization, emphasizing business-like methods, use of specialists, and functional structures. Private organizations grew with the demand for specialization. Specialists achieved status because of their skills in professions such as medicine, law, and teaching, as well as in business, labor, and agriculture. Each group, furthermore, wanted to regulate itself and to establish its own standards of competence. Thus insulated, loyalty to one's own group began to replace loyalties to the local community.

Centralization quickly spread to government organization. Local communities began losing their powers to state governments. Municipal reforms weakened wards and townships. City boards of education took over control of schools.[10] Consistent with centralization was the growth

[8] John B. Jackson, "Land as Freedom," *The Mindscape of America*, Regents of the University of California, 1975, syndicated newspaper series.

[9] Robert H. Wiebe, *The Search for Order 1877–1920* (New York: Hill and Wang, 1967) pp. xiii–iv, 12, 44, 111–29.

[10] Samuel P. Hays, "Political Parties and the Community-Society Continuum," in *The American Party Systems: Stages of Political Development* eds., William Nisbet

of the powers of executives, and an expansion of bureaucracies. In their representative function, party leaders had been far more concerned with constituent interests than with the complexities of general public policies. On the other hand, government executives became increasingly policy-conscious in dealing with a range of problems that seemed to require such solutions as restrictive regulations, subsidies, and direct services.

In addition to centralized governments, functional interest groups and bureaucracies challenged parties. Both challenges were intentional and, no doubt, inevitable. Private interest groups were replacing parties as the dominant form of political organization. Bureaucrats, who had long been thwarted by party politics, finally found it possible to go about their business and ignore parties some of the time, at least. In the process of lobbying, representatives of interest groups contributed their own expertise to the art of governing. Policies began to flow from the mutual interests of private groups and bureaucrats who sought legislation to be administered according to their special needs. Acceptance of the philosophy that a complex society could be properly governed only by those who were trained and understood modern problems, led to a revamping of the civil service. As a result, applicants were recruited on the basis of professional competence rather than of party credentials. The rise of an educated elite of experts, scientists, and bureaucrats, attempting to administer government without interference from the "politicians," was reminiscent of the preparty period before the 1830s.[11]

These momentous changes in relationships between the party system and the government disrupted the relationships between the parties and the public. As government grew into a Leviathan, it seemed to become the enemy of parties instead of their base for operations; and as people became directly dependent upon government, they were likely to see less necessity for parties.

THE PUBLIC RESPONSE

For twenty to thirty years following the Civil War, political parties were the determining factors in political life. Rallies, parades, and barbecues created excitement, offered release from the humdrum of daily living, provided a principal form of entertainment, and gave dramatic demonstrations of party spirit and solidarity. Each party was an agent of political socialization for its members. Political speeches, pamphlets, and

---

Chambers and Walter Dean Burnham (New York: Oxford University Press, 1967) pp. 166–73, 176–77; and Hays, "The Social Analysis of American Political History, 1880–1920," *Political Science Quarterly*, 80 (September 1965) 383.

[11] Robert D. Marcus, *Grand Old Party: Political Structure in the Gilded Age 1880–1896* (New York: Oxford University Press, 1971) pp. 257–65.

the party press communicated most political information and attitudes. Although most people were exposed only to their own party's messages, the information level, and the level of interest, were far higher than they were after parties lost this primary function of being "educators." [12]

In retrospect, the 1870s and 1880s appear to have been the golden age of the party system. Even at the end of the 1890s, the McKinley administration is spoken of as the "golden age" of the "great state bosses." However, by the late 1880s, political leaders had begun worrying about the electorate's disappointing response to parties and to election campaigns.[13] At what seems the peak of the party system, the rise of commercial entertainment, increasingly provided through the *media*, and new sources of information on public affairs undercut the parties. The party press disappeared into *professional journalism* whose independent editors, insisted their goal was the objective presentation of the news.

It is impossible to fix an exact point in time as the beginning of an historical movement, but the symptoms of withdrawal from the party system became apparent during the 1890s. The presidential election of 1896 has become a convenient date within that decade for distinguishing old forces from new.

In 1896, the Democrats achieved fusion with the Populist party and William J. Bryan, their presidential candidate, campaigned for the "free and unlimited coinage of silver" with the fervor of an Old Testament prophet. He lost to William McKinley, the Republican candidate, who emphasized the issue of prosperity in an increasingly industrialized nation and succeeded in appealing to the interests of both capital and labor. For the first time in twenty years, the winning presidential candidate received a majority of the total popular vote, and it was this realignment of political forces throughout the country that made the election historically significant, not the simplistic wrangling over the currency question that received so much attention.

The election was associated with other forces that boded ill for the party system. Following 1896, the separation between a Republican North and a Democratic South became more rigid. A genuine and consistent two-party system survived in only a few northern and western states. Instead of being antidotes for *sectionalism*, parties became instruments for expressing sectional differences. Millions of Americans found that having one dominant party was a protection against the "enemy" represented by

[12] Richard Jensen, *The Winning of the Midwest: Social and Political Conflict, 1888–1896* (Chicago: The University of Chicago Press, 1971) pp. 2–6; and Jensen, "Armies, Admen, and Crusaders," *History Teacher*, 2 (January 1969) p. 45 and *passim*. Marcus, *Grand Old Party*, p. 5. Stanley Kelley, Jr., "Elections and the Mass Media," in *Readings on the American Political System*, eds., L. Earl Shaw and John C. Pierce (Lexington, Mass.: D. C. Heath and Company, 1970) p. 358.

[13] Marcus, *Grand Old Party*, pp. 16, 240. Kevin P. Phillips, *Mediacracy: American Parties and Politics in the Communications Age* (New York: Doubleday & Company, Inc., 1975) pp. 173–74.

the other party. By deemphasizing party competition, people could get on about their pressing affairs without so much distraction from "petty politics."

Linked to the decline in party competition was the steady downward course of the voting rate and new behavior among some who continued to vote.

Long-Term Trends in Voting

The nineteenth-century electorate, compared with that of the twentieth, had a far lower level of formal education, was much more rural, displayed far less class antagonism, voted in far larger numbers, and responded differently when marking ballots.

In some northern states, voting in nineteenth-century presidential elections was consistently above 80 percent and sometimes above 90 percent; in state and local elections, the voting rate ranged from 60 to 80 percent. *Ticket-splitting* was low, and voters generally cast a vote for all offices to be filled. *Roll-off*, which means voting for candidates for the highest offices and failing to vote for the other offices, was low. *Drop-off*, the difference in the voting rate between presidential and midterm congressional elections, was also low. Whenever the electorate was enlarged, the voting rate increased, and landslides in presidential elections resulted from a decreased turnout.

In the twentieth century, by contrast, turnout has been in a *long-term decline*. Although it made moderate gains from the 1930s through 1960 in presidential elections, it has been in another decline since then (Figure 4.1). As parallel developments, ticket-splitting, roll-off, and drop-off have increased sharply. The trend of lower voting rates has been nation-wide, not confined to the South, and greater in rural than urban areas. The voting rate has gone down whenever there was a substantial increase in the total electorate. Principal examples have been woman suffrage in the 1920s, the enfranchisement of eighteen-year-olds, and a thirty-day residence requirement to vote in presidential elections in the 1970s. Presidential landslides have generally resulted from an increased turnout.[14]

Exceptions to some of these trends have been found in individual states. Higher voting in urban than rural areas has been questioned in

[14] Jensen, *The Winning of the Midwest*, p. 2. Marcus, *Grand Old Party*, pp. 6–8. Paul Kleppner, *The Cross of Culture* (New York: The Free Press, 1970) p. 128. Walter Dean Burnham, "The Changing Shape of the American Political Universe," *The American Political Science Review*, 59 (March 1965) 7–28; and Burnham, "Rejoinder," *The American Political Science Review*, 68 (September 1974) 1052. Angus Campbell, "Surge and Decline: A Study of Electoral Change" *Public Opinion Quarterly*, 24 (1960) 397–418. Marc V. Levine, "Standing Political Decisions and Critical Realignment: The Pattern of Maryland Politics, 1877–1948," *The Journal of Politics*, 38 (May 1976) 322–25. Michael Rogin, "California Populism and the 'System of 1896'," *The Western Political Quarterly*, 22 (March 1969) 179–96.

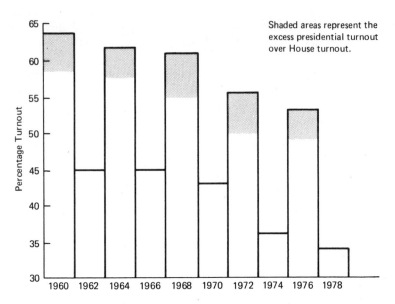

FIGURE 4.1   Percentage of Voting-Age Population Casting Ballots, Presidential and House Elections, since 1960. (Note drop-off in nonpresidential years.)

West Virginia, which ranked sixth in presidential voting between 1920 and 1968, and in Illinois, where rural areas had higher voting rates in 1970 and 1972 than urban areas.[15] Judging from 1972 survey-research data, young and middle-aged farmers had a high personal involvement in voting and in letter-writing but a low involvement in organizational activity.[16]

There is also some dissatisfaction with the assumption that nonvoting is mainly voluntary. The voting rate is determined by dividing the number actually voting in an election by the population of voting age. The *potential electorate*, those of voting age, is unrealistically high because everyone old enough to vote cannot necessarily vote. No allowance is made for failure to vote because of reasons beyond a person's control, such as illness; for aliens who are ineligible to vote; or for those who are disqualified temporarily—although their number was substantially reduced during the 1970s by easing residence requirements.[17]

Despite such qualifications, voting has declined in the twentieth century. Neither party leaders nor reformers could maintain the nineteenth-

[15] Gerald W. Johnson, "Political Correlatives of Voter Participation: A Deviant Case Analysis," *The American Political Science Review*, 65 (September 1971) 768–76. Alan D. Monroe, "Urbanism and Voter Turnout: A Note on Some Unexpected Findings," *American Journal of Political Science*, 21 (February 1977) 71–78.

[16] Michael S. Lewis-Beck, "Agrarian Political Behavior in the United States," *Ibid.*, 21 (August 1977) 543–66.

[17] William G. Andrews, "American Voting Participation," *The Western Political Quarterly*, 19 (December 1966) 639–52.

century rate of turnout. The Progressive Movement presented programs for civic improvement, for achieving "good government," and for ever-greater government responsiveness to the public. It was assumed that the reforms and increased policy outputs would heighten citizen awareness and motivate them to vote. Instead, the falling tide of the voting rate went on.

To know *what* happened to the voting rate does not explain the *motives* behind the declining percentages.

Motive: Withdrawal or Opportunity?

Increased nonvoting reflected a change in the meaning of electoral competition. A new elite opposed the traditional party leaders. However, the elite's reform-oriented communication did not stir up some voters even with new public relations techniques. Party leaders had been able to arouse a larger proportion of those of lower economic status with party-oriented appeals that relied upon such basic emotions as pride and hostility. The people who had the greatest cause for discontent were, in greatest numbers, "demobilized" and dropped out of the active electorate.[18] If they needed an ideological involvement to fill the void, they could not find it either in the reform programs or in the various species of minor parties that had no immediate prospects for winning elections.

If the decline in both voting and in party-oriented voting are evidence of long-term *withdrawal from parties*, then the party system has been deteriorating and will, it seems, eventually come to an end. If the withdrawal from parties was not entirely conscious and purposeful, how else can the phenomena be explained? One explanation is that in response to the entreaties of reformers, state legislators wrote new laws or state constitutions were amended to change the institutional structure for holding elections. Two of these *legal changes* are particularly pertinent.

Registration Requirements. States began requiring voters to register some time prior to election day. Registration was intended to help purify the ballot by preventing impersonation and repeating. Nevertheless, it requires overt activity by people to place their names on the voting rolls and making this individual effort is itself a sign of some political interest and involvement. Those who are only marginally concerned about voting may never quite get around to registering. In states where it is relatively easy to register and to vote, turnout has been higher.[19] As voter requirements have been eased over the years, registration laws are the principal remaining institutional effect and were computed to have reduced turnout

[18] Rogin, "California Populism," p. 181. Marcus, *Grand Old Party*, pp. 253, 255.

[19] Stanley Kelley, Jr., Richard E. Ayres, and William G. Bowen, "Registration and Voting: Putting First Things First," *The American Political Science Review*, 61 (June 1967) 359–79. Robert H. Blank, "State Electoral Structure," *The Journal of Politics*, 35 (November 1973) 988–94.

by about 9 percent in 1972. Even the importance of registration provisions is exaggerated because they vary so much from state to state, and changing state laws may only increase turnout among the slightly less affluent and educated by about 1 to 2 percent.[20]

Reform of the Ballot.   As difficult as it may be to comprehend today, political parties had prepared their own ballots, called "party strips," and distributed them to the voters at the polls. Each party's ballot was easily distinguishable from the other in shape and color, and voters marked them in public. With the adoption of the *Australian ballot*, beginning in Massachusetts in 1888, state governments assumed the responsibility for preparing an official ballot which listed the names of all candidates and was marked in secret by voters. The Australian ballot was adopted in two different forms. The *party-column* ballot makes it easy to vote a straight-ticket by making one mark on the ballot to complete the voting. The *office-block* ballot requires a separate mark for each candidate, whether voting a straight-ticket or a split-ticket, and was intended to encourage voting for candidates rather than for a party.

In elections from 1890 to 1908, the principal factor in ticket-splitting was the format of the ballot. The least ticket-splitting occurred with the unofficial party strip; somewhat more with the party-column; and the most with the office-block, which also increased roll-off. *Party emblems*, as part of the ballot format, apparently were an additional party guide. In party-column states there was less ticket-splitting with emblems than without them. Ticket-splitting was undoubtedly intentional, but the incidence of it was related to the form of the ballot and, therefore, to the degree of opportunity offered the voters.[21]

The extent to which twentieth-century changes in voting were independent of all institutional influences has been well argued back and forth in scholarly literature. Legal provisions do not make clear why people withdrew from parties more readily when office-block ballots were used, nor do they fully account for the long-term decline in turnout. Even though the impact of institutional changes has been slighted, no one questions that attachment to parties has undergone a phenomenal change since the 1890s. The historical trends are clear even if motives were somewhat mixed.[22]

---

[20] Steven J. Rosenstone and Raymond F. Wolfinger, "The Effect of Registration Laws on Voter Turnout," *The American Political Science Review*, 72 (March 1978) 22–45, especially 25, 33–37. See also the exchange regarding the relationship between registration laws and age differences in turnout in *Ibid.*, 69 (March 1975) 107–31.

[21] Jerrold G. Rusk, "The Effect of the Australian Ballot Reform on Split Ticket Voting: 1876–1908," *The American Political Science Review*, 64 (December 1970) 1220–38. Also V. O. Key, Jr., *American State Politics: An Introduction* (New York: Alfred A. Knopf, 1956) pp. 211–12.

[22] Walter Dean Burnham and Jerrold G. Rusk, "Communications," *The American Political Science Review*, 65 (December 1971) 1149–57. Burnham, Rusk, and Philip E. Converse, "Comments and Rejoinder," *The American Political Science Review*, 68

The Party Factor in Turnout

It is quite understandable that the close association of the party system with elections and voting has made parties crucial as an explanation of the voting rate. The American record seems to confirm the conclusion that an appeal to vote which is not party-oriented will fail to stop a declining trend in turnout.[23] When parties were strong, they aroused and mobilized voters. As appeals from parties carried less weight, voters had to activate themselves. Instead of speaking of elections in terms of mobilization, we now speak of *participation*.[24]

The change in the electorate's attitudes has produced other changes in terminology. In the years of high voting rates, we think of people being *members* of their parties. The term frequently used now is party *identification*, which was adopted in the first major publication of the Survey Research Center.[25] People can withdraw from membership and still maintain a sense of identification, but this changed relationship amounts to more than a mere change in terminology.

If party membership meant a sense of formal affiliation, comparable to joining an organization and being personally associated with it, party identification is more nearly "psychological." It is a sense of attachment, to the extent that parties are reference groups which provide both a screen through which their identifiers perceive political reality and a cue for their voting behavior.[26] Party identification becomes comparable to a religious affiliation. For some people, it may have little day-by-day meaning and for others, it may provide a constant sense of identity.[27]

The concept of party identification makes a political party something that exists because people have certain attitudes toward it and various associations with it. Unlike party membership, party identification is not a firm guide in voting.

Still, the historical association of parties with regularity of voting does have an element of "chicken-and-egg" reasoning. Because of a

---

(September 1974) 1002–57. Douglas Price, "Micro- and Macro-Politics: Notes on Research Strategy," in *Political Research and Political Theory* ed., Oliver Garceau (Cambridge, Mass.: Harvard University Press, 1968) pp. 115–19.

[23] Marcus, *Grand Old Party*, p. 9.

[24] James F. Ward, "Toward a Sixth Party System? Partisanship and Political Development," *The Western Political Quarterly*, 26 (September 1973) p. 407.

[25] Angus Campbell, Gerald Gurin, and Warren E. Miller, *The Voter Decides* (Evanston, Ill.: Row, Peterson and Company, 1954) pp. 88–89.

[26] Angus Campbell, Philip E. Converse, Warren E. Miller, and Donald E. Stokes, *The American Voter* (New York: John Wiley & Sons, Inc., 1960) p. 121. V. O. Key, Jr., *Public Opinion and American Democracy* (New York: Alfred A. Knopf, 1963) pp. 243–47.

[27] Kenneth Prewitt and Norman Nie, "Review Article: Election Studies of the S.R.C.," *British Journal of Political Science*, I (1971) 486–87. Warren E. Miller and Teresa E. Levitin, *Leadership and Change: Presidential Elections from 1952 to 1976* (Cambridge, Mass.: Winthrop Publishers, Inc. 1976) pp. 31–32.

weakening attachment to parties, they lost their dominance in political life; when they lost their dominance, attachments became weak. We emphasize political parties in the past because we see them as being strong, but we do not know if other factors were also strong.

Even the striking difference in the flow of *political information* can be interpreted two ways. In the twentieth century there has been a tremendous increase in the flow through the *media*, exerting an influence upon those with little political interest and with weak party identification. If these people should be stimulated by the publicity in one particular election, they are likely to vote for the candidate favored by this short-term influence. If they are not exposed to the media, they either do not vote or vote their weak party identification. In the nineteenth century, the flow of information was weak and there was less likelihood of any strong short-term forces, so apoliticals voted for their party.[28]

If this was the situation, the power of party was overemphasized, but this situation may only characterize the twentieth century. In the nineteenth century people cast a party vote because they were more directly involved with their parties and there was more flow of *partisan* information in newspapers, speeches, and discussion. Now, apoliticals respond, if at all, to media projection of images, for there is little party communication except through the media. Information flow used to be inseparable from parties. Now, it is not.[29]

Extensive investigations of *nonvoting* have related turnout to a variety of factors. It has been linked to *social characteristics*, to *attitudinal factors*, to rational individual calculations of the *costs and benefits* involved, and to *cultural traditions*. With the twentieth-century party system, there is no one explanation for everyone's decision to vote, and controversy surrounds the theory of turnout.[30] The voting rate is consistently highest in the states where the parties are competitive. However, for the states as a whole, increased competition in gubernatorial elections accounted for little increase in turnout.[31] In a traditionally competitive state like Indiana,

[28] Philip E. Converse, "Information Flow and the Stability of Partisan Attitudes," reprinted in *Political Opinion and Behavior: Essays and Studies*, 2nd ed., eds., Edward C. Dreyer and Walter A. Rosenbaum (Belmont, Ca.: Wadsworth Publishing Company, Inc., Duxbury Press, 1970) pp. 407–26.

[29] Charles Sellers, "The Equilibrium Cycle in Two-Party Politics," in *Electoral Change and Stability in American Political History*, eds., Jerome M. Clubb and Howard W. Allen (New York: The Free Press, 1971) pp. 170, 176–77.

[30] Paul F. Lazarsfeld, Bernard Berelson, and Hazel Gaudet, *The People's Choice* 2nd ed. (New York: Columbia University Press, 1948). Anthony Downs, *An Economic Theory of Democracy* (New York: Harper & Row Publishers, 1957). Daniel J. Elazar, *American Federalism:A View from the States*, 2nd ed. (New York: Thomas Y. Crowell Company, 1972) pp. 130–34. Benjamin I. Page, "Elections and Social Choice: The State of the Evidence," *American Journal of Political Science*, 21 (August 1977) 652–53.

[31] Virginia Gray, "A Note on Competition and Turnout in the American States, *The Journal of Politics*, 38 (February 1976) 153–58.

party competition increased turnout over and above other factors such as socioeconomic status.[32]

In the 1950s, voting increased with the intensity of *partisan prefer-ence*. Perceiving an election as close increased voting among those with high intensity, but not among those with low intensity. Yet, many who voted did not have a high intensity of partisan preference. Voting was also related to *interest* in the campaign, *concern* with the outcome, a sense of *efficacy* in voting, and a sense of *citizen duty* to vote. These four in addition to the intensity of partisan preference explained twice as much voting as intensity of partisanship alone.[33]

Among those lower in education, income, and occupation, high partisan intensity gives a greater boost to voting than it does among those of upper socioeconomic status; and the lower in status are more likely to have a strong party identification. Nevertheless, the upper status, overall, have a higher voting rate; and those among them who vote tend to be consumers of political information in the media. The best turnout among lower socioeconomic voters is in highly publicized elections, as those for President, while people with higher socioeconomic characteristics also maintain their relatively high voting rate even in city elections where there is relatively little publicity. The decline in voting, in general, has been most marked among those of lower status who have low levels of information and weak party identification.[34]

The American electorate now is often labeled apathetic because of its low voting rate. There is no way of knowing the independent signifi-cance, if any, of social, psychological, and rational factors when parties were the major force in elections; but we do not think of voters being apathetic at that time. Knowing that a high group voting rate today is not necessarily the result of strong party identification does not keep us from inferring that a strong attachment to a party accounted for the high nineteenth-century voting rate among all groups. We have to rely upon inference because, without survey data, we cannot be sure.[35]

Could a high nineteenth-century voting rate have been maintained by use of corrupt methods? Decline in voting coincided with attempts to eliminate such practices as repeating, stuffing ballot boxes, and fraudulent

---

[32] C. Richard Hofstetter, "Inter-Party Competition and Electoral Turnout: The Case of Indiana," *American Journal of Political Science*, 17 (May 1973) 351–66.

[33] Campbell and others, *The American Voter*, pp. 101–7. Lester W. Milbrath and M. L. Goel, *Political Participation: How and Why Do People Get Involved in Politics?* 2nd ed. (Chicago: Rand McNally College Publishing Company, 1977) p. 54.

[34] Sidney Verba and Norman H. Nie, *Participation in America* (New York: Harper and Row, 1972) pp. 218–20. Arnett A. Elliott, Thomas C. Hood, and Jack E. Holmes, "The Working Scientist as Political Participant," *The Journal of Politics*, 34 (May 1972) 399–427. Milbrath and Goel, *Political Participation*, p. 94.

[35] Philip E. Converse, "Comment," *The American Political Science Review*, 68 (September 1974) 1024–27.

counting of votes.[36] It seems unlikely, however, that corrupt practices inflated the total vote enough to account for the high turnout. An examination of both major and unpublicized cases of election fraud, bribery, and coercion in the Midwest during the 1880s and 1890s showed them based more upon rumors and partisan charges than upon solid documentation.[37]

Another possibility is that voters were somewhat "captive audiences" of the two parties in the sense that there was less opportunity to escape or ignore party activities. The extreme emotional appeals during the nineteenth-century campaigns, playing upon the hopes and fears within each coalition, may have been needed to mobilize even party-oriented voters.[38] When people could escape from party influence, some of them turned to other pursuits and began ignoring elections.

Considering the way Americans live now, politics has to compete for their time and attention. Turnout in the twentieth century may be "normal" for this century, or "normal" for any system other than that of the nineteenth century which, in retrospect, seems to have been unique.

THE REFORMERS' ATTACKS

Weakening individual attachments to parties did not represent a concerted and purposeful movement but a gradual tendency that became more and more evident. Both failure to vote and ticket-splitting appeared to be part of a pattern of disregarding parties, a reaction toward them which was more negative than positive. Reformers, by attempting to bring government directly to the people, offered something positive, but the case for reform was bolstered by the negative picture they painted of parties.

At all government levels, reformers stereotyped party organization as the system of the "boss and the machine" which were then identified as the sources of evils in government. They gave wide publicity to exposés of unsavory, if not always illegal, activities, and this image of parties has been kept alive ever since. Ironically, the big-city organizations, so thoroughly discredited by reformers, were one illustration of parties attempting to copy the centralized organizational style; but this sort of adaptation was not acceptable. Graft and corruption were favorite topics, and lively reading made for an easy black-and-white distinction between what was good and what was bad. Emphasizing the negative effects of parties coupled with the drive for efficiency led to the conclusion that parties should be abolished in favor of nonpartisan elections at the municipal level.

[36] William H. Flanigan, *Political Behavior of the American Electorate*, 2nd ed. (Boston: Allyn and Bacon, Inc., 1972) pp. 19–20.

[37] Jensen, *The Winning of the Midwest*, Chapter 2.

[38] Flanigan, *Political Behavior of the American Electorate*, pp. 19–20.

To distinguish between negative and positive motives in the withdrawal from parties can be carried too far. While some people ceased to be interested, others, by attacks upon parties, helped to create the climate of opinion conducive to reform. There is no doubt that the time was ripe for change. In fact, the rapid success of the *Progressive Movement* raises the question of whether its leaders found a ready-made following and set out to achieve something that was already beginning to happen. The objective of increasing the public's control over public affairs seems so thoroughly American that one wonders if the Progressives' contribution was not so much persuasion as their prestige and communication skills.

The stated purposes of reform may have sounded more threatening than they actually were meant to be, and their effects may have gone beyond what some had intended. Once the reform spirit was turned loose, like the genie escaping from a bottle, it could not quickly be contained. For a time, all reforms seemed irresistible. Even the proposal for direct election of United States senators, which antedated the Progressives, was soon adopted as a step toward greater democracy and a further restriction upon parties—although the change itself was procedural and not a limitation upon the power of parties in the government.[39]

The Extent of the Reforms

The attacks upon parties may have created a misconception about the nature of party organization and have distorted evaluations of the reforms themselves. It should not be difficult to concede that what we accept as fact may be, to some extent, illusion.

Distinguishing between fact and illusion raises questions about the apparently universal view in this country of what party organization used to be and how much it has been weakened by reforms. What reformers insisted upon calling "machines" still exist even if only the Democratic organization in Chicago fully measures up to the prototype. Obviously, all local party organizations do not perform this way but then many of them never did. If reformers did not eliminate all "machine" politics, how much success did they achieve? In fact, what was there to be achieved? Which was the greater illusion, the existence of "machines" or the success of the reforms?

What has never been made clear is why certain *social conditions* are associated with "machines" in some places but not in others. Party organization is supposed to thrive on poverty, but rural poverty in the North was not found to be enough by itself to lead to "machine-style party organizations, with their twin emphases on service and mobilization."

[39] David J. Rothman, *Politics and Power: The United States Senate, 1869–1901* (Cambridge: Harvard University Press, 1966) p. 256.

It was speculated, therefore, that "machines" would more likely appear where a large part of the population depended upon extensive government services.[40]

If cities were more likely to produce "machines" because of the greater numbers of people in need of government services, why have not all cities had "machines"? Four possible conclusions regarding the decline of big-city party organizations have been suggested

1. The decline is real but not due to affluence and assimilation within the population.
2. "Machines" still exist but no longer perform traditional functions.
3. They still perform the functions but cannot cope with the demands.
4. We have exaggerated the extent to which the functions were ever performed.[41]

It was noted in Chapter 2 that the leaders of the parties' committees may have been acclaimed for successes they did not achieve. It may also be true that they have been condemned for doing things that they did not do as often as they were supposed to. It is possible that the vitality of party organization was overemphasized in the past and is underemphasized in the present. People may have misjudged the effects of reforms because they misinterpreted the nature of the organizations. Perhaps the facts and the illusions can never be entirely sorted out.

Reform, not Revolution

The *Progressive Movement* cannot be judged entirely on what the reforms achieved in the purification and democratization of politics. Those on the outside were also engaged in a political fight to get "in." Venality and addiction to power were not exclusively the sins of the "bosses," for the reformers were susceptible to the same temptations once they were in office. Some of the "bosses" were not angels and neither were all of the reformers.[42] However, they could justify their attempts to capture both parties as a means for making them policy-oriented and responsive. It would seem that, once the parties were reformed, they could be trusted. The reformers did not see it this way. They wanted the power of parties restricted so they would remain dependent upon the reformers. This insistence naturally followed from the single-minded concept which domi-

---

[40] Paul Allen Beck, "Environment and Party: The Impact of Political and Demographic County Characteristics on Party Behavior," *The American Political Science Review*, 68 (September 1974) 1241.

[41] Raymond E. Wolfinger, "Why Political Machines Have Not Withered Away and Other Revisionist Thoughts," *The Journal of Politics*, 34 (May 1972) 387.

[42] See, for example, Leo Hershkowitz, *Tweed's New York: Another Look* (New York: Doubleday, 1977).

nated the Progressives. They believed that the public good could be achieved only in their way and by their standards. They could not accept the legitimacy of other means for achieving the good society. It was only logical, therefore, that Progressives rejected the pluralism of interests that were inseparable from coalition party politics.[43]

Party leaders could disparage attempts to make political operations more genteel by turning them into "high-toned" discussions, but the leaders had few options in resisting their attackers. Finding a strategy to counter the reformers was particularly complicated because they and the party leaders differed more in style and rhetoric than in basic ideology.

The Progressives' attacks upon party organization were undertaken on behalf of the *real* American principles, not on behalf of a new set of alien principles. Neither within the party cadres nor generally, among the leaders of reform was there any disposition to radicalize the political system. It seemed illogical for party leaders to turn to radicalism in order to mobilize the segments of the electorate which were dropping out of politics and refusing to vote. The day of the Populists, who had appeared radical within the two-party system, was already over. Why go back to a battle which had been fought and attempt to recapture the mood of those who had been vanquished?

For a *strategy of radicalism* to work, the party leaders would have had to go beyond agrarian discontent into the political quicksand of urban discontents among industrial workers and especially, the new immigrants. These things they could not do. In the first place, most leaders were not equipped to be crusaders in a cause for social reawakening. In the second place, the two parties became locked into their sectional mold in the 1890s and could see no way to break out.

It was the party system that was challenged, and it was the parties that had to adapt.

THE PROCESS OF ADAPTATION

The American party system, to a great extent, had been organized for and represented constituents in their "island communities." It was to be expected that, as Americans entered more fully into a national life, the party system would be reexamined and reevaluated. Could this system which arose with the industrial revolution adapt to a maturing industrial society? The early leaders of the nation had attacked parties for being divisive and for advancing private selfishness at the expense of the public good. Reformers at the end of the nineteenth century attacked parties for

[43] James W. Ceaser, "Political Parties and Presidential Ambition," *The Journal of Politics*, 40 (August 1978) 731.

obstructing legitimate private objectives and for subverting democracy by corrupting the political process.

The Political System and Society

The capacity of the party system to adapt to stages of *national growth* presents an intriguing contrast between the perpetual motion of the party system and the dynamic nature of American society.

American settlers, as Samuel Huntington pointed out, brought with them the English sixteenth-century institutions which "were still partially medieval in character." There were, for example, the beliefs in everyone being subject to law, in executive and legislative powers as checks upon each other, and in the separation of local governments from the central government. These institutions became fixed, making the American political system "a curious anachronism" which is "unique, if only because it is so antique." American society, which Louis Hartz found to be untainted with "feudal and clerical oppressions of the Old World," was governed through a political system with medieval roots. The society itself is oriented toward change and prizes the new over the old. Changes can be made with relative ease because the absence of feudal social institutions means there were no classes with a vested interest in the status quo. America is distinguished by being a new society, but an old state.[44]

Party Survival

The reform movement had insisted that the party system adapt to the industrial society both by embracing the new issues and by overhauling the party mechanism. Parties were expected to govern differently while representing new interests, but parties could not adapt to the point of ceasing to be parties.

The continuity of the party system may give the appearance that it has adapted to changes with all deliberate hesitation. Yet, the continuity itself is the best evidence that the parties have been responsive forces; otherwise, they would not have survived. They could adapt because they were not agents of fixed ideologies or of doctrinaire commitments. Far from being rigid, "it is the political party structure that has shown the greatest resilience on every level, the most impressive capacity to absorb new social and economic experience without major structural alternation."[45]

Whatever the exact truth about the significance of reforms upon

[44] Samuel P. Huntington, "New Society, Old State," in *The American Political Experience: What Is the Key?* Edward Handler, ed. (Lexington, Mass.: D. C. Heath and Company, 1968) pp. 90–103.

[45] Marcus, *Grand Old Party*, pp. 20, 250.

big-city party organizations, the *adaptive qualities of parties* were severely tested by popular withdrawal and the removal of incentives underlying party organizations, notably patronage and local personal services. The rise of middle-class affluence and the extensive growth of government welfare services seemingly weakened these supports. Restrictions upon immigration undoubtedly hurt some city organizations. Nevertheless, all was not lost. Beginning with World War II, waves of black and Puerto Rican immigrants arrived in northern cities. Democratic big-city organizations, supposedly in the doldrums since the time of the New Deal, grew stronger in some cities when they became intermediaries between the federal government and constituents, by providing information and interceding on behalf of those in need.[46]

However their foundations may have been shaken, *parties survived.* They have proved to be too useful to have been destroyed in one cataclysmic orgy of reform. Parties fell prey to the many distractions of American society and to hostility toward what came to be seen by many as meaningless partisan politics. There really is no problem here of deciding between the "chicken-and-the-egg." The supporters did not lose their parties. It was the parties that began losing their supporters. Local party leaders were still willing and eager to haunt the street corners, pass on the word to the faithful, and organize rallies. Most Americans preferred having parties but wanted to be able to ignore them much of the time.

There is no question that the *reform movement,* separate from popular withdrawal, made its mark on the party system as a whole. The reformers, with general support from the media, had the advantage of momentum and the unanswerable contention that government was to serve the "people," not the "interests." As a result, party leaders were placed in an increasingly untenable position: There was no end to proposals for change, and the leaders risked being undercut by accepting them or being damned for resisting them.

How the party system has adjusted to some of the specific changes is reserved for the next chapter.

---

[46] Bruce M. Stave, *The New Deal and the Last Hurrah* (Pittsburgh: University of Pittsburgh Press, 1971). Elmer E. Cornwell, Jr., "Bosses, Machines and Ethnic Groups," *The Annals,* 353 (May 1964) 27–39. James Q. Wilson, *The Amateur Democrats* (Chicago: University of Chicago Press, 1962). Wolfinger, "Why Political Machines Have Not Withered Away," pp. 383–86.

5

The Impact of Reforms

Presumably, the intentions behind a reform are to make improvements, but the intentions behind reforms of the party system were not necessarily to improve the parties themselves. If there were some unintended effects of reforms which weakened parties, it is unlikely that very many paid attention to them. The possibility that the party system has been hurt in this way will be confined to reforms of those political processes that have aroused the greatest concern: nominations, presidential elections, and control of the sources and amounts of money spent in politics.

THE DIRECT PRIMARY

Party leaders naturally looked upon the *nomination process* as being within their jurisdiction. The *party organization*, as pointed out in Chapter 2, grew out of the *convention system*. Unfortunately, the theory that nominating conventions were representative of the rank-and-file party members eventually became discredited. Many neglected to attend the local meetings or caucuses where delegates were elected, and sometimes it was not easy for them to take part because of various strategems devised by party leaders to insure their own control. Delegates in some cases were hand-picked by leaders in order to control nominations and make other decisions in their own interests.

The *direct primary* made the nomination process a public election where voters choose each party's candidates directly. The principal objectives were to put a stop to "boss" control over nominations, permit anyone in either party who aspired to be a candidate, to enter the primary, and to let the voters make the nominations. The hopes of the reformers were as clear as they were sincere, but their hopes were never fully realized. They did not correctly assess the responses of voters and candidates nor the state of party competition.

The Voters

It is significant that the direct primary was often justified as a means of strengthening the party system because the parties would be invigorated by individual participation at the grass-roots. If parties had commanded greater support in the early twentieth century or had voluntarily adopted the direct primary, the expectations may have come closer to realization.

Instead of grasping the opportunity to take part in making their respective parties' nominations, voters were ceasing to vote even in general elections. Turnout for primaries has almost uniformly been lower than for general elections.[1] Although the voting rate at both elections depends upon attitudes, interest, and socioeconomic status, state laws have a special influence upon primaries. In the *open-primary* states, voters can choose the ballot of either party, and no record is made of the party the voters select. In *closed-primary* states, there may be restrictions on changing parties from one election to the next, and there is a record of the party each voter selects. Only one or two states permit a voter to vote in both parties' primaries. The open-primary offers greater flexibility and has been associated with higher turnout, but voters may feel their ballot is not entirely secret in either because they are usually identified by parties when they vote.

In one-party states, far more people vote in the dominant party's primary although, in the South, the voting rate varies widely from state to state. It is higher in those with the least party competition. Primary voting is higher in the West and Border states than in the Midwest and Northeast, but turnout is somewhat erratic and cannot be accounted for by any one single factor.[2] Total primary turnout is not necessarily higher in two-party states than in one-party states.

There is a possibility that the low-voting rate has had an unforeseen effect. The voters in a party's primary are usually the dedicated, hard-core identifiers and may not be representative of the party as whole. If so, the electorate at a primary may not only nominate candidates who are unrepresentative of their parties but even more unrepresentative of the total electorate. The evidence on this point, however, is both scanty and conflicting.[3]

---

[1] Austin Ranney, "Parties in State Politics," in *Politics in the American States: A Comparative Analysis* 2nd ed., eds., Herbert Jacob and Kenneth N. Vines (Boston: Little, Brown and Company, 1971) pp. 96–98.

[2] Malcolm E. Jewell, "Voting Turnout in State Gubernatorial Primaries," *The Western Political Quarterly*, 30 (June 1977) 236–54.

[3] V. O. Key, Jr., *American State Politics: An Introduction* (New York: Alfred A. Knopf, 1956) pp. 145–65. Austin Ranney and Leon D. Epstein, "The Two Electorates: Voters and Non-Voters in a Wisconsin Primary," *The Journal of Politics*, 28 (August 1966) 598–616. Austin Ranney, "The Representativeness of Primary Elections," *Midwest Journal of Political Science*, 12 (May 1968) 224–38.

The Candidates

Encouraging healthy *intraparty competition* in the nomination process was one of the most important anticipated benefits of the direct primary. Experience with party conventions had shown that the organization leaders could nominate their preferred candidates by discouraging competition from others who wanted to be nominated. Experience with the direct primary has shown that political logic can be just as effective in discouraging competition for a nomination, for primary competition is related to the degree of party competition and to incumbents running for renomination.

These two factors, in particular, hold down primary competition for seats in the House of Representatives, as shown in Table 5.1. First of all, party competition has declined as shown by the increased number of safe districts, that are defined in the Table as those where the winning candidate in the general election received 60 percent or more of the total vote. A *primary* is classified as *competitive* if the winner received less than two-thirds of the total primary vote. In safe districts, the only meaningful choice for voters is a contested primary in the dominant party, but there was primary competition in only 9.1 percent of safe districts in 1964–1974, compared with 22.2 percent between 1944 and 1950. Even if incumbents had competition, the number defeated in primaries declined by more than half.

TABLE 5.1 Direct Primary Competition in Safe Districts, House of Representatives, for Years 1944–1950 and 1964–1974.

	1944–1950 *	1964–1974 **
Number of safe districts	965	1,691
Number of safe districts with competition	214	154
Percentage with competition	22.2%	9.1%
Number of Incumbents defeated	35	16

* Based on data in Julius Turner, "Primary Elections as the Alternative to Party Competition in 'Safe' Districts," *The Journal of Politics*, 15 (May 1953) 197–210.
** Based on data in Harvey L. Schantz, "Julius Turner Revisited: Primary Elections as the Alternative to Party Competition in 'Safe' Districts," *The American Political Science Review*, 71 (June 1976) 541–45.
Note: Two other trends between the two groups of years: Metropolitan districts had become less competitive than rural districts; general elections had become more competitive and primaries less competitive in the South.

In addition to the depressing effects upon primary competition of weak party competition and the candidacies of incumbents, there is less competition within a party when its organization is strong. However, the leaders of an organization may occasionally encourage a primary contest to settle an internal factional fight. There is more competition for higher offices than for lower, less prominent offices. In a majority of primary contests, winners receive 60 percent or more of the vote so that opposition does not necessarily mean close competition. Redrawing legislative district lines may increase competition.[4]

Parties and Party Competition

The extent of party competition helps to account for the amount of competition in direct primaries. Viewed the other way around, does the direct primary encourage or discourage party competition?

The direct primary may have reduced party competition in comparatively small legislative districts where one party was already dominant. There is intense interest and activity in preparation for a primary within the dominant party, but the weaker party may not even hold a primary because its prospects are so poor that no one wants to be a candidate. The result is further degeneration of the weaker party because its local leaders have nothing to do. With neither local nor state nominating conventions to keep up enthusiasm and keep committee members busy, local organizations begin to "atrophy," as "institutional decay follows deprivation of function." Having lost its role to provide opposition, the weaker party is in danger of losing its capacity to govern in case it ever should win an election.[5] However, other studies either found no effects upon the weaker local party or speculated that party competition may have been strengthened by the direct primary.[6]

[4] Lester G. Seligman, Michael R. King, Chong Lim Kim, and Roland E. Smith, *Patterns of Recruitment: A State Chooses Its Lawmakers* (Chicago: Rand McNally College Publishing Company, 1974) pp. 56–61. John R. Owens, Edmond Costantini, Louis F. Weschler, *California Politics and Parties* (London: Collier-Macmillan Limited, 1970) pp. 92–93, 296. Malcolm E. Jewell, *Legislative Representation in the Contemporary South* (Durham, N.C.: Duke University Press, 1967) pp. 120–30. William H. Standing and James A. Robinson, "Inter-Party Competition and Primary Contesting: The Case of Indiana," *The American Political Science Review*, 52 (December 1958) 1066–77. Key, *American State Politics*, pp. 107–16, 171–81.

[5] *Ibid.*, pp. 181–96. Also Standing and Robinson, "Inter-Party Competition and Primary Contesting," 1071.

[6] Duane Lockard, *New England State Politics* (Princeton, N.J.: Princeton University Press, 1959) pp. 188–89. Walter Dean Burnham, "The Changing Shape of the American Political Universe," *The American Political Science Review*, 59 (March 1965) 19–20. Leon D. Epstein, *Political Parties in Western Democracies* (New York: Frederick A. Praeger, 1967) pp. 210–11.

Leaders of the party committees normally prefer *uncontested primaries* for fear that a contest will divide the party in the general election. Impartial investigations of the effect of a divisive primary both support these fears and contradict them. In part, these mixed findings result from lumping both strong and weak party organizations together. It is even argued that, if a party is strong, a good fight may help to rally the party and appeal to independents.[7]

The degree of party competition and the strength of party organization existing before the direct primary were related to the speed of adopting the primary itself. When it was adopted, it seemed to undermine party organization most where it was already weak and had the least effect where organization was already strong.

In one-party states, the direct primary was accepted as a means for giving voters a genuine choice in elections; in some southern states, during the 1880s and 1890s, the Democratic party used primaries voluntarily before they were required by law. Two-party states with relatively weak organizations, particularly in the West, readily adopted the primary.

Political leaders in two-party states, with relatively strong party organizations, resisted. In Delaware, conventions still nominate candidates for state-wide offices. Some states provide for a party convention or committee to designate a candidate to run in a primary, but other candidates are legally entitled to enter the primary to oppose the designated choice of the party. In Connecticut, a primary is held only if an opponent challenges the party-designated candidate. In Illinois, each party, without legal authorization, designates a slate of candidates for state-wide offices.[8]

Even if, as some may suspect, direct primaries contributed to the decline of party competition, they have certainly not prevented the revival of competition in one-party states and may even have been an aid to candidates of the minority party. In fact, it is precisely this emphasis upon candidates that was intended although some of the results, such as image-projection, were not anticipated. The direct primary, by diluting party influence in the nominating process, drew attention away from parties as institutions and focused upon the personal qualities of individuals seeking nominations.

---

[7] Andrew Hacker, "Does a 'Divisive' Primary Harm a Candidate's Election Chances?" *The American Political Science Review*, 59 (March 1965) 105–10. Donald Bruce Johnson and James R. Gibson, "The Division Primary Revisited: Party Activists in Iowa," *The American Political Science Review*, 68 (March 1974) 67–77. James E. Piereson and Terry B. Smith, "Primary Divisiveness and General Election Success: A Re-examination," *The Journal of Politics*, 37 (May 1975) 555–62.

[8] Richard J. Tobin, "The Influence of Nominating Systems on the Political Experiences of State Legislators," *The Western Political Quarterly*, 28 (September 1975) 553–66. Richard J. Tobin and Edward Keynes, "Institutional Differences in the Recruitment Process: A Four-State Study," *American Journal of Political Science*, 19 (November 1975) 667–82.

PRESIDENTIAL NOMINATIONS

Presidential nominations are in a class by themselves, unlike all other nominations, which are held within states. Delegates from all of the states, as well as the District of Columbia and the territories, choose presidential candidates at national conventions.

Convention Leadership

It is remarkable when party processes are discussed, that we sometimes seem to forget that parties are factions existing in varying degrees of unity. Perhaps it is not really forgetfulness, but an assumption that with American parties, nothing much can be accomplished without the exercise of invidious authority. In any event, it has proved difficult to reconcile the role of leadership with the independent role of delegates and thus, to accept national conventions as representative bodies.

There is a tendency to see the centralizing force of leaders and to overlook the fragmenting force of people. But a 1952 project, the most thorough examination of major party conventions ever made, concluded that there was more evidence of confusion resulting from indecision among delegates than there was evidence of leaders telling their respective state delegations how to vote. The lack of unanimity in most states "left much to be desired from the point of view of those who were trying to weld their respective delegations into teams that could be effective on behalf of a candidate or a cause." [9]

A contested presidential nomination breeds an uncertain situation which cannot be resolved by dictatorial leaders imposing decisions upon delegates. Many delegates have a sense of responsibility and want to do what is in the party's interest and, at the same time, reflect party sentiment. The passage of time in the whole process is often critical. What the party at home seemed to say it wanted when delegates were chosen may not be what it seems to want when a convention meets. Delegates sometimes find themselves committed to a candidate who suddenly has no prospects of being nominated. The more fluid the situation, the worse it is. [10]

Conventions only appear to run smoothly when there is no contest for the nomination, usually when an incumbent President is to be renominated. Yet, in the case of two accidental presidents, Truman in 1948 and Ford in 1976, the conventions were very much divided, and Ford just

[9] Paul T. David, Malcolm Moos, and Ralph M. Goldman, *Presidential Nominating Politics in 1952: The National Story* (Baltimore, Md.: The Johns Hopkins Press, 1954) p. 191.

[10] Eugene B. McGregor, Jr., "Rationality and Uncertainty at National Nominating Conventions," *The Journal of Politics*, 35 (May 1973) 450–78.

barely managed to win. The domination of parties by their presidents is one variant of convention leadership, but it is indicative of a major change which has taken place in presidential nominations.

Candidate Leadership

There has been no decline in the roles of leadership and organization in conventions, but the roles are more and more performed by *candidates* than by leaders of the party's committees. This change in the source of leadership seems to have occurred so gradually that it did not become conspicuous until the 1950s.

What was happening could have been overlooked because superficially, nothing particularly new was happening. Candidates traditionally had their own organizations. Both Abraham Lincoln and William Seward were well organized at the Republican convention in Chicago in 1860. Mark Hanna has achieved historical notoriety from the 1896 Republican convention, but he was the manager of William McKinley's organization, not the "boss" of a centralized party. Woodrow Wilson's personal organization in 1912 finally triumphed over the organizations of competing Democrats as did the organization of Franklin Roosevelt in 1932.

It used to be that candidates had personal organizations purely for the purpose of winning the nomination. Then, the winning candidate's campaign manager often became the chairman of the national committee, and the personal organization was "blended" into the national committee. Now, when candidates are nominated, they continue to keep their personal organization separate because they want to go into the general election campaign with their own teams intact. Kennedy, Nixon, and Carter have been good examples. It would often be impractical to attempt to make the two organizations into one because candidates now attract workers who have no party antecedents or connections and may even be antagonistic to the party system.

Presidential Primaries. In large part the transition from *party leadership* to *candidate leadership* came about because of a reform in the method of choosing delegates. To prevent their being picked by the party committee leaders, states began to adopt the presidential primary so voters could *choose delegates directly*. In 1976, nearly three-fourths of the delegates in both parties were chosen in presidential primaries. There can be no doubt that these primaries draw attention away from the party significance of the process. In those states where, in addition to electing delegates, voters can express a preference directly for a candidate in the so-called "beauty contest," the importance of candidate image is magnified at the expense of the selection of delegates. The media recognize the main interest in personalities by emphasizing the vote in the "beauty contest" rather than the number of delegates a candidate wins.

Even with this personalizing of the presidential-nomination process, turnout at presidential primaries tends to be as low as turnout in direct primaries, for the two are usually held on the same day. Therefore, voters in presidential primaries, as in direct primaries, may be unrepresentative of the rank-and-file party identifiers.[11] More people vote in presidential primaries than in party caucuses or conventions, which is the alternate method for electing delegates in some states. Neither method is clearly more representative of a party than the other nor, for that matter, of the whole electorate, either. The advantage of the *caucus* or *convention* is that party activists have the opportunity to make decisions about issues, candidates, and delegates at one and the same time. The choice is between gross numbers who participate in primaries as opposed to the advantages, in caucuses and conventions, of party building, and of reliance upon people who represent a range of intraparty views in their approach to a party activity.[12]

Polling. Interlocked with primaries are *public opinion polls*. Candidates rely upon their high rating in polls to win primaries and count upon winning primaries to increase their standing in polls. In 1968, Nelson Rockefeller used polls to overcome his weakness with Republican delegates. He depended upon a "heavy media campaign which, it was hoped, would influence the public and then be reflected in public opinion polls, which, in turn, would influence the delegates." [13]

Both polling and primaries lengthen the campaign period because they encourage unknown candidates, like McGovern in 1972 and Carter in 1976, to begin their campaigns one to two years before the convention in order to have a chance to win. The same practice was followed by the Republicans when they no longer held the White House; Representative Philip Crane announced his candidacy for 1980 in August, 1978. Once candidates become known and can claim some support, the snowballing effect attracts still more supporters, increases pressure on delegates, and makes it easier to raise money.[14]

Polling in primaries, however, is less reliable than in general elections. It is more difficult to identify who will actually vote. Party identification is not a factor since the competing candidates are members of the same party, and candidate popularity is often unstable. Rating can change in

[11] Nelson W. Polsby and Aaron Wildavsky, *Presidential Elections: Strategies of American Electoral Politics*, 4th ed. (New York: Charles Scribner's Sons, 1976) pp. 224–26. Austin Ranney, "Turnout and Representation in Presidential Primary Elections," *The American Political Science Review*, 66 (March 1972) 21–37.

[12] Thomas R. Marshall, "Turnout and Representation: Caucuses Versus Primaries," *American Journal of Political Science*, 22 (February 1978) 169–82. *Openness, Participation and Party Building: Reforms for a Stronger Democratic Party*. Report of the Commission on Presidential Nomination and Party Structure, Democratic National Committee, January 25, 1978, pp. 10–21, 29–30.

[13] Herbert E. Alexander, *Financing the 1968 Election* (Lexington, Mass.: D. C. Heath and Company, 1971) p. 115.

[14] Polsby and Wildavsky, *Presidential Elections*, pp. 115–16.

response to various campaign developments. In the 1972 Democratic presidential primary in California, a statewide poll gave McGovern a 20 percent advantage over Humphrey, but McGovern defeated Humphrey in the primary by only 6 percent.[15] Nevertheless, polls and primaries combined have become better predictors of the winning nominee than bargaining and evaluations among party leaders at conventions.[16]

Media.   The way the public sees candidates ultimately depends upon how they appear through the media. Not only are reporters, willingly or unwillingly, a direct factor in convention decision-making, but also *television coverage* of conventions has carried the influence much further. Television has been the most important single factor in building candidates' images and altering convention procedures, especially in shortening the length and number of convention sessions. To the networks, national conventions are shows, and the networks battle for audience ratings in their coverage. A viewer may gain the impression that conventions are really held to provide television spectaculars. Now, instead of attacking conventions for being "boss-dominated," they are sometimes belittled because they are not under party control.[17]

Preeminence of Candidates.   Making the nomination process a kind of presidential sweepstakes lengthens the campaign period but shortens the conventions. After a long race, we want a quick decision at the finish. First-

TABLE 5.2   Number of Ballots Taken in Major-Party Conventions
to Nominate Presidential Candidates, since 1856.

Number of Conventions

Number of Ballots:	Nineteenth Century		Twentieth Century	
	D	R	D	R
1	4	5	15	16
2–10	4	5	2	4
11–50	2	1	2	0
over 50	1	0	1 *	0

* Highest number of ballots: 103 in 1924 Democratic Convention.

[15] Harold Mendelsohn and Irving Crespi, *Polls, Television, and the New Politics* (Scranton, Pa.: Chandler Publishing Company, 1970) pp. 109–20. Martin Mayer, "What Did We Learn from the Polls This Time?" in *Politics USA,* 4th ed., eds. Andrew M. Scott and Earle Wallace (New York: Macmillan Publishing Company, Inc., 1974) p. 215.

[16] William H. Lucy, "Polls, Primaries, and Presidential Nominations," *The Journal of Politics,* 35 (November 1973) 830–48. James D. Davis, *Springboard to the White House: Presidential Primaries* (New York: Thomas Y. Crowell Company, 1967).

[17] Mendelsohn and Crespi, *Polls, Television, and the New Politics,* pp. 297–301, 308, 312.

ballot nominations were fewer than one-half of all nominations in the nineteenth century but over three-fourths in the twentieth, and all nominations have been made on the first ballot since 1956 (Table 5.2). The gathering of delegates, when most of them are already committed to a candidate, appears to be a meeting to *ratify a decision* rather than an assembling for the purpose of resolving conflicts. Even the aura given to a nomination in a convention conveys a mastery of a party by the successful candidate instead of a decision in the name of the party.

The previously noted effect of the direct primary to magnify candidates at the expense of their parties has reached fruition in national conventions. We find the same kind of result with or without reform of the nominating method.

The Role of Delegates

During the 1972 contest for the Democratic presidential nomination, Hubert Humphrey may have sounded like the nostalgic voice of conventions-past when he asserted: "This nomination is not going to be decided by television cameras, pollsters, pundits or the press, It's going to be decided by the delegates." [18] If delegates were immune from the influences to which the whole nation is exposed, they could not be depended upon to make nominations. Conversely, if nominations are to be made by primaries, polls, and the media, what need is there for delegates—except to register a predetermined result?

Delegates, as a group, are politically active and experienced. They know the candidates or, at least, see them in person and are more likely to evaluate them in terms of party and policies. National conventions may be one of the few remaining counterweights to media images. Delegates to both Democratic and Republican conventions have been found to be *issue-oriented* and to reflect party differences on issues.[19] Delegates want to nominate a winning candidate, so their resistance to popular influences can be overemphasized. When the trends are so strongly toward style and images, however, delegates are one remaining source for evaluating the qualities as well as the electability of candidates.

[18] Quoted *St. Louis Globe-Democrat*, June 10, 1972.

[19] Gene Wyckoff, *The Image Candidates: American Politics in the Age of Television* (New York: The Macmillan Company, 1968) p. 239. Edmond Costantini, "Intraparty Attitude Conflict: Democratic Party Leadership in California," *The Western Political Quarterly*, 16 (December 1963) 956–72. Herbert McClosky, Paul J. Hoffman, and Rosemary O'Hara, "Issue Conflict and Consensus among Party Leaders and Followers," *The American Political Science Review*, 54 (June 1960) 406–27. John W. Soule and James W. Clarke, "Issue Conflict and Consensus: A Comparative Study of Democratic and Republican Delegates to the 1968 National Convention," *The Journal of Politics*, 33 (February 1971) 72–91.

National Conventions and the Parties

To see national conventions as nominating candidates and nothing else is to miss their full significance. Conventions provide the occasion for healing rifts within the coalition, for unifying discordant factions, for providing the glue that holds parties together. A convention brings into one place at one time the active leaders of the party because there is something important to do and they have to do it together or they will cease to be a party. Conventions make it possible for the peculiarly decentralized American parties to have a national existence. Nominating presidential candidates in conventions, even if the candidates overshadow the party, means the nomination is still made under party auspices.

Although national conventions continue to serve party purposes as a national meeting-ground, party involvement in the nomination process has weakened as party organizations have been undermined. State committee leaders have less interest in presidential candidates because, with the growth of ticket-splitting, presidential coattails are much weaker in winning local and state elections. Whether delegates are chosen by primaries or by caucuses and conventions in the states, the state party leaders now play more nearly an administrative role than a decision-making role within the party. The leaders of the state and local committees no longer have the ability they once had to resolve conflicts in national conventions.[20]

When conventions in the past became deadlocked, candidates were chosen as a result of *interfactional bargaining*. This process, even without deadlocks, still generally continues because failure to patch up the coalition by the time the nomination is made increases the risk of factional separation and, therefore, of defeat in the coming election. The danger of greater separation has not arisen from making nominations on the first ballot, nor from reforms imposed upon parties from outside, but from rules changes made by the party itself. These changes were themselves evidence of factional separation resulting from greater emphasis upon ideological positions than upon winning elections.

Rules changes in the Democratic party in 1972 and 1976 reflected the separatist tendencies of the activists-purists and made it more difficult to exercise leadership and unify the party. In order to open up the party to wider participation, fewer party officials and public office-holders were chosen as delegates or alternates. For instance, the percentage of Democratic United States senators declined from 90 percent in 1956 to 36 percent in 1972 and 18 percent in 1976; and Democratic House members, from a high of 46 percent in 1964 to 15 percent in 1972 and 1976. All Democratic governors were delegates or alternates in 1956, but only 80 percent of them were selected in 1972 and 47 percent in 1976. Conversely, the proportion

[20] *Openness, Participation and Party Building*, pp. 24–27.

of delegates and alternates representing minorities rose from 1.58 percent in 1956 to 15 percent in 1972; women, from 9 percent in 1956 to 40 percent in 1972; and those under 30 years of age from approximately 1 percent in 1956 to 22 percent in 1972.

After Carter became President, an effort was made to insure more leadership representation while still encouraging wide participation. A Commission appointed by the Democratic National Committee proposed for the 1980 national convention that, in each state, 10 percent of the total number of publicly-elected and at-large delegates should be party leaders and elected officials, with priority given to governors, chairmen or chairwomen and vice-chairmen or vice-chairwomen of the state committee, United States senators, and House members.[21]

Refusal to compromise, of course, cannot be cured by rules alone. Goldwater was nominated in 1964 by a faction that captured the convention without benefit of changes in the rules.[22] Separatism can become inescapable if factions are simply incompatible in ideology and in attitudes toward their party. Yet the divisions over issues that have characterized both parties have had different implications for separatism. The McGovern followers, compared with professionals in the Democratic party, were found to be weaker supporters of the party in both 1972 and 1974.[23] Goldwater delegates, at least in California in 1964, were more strongly Republican than the Rockefeller delegates.[24]

The *objective of rules* for the selection of delegates and the conduct of conventions is to insure that an entrenched party hierarchy cannot prevent people from participating in good faith. In addition, rules help to insure that a party will not be captured by quasi-party members who will only play the game on their own terms.

Members of the party who work throughout every year are entitled to make some decisions. They attend to the grubby business of human relationships when nothing exciting is going on. They find meaning in the monotony of keeping the party committees functioning when most

[21] *Ibid.*, pp. 18–19, 50. Polsby and Wildavsky, *Presidential Elections*, p. 228. Denis G. Sullivan, Jeffrey L. Pressman, and F Christopher Arterton, *Explorations in Convention Decision Making: The Democratic Party in the 1970s* (San Francisco: W. H. Freeman and Company, 1976) pp. 23–25, 37, 39–40, 63–64, 103. Thomas H. Roback, "Amateurs and Professionals: Delegates to the 1972 Republican National Convention," *The Journal of Politics*, 37 (May 1975) 433–67. See, in general, Austin Ranney, "Changing the Rules of the Nominating Game," in *Choosing the President*, James David Barber, ed. (Englewood Cliffs, N.J.: Prentice-Hall, Inc., 1974) pp. 71–87.

[22] *Ibid.*, p. 82. Aaron Wildavsky, "The Goldwater Phenomenon: Purists, Politicians, and the Two-Party System," *The Review of Politics*, 27 (June 1965) 386–413.

[23] Sullivan and others, *Explorations in Convention Decision Making*, p. 47. See also John W. Soule and Wilma E. McGrath, "A Comparative Study of Presidential Nomination Conventions: The Democrats 1968 and 1972," *American Journal of Political Science*, 19 (August 1975) 501–18. Robert A. Hitlin and John S. Jackson III, "On Amateur and Professional Politicians," *The Journal of Politics*, 39 (August 1977) 786–93.

[24] Edmond Costantini and Kenneth H. Craig, "Competing Elites within a Political Party: A Study of Republican Leadership," *The Western Political Quarterly*, 22 (December 1969) 879–903.

people find more interesting things to do. Those who tend the store during slack seasons should not be fired when all of the advertisements go out announcing the glamorous event of a nomination. A party does not become representative by neutralizing its leaders but by maintaining a balance between the year-round activists and the quadrennial activists.

PRESIDENTIAL ELECTIONS

In Chapter 1 we concluded that the electoral-college system was not the reason for our having just two major political parties but that the electoral-college system has been adapted to the two-party system.

It may help to review quickly the way the system works. The United States Constitution provides that each state cast as many electoral votes as it has members in both houses of Congress. The presidential candidate who receives a majority of all the electoral votes cast, is elected. If no candidate has a majority, the House of Representatives chooses the President from the three candidates having the largest number of electoral votes. For this purpose, each state has one vote in the House, and a majority of all states is necessary to elect the President. Electoral votes cast by a state do not reflect its population in one respect because every state has two senators. However, electoral votes do partially reflect a state's population because every ten years after the federal census is taken, members of the House are reapportioned to the states according to their population.

To change the present system, either by abolishing electoral votes or changing the way they are cast, can alter the political climate without necessarily threatening the system itself. Furthermore, each one of the proposed changes would make a distinctive difference, as we shall see.

Proposals for Change

The most widely discussed reform of the presidential-election process is *direct election* of presidents. If this change were made, there would be no electoral votes, and every voter would have one vote whether in Ohio or Wyoming. State lines would officially disappear, and all popular votes would be lumped into totals for the various candidates.

Two other proposed reforms have been advocated over the years, the *district* and *proportional* methods. Both would keep electoral votes, but the votes would be counted differently. With the *district method*, voters in each congressional district would elect one presidential elector and two electors would be elected by the statewide vote. Thus the unit vote on the state level would be reduced to just two electoral votes but there would be a unit vote from each congressional district. There would be an equality in voting to the extent that each voter in the country would be voting for three electors. A state's vote could still be cast as a unit if one party carried all of the districts. With the *proportional method*, each party in each state would receive the proportion of the electoral votes that it received of the popular votes, making it impossible for a party to receive all of a state's electoral votes.

Either direct or proportional election would place a premium upon the margin of a state's vote a party received. Accordingly, the Democrats would be encouraged to expend greater energy in Democratic states and areas to get out the maximum Democratic vote, and the Republicans, likewise, in Republican states and areas. The district method would shift the emphasis to individual congressional districts. The population of each district in the same state is now generally equal because of the doctrine of one-person, one-vote, enforced by the Supreme Court, but the districts could still be *gerrymandered* in favor of one party or the other. Therefore, many districts would not likely be competitive in presidential elections although the dominant party would be encouraged to get out the maximum vote to help carry the whole state.

Votes and Political Power

A shift in presidential campaign strategies, resulting from any of these proposed changes, promises a comparable shift in the location of *voting power*. As the nation has become more urban, presidential candidates have appealed more strongly to urban minorities, whether organized or unorganized, which are believed to be susceptible to group appeals. Consequently, the present operation of the electoral-college system gives special advantages to *blocs* of voters in the *large cities* of *large states*. Using any of the three proposed reforms, a heavy concentration of voters would continue to receive special attention, but the calculations in bidding for their votes would have to be affected by the fact that the big-city states could no longer be looked upon as a unit.[25]

All three proposals would have the effect of *fragmenting* the voting power of the largest states, where the vote is often so close that neither party enjoys much of a popular-vote margin over the other. Advocates of the district and proportional methods have based their arguments on the desirability of reducing the power of large-state voters. Curiously, supporters of direct election, which would have the same effect, have discussed it in terms of advancing democracy by creating equality through the device of one-person, one-vote. In any election method, some votes are easier to acquire than others, and some are more eagerly sought depending upon the weight given to the votes.

[25] Polsby and Wildavsky, *Presidential Elections*, pp. 244–45. Neal R. Peirce, *The People's President: The Electoral College in American History and the Direct Vote Alternative* (New York: Simon and Schuster, 1968) pp. 282–83. Wallace S. Sayre and Judith H. Parris, *Voting for President: The Electoral College and the American Political System* (Washington, D.C.: The Brookings Institution, 1970) pp. 61–73, 79, 82.

With the present system, it appears that the individual voter in the smallest states is benefited because of the failure of the electoral votes fully to reflect state populations. By one method of calculation, a voter in Alaska, which has three electoral votes, is equal to four or five voters in California which has the maximum of 45 electoral votes. Calculated another way, each California voter, by being able to vote for 45 electors is two to three times as powerful as the Alaska voter.[26]

All of this discussion is more theoretical than political. The power of the voter in the abstract should be distinguished from the power of the voter in reality. What do state lines do to the power of voters as opposed to taking down state barriers? Existing political calculations are based upon voters being isolated, so to speak, by states and therefore, upon the meaningfulness of votes when they are tabulated state-by-state. Advocates of direct election are not talking about isolated individuals casting a vote, but about voters as coalitions of interstate interest groups. Once voters are no longer contained by state lines, calculations would be different because the power of a voter would then depend upon the number of voting allies throughout the country, not upon the size of the state in which the votes are cast.[27]

Campaign strategies with any of the proposed methods of reform could be subjected to the same questions raised about current strategies. Long before computer analysis was brought into political campaigns, the general plan in running for president was to concentrate on the large states, even though they are under-represented in the electoral college. The smaller states do not receive special attention simply because they are over-represented. No one has really been sure that concentrating upon large states is an entirely valid strategy, but people who plan campaigns still proceed on this assumption.[28]

The Mechanics of a Majority

One advantage of the *general-ticket system* now in use is the ease of creating a majority in the electoral college for one presidential candidate. The importance of the present mechanics becomes more striking when we

---

[26] J. F. Banzhof III, "One Man, 3.312 Votes: Mathematic Analysis of the Electoral College," *Villanova Law Review*, 13 (1968) 303. The mathematics is further discussed in Steven J. Brams and Morton D. Davis, "The 3/2's Rule in Presidential Campaigning," *The American Political Science Review*, 68 (March 1974) 113–14. Calud S. Colantoni, Terrence J. Levesque, and Peter C. Ordeshook, "Campaign Resource Allocations under the Electoral College," and "Rejoinder," *The American Political Science Review*, 69 (March 1975) 141–61.

[27] Carleton W. Sterling, "The Electoral College Biases Revealed: The Conventional Wisdom and Game Theory Models Notwithstanding," *The Western Political Quarterly*, 31 (June 1978) 162–63.

[28] Alexander M. Bickel, *Reform and Continuity: The Electoral College, the Convention and the Party System* (New York: Harper Torchbook, 1971) p. 5.

must decide what percentage of the vote should be required for election in the case of any of the three proposed reforms.

There is an unavoidable dilemma between two alternative methods. If the candidate with a plurality of the vote is accepted as the winner, a President could be elected with such a small percentage of the vote (conceivably as small as 35 percent) that his legitimacy might be questioned. If a specific percentage of the vote is required for victory, 50 percent seems unrealistic, particularly with the direct or proportional methods. Therefore, proponents of reform have settled on 40 percent as a compromise figure, low enough for a candidate to be able to attain it and high enough to assure legitimacy. The danger lies in creating more fragmentation by encouraging more candidates or parties to compete. The more of them there are, the less likely any one can win even 40 percent. Fears about legitimacy and fragmentation may very well be exaggerated. If the voters continue to respond as they have, there should be no weakening of the two parties. It would be perfectly safe to assume that the candidate with the most votes will have either a majority or such a high plurality that the people would unquestionably accept the outcome.

Election Methods and Objectives

What begins as a straightforward attempt to reform presidential elections can involve the whole distribution of political power in the country. No matter how simple an objective may be, achieving it can become complicated. Table 5.3 is an attempt to anticipate the changes that would occur

TABLE 5.3   **Presidential Elections: The Objectives and the Methods.**

Objectives	Present Method	Proposed Methods		
		Direct	District	Proportional
Majority required to elect	yes	no *	yes *	no *
Equalize power of a vote nationally	no	yes	yes	no
Encourage two-party system	yes	yes/no	yes	yes/no
Reduce influence of large states	no	yes/no	yes	yes
Preserve identity of a state's vote	yes	no	yes	yes

* Not inherent in the method, depends upon a specific proposal. yes/no—indeterminate or controversial.

with each of the three proposals, compared with the present system. Obviously, the Table includes neither all conceivable objectives nor all of the possible results, and some results are shown to be indeterminate or controversial.

The two greatest weaknesses of the present system are the "faithless" elector who refuses to vote for his party's presidential candidate, and the unlikely possibility of a minority president who receives fewer popular votes than his opponent. The "faithless" elector can be eliminated by abolishing presidential electors and having each state's vote cast automatically by some state official. A suggestion for insuring against minority presidents is to combine the abolition of presidential electors with a bonus of fifty or one hundred electoral votes added to the candidate with the plurality of popular votes.[29] Ways can be found to eliminate some of the disadvantages without losing the advantages.

Quite simply, the overall advantage of the present system is that it works as an election method and achieves most of the objectives of different political interests.[30] The presidential candidate with the strongest national following wins and often has a majority of the popular vote as well. The choice lies between what we know and the uncertainties of a method we can devise.

POLITICAL MONEY

It is impossible to run for public office without spending money, yet there is no more sensitive political subject than the *sources*, the *amounts*, and the *implications* of these expenditures.

Political money is a problem both for the public and for fund-raisers although the two see the problem differently. Most of those responsible for financing campaigns would, no doubt, prefer a source of fixed and dependable income without having to beg, cajole, or threaten. The only solution for them would be a system of party dues or regular contributions from a large number of people, characteristic of mass parties. In the early days of the party system, when ownership of property was the primary voting qualification, it was natural to depend upon the well-to-do for contributions. This method of collecting money proved to be so effective that it continued even when the principles of democratic suffrage were adopted.[31]

As the importance of money in politics became greater, people failed

---

[29] Neal R. Peirce, "Bonus Plan Alters Electoral College," Washington Post Service, *The Miami Herald*, March 19, 1978, p. 3E.

[30] Polsby and Wildavsky, *Presidential Elections*, pp. 242–53.

[31] Alvan Kass, *Politics in New York State 1800–1830* (Syracuse, N.Y.: Syracuse University Press, 1965) p. 26.

to distinguish among motives for contributing. The size of a contribution is not necessarily indicative of an illegal or unethical intent. W. Clement Stone did not need to contribute $2 million to the Nixon campaign in 1972 to buy influence. No one is likely to contribute ten dollars or $2 million without feeling some compatibility with the candidate. The growth of the powers of the federal government has had its own peculiar effect upon motives. Heads of corporations made illegal contributions to the Nixon campaign in 1972 to buy protection, a form of insurance against the use of government power. The motive for giving was less suspect than the means used to motivate the giving.

Money as a Campaign Resource

Money in the amount of hundreds of millions spent in one election year appears astronomical. But it is not as excessive as it seems, considering such factors as the number of officials elected, the length of campaigns, the need to reach more people through the high-priced facilities of the media, and the nearly doubling of costs because of both primary and general elections. Expenditures also vary with the state and with the extent of competition in a campaign. It is still true that the real costs of campaigns have not increased compared with the nation's price level and income. The $540 million spent for all campaigning in 1976 was less than 1 percent of all government budgets—federal, state, and local.[32] All the same, the fear remains that elections can be bought, a danger that is certainly not confined to the United States. Political corruption abounds in many countries, not just capitalistic systems, and is similar in kind, if not in degree, in the U.S.S.R.[33]

The problem really is to identify the importance of money in campaigns. Probably the popular view is that the most money wins elections, but the most money does not always win. It is a tale told over and over again that Republicans since 1932 have usually outspent Democrats in presidential elections. Yet, Democrats won nearly twice as many of these elections from 1932 to 1972 as Republicans. Could the Democrats have beaten Eisenhower or Nixon with more money? If the Republicans had spent even more, could they have won more of these elections? It may be

---

[32] Daniel J. Elazar, *American Federalism: A View from the States*, 2nd ed. (New York: Thomas Y. Crowell Company, 1972) pp. 134–35. Alexander Heard, *The Costs of Democracy* (Chapel Hill, N.C.: The University of North Carolina Press, 1960) pp. 5–6. The most extensive research on presidential campaign spending has been done by Herbert E. Alexander and the Citizens' Research Foundation. In addition to publications on individual presidential years, a general source is Alexander, *Financing Politics: Money, Elections and Political Reform* (Washington, D.C.: Congressional Quarterly Press, 1976). Also Alexander interview in *U.S. News & World Report*, October 16, 1978, p. 29.

[33] John M. Kramer, "Political Corruption in the U.S.S.R.," *The Western Political Quarterly*, 30 (June 1977) 213–24.

difficult to find anyone, except the losing candidates and their closest supporters, who would answer "yes".[34]

It seems that candidates themselves always believe they need more money whether their campaign budgets are in hundreds of dollars or in millions of dollars. It is difficult to find candidates who do not think they are being outspent. There is no way of being sure, but it is quite likely, that insufficient money is not nearly as serious a problem as the useless spending of money. A campaign is a short-term, hectic operation. There is seldom time or inclination to analyze and allocate money in the most rational manner. Information is incomplete, and fear of losing dominates decisions.

The greatest puzzle about campaign expenditures is why money is not more effective in winning elections. The answer is to be found in the resources candidates possess besides the money they raise and spend themselves.

Other Resources

Money is such a dramatic and highly publicized subject that its importance is magnified while other campaign resources are easily overlooked.

One of these resources is money not handled by candidates, but *government money*, spent through legislative appropriations. Federal money flows out for what seems to be every conceivable purpose, but government officials are more inclined to spend during election years. The theme of most incumbents' campaigns is "See what I've done for you lately." Government money, though not ordinarily thought of as candidates' campaign costs, helps to create a tone of greater satisfaction within the electorate. It pacifies, if it does not please, various economic interests and politically important groups. Government money may not necessarily win any specific election, but there is hardly a person in politics who doubts that spending, or not spending, has an effect upon voting.

People who run for reelection have a very genuine resource: *incumbency*.[35] This advantage varies somewhat with different offices, but it still gives candidates a head start in a campaign. The resource of incumbency means in some cases that incumbents do not have to raise and spend as much money as their challengers. Members of Congress have a distinct advantage in being able to communicate directly to constituents at taxpayers' expense by use of the franking privilege, except for a period of six months before an election. It can hardly be entirely coincidence that in California legislative and congressional elections in the 1970s, and in all House elections in 1972, the more a challenger spent, the smaller the in-

---

[34] Polsby and Wildavsky, *Presidential Elections*, pp. 52–56.
[35] See the discussion of incumbents in Chapter 8.

cumbent's margin of victory.[36] It is definitely no coincidence that challengers often have more difficulty raising money than incumbents.

An unfailing resource in politics is *publicity* in the media. This is most likely to favor incumbents because they are in a better position to make news and to have continuing exposure. Presidents have a built-in advantage because they are always news and normally can have access, upon request, to the television networks.

The *political party* is still a resource of great importance. Candidates receive support simply because of the party name. In some parts of the country, party organization work wins votes in the precincts by reminding people who the party candidates are.

As the effectiveness of party organization has declined, *endorsements* and *volunteer work* by private groups have become more significant. There is a distinction between campaign contributions by groups, which is political money given to candidates, and the contribution of votes made possible by support from group membership. No group is likely to vote as a unit unless its members sense a direct threat, like a truck company whose officials and employees oppose new weight restrictions on highways. But, support from large groups, like labor unions, can be crucial in some races. Rather than having to raise big sums of money for advertising, a candidate has only to cultivate a large body of voters already receptive to the candidate's campaign. Small groups of supporters, such as students, may make up for their lack of numbers by their intense and persuasive campaigning.

Group support usually involves both *direct campaign contributions* to candidates and indirect, "in kind," contributions in expenditures of money and man-hours by the group itself. *Indirect contributions* can be more effective and cannot be equated in dollars-and-cents. The direct contributions of labor unions are sometimes comparatively small, but their indirect contributions range from support in union newspapers, to registration and get-out-the-vote drives. They also perform the functions of the Democratic party organization itself in some parts of the country.

Regulation by federal and state law is indicative of the attention given to money contributed to, and spent, by candidates.

Regulations

Basically, there are two alternatives in the attempt to control the raising and spending of money by parties or candidates: Set *legal ceilings* on the amounts or rely upon *detailed reporting* to expose questionable and illegal practices. Generally, governments use both kinds of regulations, including

[36] Stanton A. Glantz, Alan I. Abramowitz, and Michael P. Burkart, "Election Outcomes: Whose Money Matters?" *The Journal of Politics*, 38 November 1976) 1033–38.

restrictions or prohibitions upon contributions from specified sources such as corporations and labor unions.

In the history of regulating campaign finance, the *Federal Elections Campaign Act of 1974* contained some remarkable features. Presidential nominations are financed by federal money raised directly from those taxpayers who contribute one dollar to a Presidential Election Campaign Fund on their income-tax returns. The Act also created a Federal Elections Commission as an independent regulatory agency with powers to enforce criminal penalties, with a maximum fine of $50,000.

To be eligible for federal money, a candidate for the presidential nomination must raise at least $5,000 in each of twenty states through individual contributions of $250.00 or less. The Federal Elections Commission then matches a candidate's money up to a maximum of $5 million so that the most a candidate can spend for the nomination is $10 million. A candidate must receive at least 10 percent of the vote in three consecutive primaries or federal funding is cut off. Major-party candidates cannot raise money after their nominations but must operate their general-election campaigns solely on federal money. The Federal Election Commission allotted $22 million to each candidate in 1976.

Minor parties do not fare so well. They are eligible for federal money in the general election only if they received 5 percent of the total presidential vote in the previous election. Therefore, in 1976, minor parties were not eligible for federal money, and none will be eligible in 1980 because no minor party candidate received 5 percent of the vote in 1976. Independent presidential candidates who run without a party name, as Eugene McCarthy did in 1976, will have to finance their campaigns solely by themselves.

The Supreme Court made some significant changes in the 1974 Act. It held, as a matter of constitutional principle, that candidate expenditures, not contributions, can be limited by law. However, a candidate's expenditures for nomination and election can be limited only if the candidate chooses public financing. If candidates forego public financing, they can spend whatever amounts they can raise.

Congress had also provided that an individual may give no more than $1,000 to a candidate in a primary or a general election and no more than $25,000 to all candidates in any one calendar year. No political committee or other group is able to contribute more than $5,000 in any primary or general election. The Supreme Court did not disturb these provisions but held that an individual or a group on its own can spend without limit as long as the money is separate from a candidate's expenditures. During the general election campaign, for example, an individual or a group can spend thousands of dollars to help elect a presidential candidate but cannot buy him a meal.

Certain generalizations can be made regarding the applicability and effects of the Act of 1974 as amended by the Supreme Court:

Public Financing. The public financing of presidential nominations requires candidates to start their campaigns long before the national conventions in order to raise money in small contributions. Even if candidates choose the option of raising all of their money, they have to begin early in order to compete for *contributions* and *publicity*. A special advantage is that a candidate can keep money left over from an unsuccessful campaign and use it in another campaign four years later.

Small Contributions. By requiring that money be raised in small contributions, the law makes *professional fund-raisers* and *direct-mail specialists* the new elite in the business of financing campaigns. They replace the former large contributors. Under the law presidential candidates are permitted to spend as much as 20 percent beyond the legal limits for the cost of fund-raising. To raise large amounts in small contributions requires money to begin with and involves financial risks. A direct mailing of a million letters from a computerized list can cost over a quarter of a million dollars. Lists of known contributors become an important resource, and fund-raisers exchange or buy and sell them. In order to attract large numbers of small contributors, it appears that candidates must build a well-identified constituency by taking strong stands on controversial issues. Examples of such candidates have been George Wallace, George McGovern, and Ronald Reagan.

Limits on Campaign Spending. The Supreme Court, in effect, removed limits on campaign spending by freeing individuals and groups from restrictions upon their *indirect expenditures*. There are also no limits upon individual contributions to *organizations* which carry on their own campaigns. Labor unions can continue to use their traditional resources through the Committee on Political Education (COPE). Every conceivable group or business is free to spend voluntary funds through its own political action committees (PAC), be they corporations, trade associations, banks, utilities, or fast food chains. Estimates of the number of PAC's which will ultimately be created run as high as 16,000.

Fiscal Responsibility. Presidential candidates, who long ago were made independent of their parties in raising and spending money, now have no control over or responsibility for all of the money spent on their own behalf. Instead of campaign money being centralized, it has been further dispersed in private hands. This *decentralization*, furthermore, is institutionalized by encouraging a multitude of separate groups to act on their own.

What Happened to the Parties?

Laws regulating political money first appeared in the twentieth century when candidates were becoming the center of attention and the intention was to limit their spending. If laws had been passed in the nineteenth century, they probably would have applied to political party organizations as well. It is intriguing to speculate whether the leaders of party committees would have maintained their positions of strength by their control over money if regulations had applied principally to parties. When the laws were enacted, they emphasized what reformers wanted, the individual responsibility of candidates directly to the public. The parties themselves were shunted aside.

Regulations of parties came largely through restrictive provisions applying to committees which support candidates. The Act of 1974, in addition to restrictions, offers party committees a greatly expanded role in financing campaigns. State and national party committees can spend $10,000 in each congressional district for House elections and two cents multiplied by a state's voting age population in each Senate election. Except as restricted by state laws, party committees can finance state and local elections. The Elections Commission ruled in 1976 that each state and local party committee could raise and spend $1,000 for its presidential candidate and that each national committee could likewise raise and spend about $3.2 million.

The parties are also brought into the public financing system with $2 million available for each national convention if the party's national committee requests the money. In 1978, in addition, Congress extended to all political committees, including the two parties' national committees, the 2.7 cent postage rate for bulk mailing. This is the same rate used by non-profit organizations, such as Common Cause and the National Rifle Association, for their political mailings. This mailing rate should prove to be a substantial saving, considering that direct-mail campaigns have cost as much as 30 cents a letter.

The authorization for expenditures by national committees in congressional elections is a significant responsibility because candidates can be expected to press their committees for the money. The result is a complete reversal of the trend to submerge parties and raises the prospects for some genuine revival of party activity.

THE IMPORTANCE OF REFORMS

When we consider the total impact of reforms, whether singly or together, they really do not account for the status of political parties in the twentieth century. It is true that parties have been most directly challenged where it has hurt most, in the nominating processes. *Primaries*, both for making nominations within the states and for choosing delegates to national conventions, have had the most influence in weakening parties as institutions. When all of this is conceded, the fact remains that, if parties had been strong to begin with, they would not necessarily have been hurt by these reforms; that popular participation in primaries might have been higher; and that interest in candidates might have been more party-oriented.

The weakening effects of reforms might have been reflections, not causes, of popular withdrawal from parties. The public gives evidence of being more attracted to candidates as persons than to an institutionalized political system.

This shift in emphasis from structure and institutions to popular personal images is inseparable from the influence of the *mass media* of communication. The media present personal conflicts and qualities much more readily and effectively than substantive issues or impersonal forces. This media characteristic is partly inescapable. In the frenzied business of reporting the daily news, it is difficult to portray either the subtlety or the depth of institutional development. The characteristic is also partly from choice: What is reported is built around what the public is understood to want to see and hear.

Many developments within the party system were, therefore, beyond the power or responsibility of either reformers or party leaders. At the outset of the communications revolution, some of the reformers were more adaptable to the mass media. But, as a group they were either oblivious or resentful of the new breed of mass communications specialists who were to play a far greater role than reformers in usurping party functions.

The revolution in the means of communication and its effects upon the manner of seeking votes, to be discussed in the next chapter, will complete the story of the challenges to the party system.

6

The Winning of the Votes

One of the legacies of elections in democratic societies is a constant preoccupation with the means for *persuading* one person to vote for another person. Judging from experience, people are not likely to vote for strangers, so persuasion begins with means for making a candidate familiar to the voters through advertising. Methods of advertising have changed remarkably over the years, but the objective has remained constant.

As long as elections were primarily for officials elected locally, voters could become personally acquainted with candidates. The need for advertising, as we think of it, did not arise until candidates were elected to higher offices. The more physically remote the offices were from voters, the greater the problems of candidates becoming familiar. The hopelessness of expecting the individual voter to be aware of qualified candidates for President of the United States was one of the reasons the delegates at the Constitutional Convention created a special presidential electorate in each state. They hoped presidential electors would be in a better position than the public-at-large to be familiar with national leaders.

The whole concept of *campaigning* was radically changed when political parties appeared. Although a campaign period had been an accepted part of the election sequence, parties gave continuity to political competition. The official campaign period became distinguished only by the increased tempo and intensity of activity. Parties conducted campaigns on behalf of the whole party ticket so that candidates and parties were constantly advertised together. As a result, voters could become instantly familiar with candidates whom they knew nothing about personally.

POLITICAL COMMUNICATION

Campaigning has depended upon the possibilities for exploiting available communication media. When government was mainly local, candidates could ask their friends to vote for them. In time, the printed word became essential for, even in rural America, all campaigning could not be a personal, one-to-one, relationship between the candidate and the voter.

The Era of the Parties

Reliance upon printed communication led to the *party press*, which actually preceded parties themselves. Alexander Hamilton and others founded *The Gazette of the United States* in 1789 to present the Federalist point of view. In 1792, Jefferson, Madison, and others who opposed the Federalists, countered with *The National Gazette*. These newspapers set the precedent for government subsidizing partisan journalism by awarding printing contracts and giving editors patronage appointments.[1] In the late 1820s, the Jacksonians created a nation-wide system of approximately 600 newspapers with a total publication cost of half a million dollars a year.[2]

Political campaigning had been leisurely and even relatively gentle when few were to be elected and few turned out to vote. As the society and its government grew in size, running for office turned into a frantic and many-faceted activity. Democratization of the suffrage created a mass electorate and, as the numbers climbed, candidates were under increasing pressure to find more effective means for communication. The means seemed to appear in response to the demands.

Political leaders were not always quick to catch the nuances of these new means but, once recognized and accepted, they were fully exploited. One of the results of the *telegraph*, which made it possible to send news across the country in a matter of hours, was the danger of making contradictory statements to different audiences. This sobering realization was far outweighted by the stunning advances in the ability to communicate over great distances without having to mount a horse. If a speaker had to watch what he said, he knew that what he did say could be quickly transmitted far and wide. *Newspapers and magazines* brought all manner of political events to national attention if the events were important enough. Abraham Lincoln was certainly indebted to these means for capturing national attention during his debates with Stephen A. Douglas in 1858.

The nineteenth century became a party era because parties gave character and tone to campaigning, and elections were largely won or lost depending upon the party's success in mobilizing loyal partisans. This style of campaigning was appropriately labeled "militarist." Voters were fired up for combat at the polls in the manner of troops being drilled on a

---

[1] James E. Pollard, *The Presidents and the Press* (New York: The Macmillan Company, 1947) pp. 8–10. Noble E. Cunningham, *The Jeffersonian Republicans: The Formation of Party Organization, 1789–1801* (Chapel Hill, N.C.: The University of North Carolina Press, 1957) pp. 13–19.

[2] Robert V. Remini, *The Election of Andrew Jackson* (New York: J. B. Lippincott Company, 1963) pp. 76–77, 129.

parade ground, and elections took on the appearance of clashes between two armies arrayed against each other on the political field of battle.[3]

The Era of the Mass Media

As early as the middle of the nineteenth century, it was possible to detect what Daniel Boorstin called the "Graphic Revolution" in communications as the printed word was more rapidly reproduced, and news became a commodity to be sold. "By a giant leap Americans crossed the gulf from the daguerreotype to color television in less than a century." [4] Out of the Graphic Revolution, came both new means and new purposes for communication. Advertising to sell intangibles as well as tangibles became "public relations." Corporations hired professional writers with newspaper backgrounds to create positive business publicity in order to counteract the effects of the reformers and "muck-rakers." Gradually, *public relations* became an integral part of corporate organization, and concern with companies' images broadened to a concern for the public's likes and dislikes about products. In this way, commercial marketing research was born.[5]

Advertising to create a positive institutional image soon spread to other groups—professional, charitable, religious, educational. Government agencies turned to public relations to sell themselves both to the public and to legislators who appropriated the agencies' funds. The federal bureaucracy's involvement became so extensive that as early as 1913, Congress prohibited agencies within the executive branch from making expenditures for "publicity experts" unless the money was specifically appropriated for the purpose. To evade the legislation, agencies hired experts under other titles, and publicity was camouflaged with names such as "information" or "record-keeping." [6]

Mass Communications and the Parties

Nineteenth-century party leaders, in the main, were not prepared for these revolutionary changes. Election battles relied upon party loyalties. Appeals to voters in the other party risked disturbing the loyalties within your own

[3] Richard Jensen, *The Winning of the Midwest: Social and Political Conflict, 1888–1896* (Chicago: The University of Chicago Press, 1971) p. 11; and Jensen, "Armies, Admen, and Crusaders: Types of Presidential Election Campaigns," *History Teacher,* 2 (January 1969) p. 34.

[4] Daniel J. Boorstin, *The Image* (New York: Harper and Row, Colophon Books, 1961) p. 13.

[5] Stanley Kelley, Jr., *Professional Public Relations and Political Power* (Baltimore, Md.: The Johns Hopkins Press, 1956) pp. 9–13; and *passim* for the following discussion.

[6] James L. McCamy, *Government Publicity* (Chicago: University of Chicago Press, 1939) pp. 6–8.

party.[7] Leaders who thought in terms of single constituencies and dealt with individuals on a person-to-person basis found it difficult to adopt the impersonal approach to mass persuasion. But this whole political way of life began to erode as the "militarist" style of campaigning gave way to a "merchandising" style. Early in the twentieth century, parties sometimes hired *press agents* who were descended from the editors of party newspapers and were to be the ancestors of political consultants. But, most party leaders resisted such innovations.

Intimate connections between the professions of politics and journalism, as well as the rise of public relations helped candidates break away from parties to go it on their own. Prominence and personal images became assets to candidates. At last the Progressives could not only attack "bosses and machines" but also sever their connections with them. In 1912, Theodore Roosevelt divided the Republican party and then bolted to become the Progressive party candidate for President. The effectiveness of Woodrow Wilson's public relations played a considerable part in making him one of the heroic Progressives in classic mold.

The government's success with professionally directed promotional campaigns during World War I convinced many political leaders of the effectiveness of the new methods for winning votes as well. The Republicans used *advertising* experts both in their 1918 congressional and 1920 presidential campaigns. Herbert Hoover has been portrayed as being ahead of his time in the use of public-relations techniques. He, in turn, became a victim of the extremely skillful attacks of Charles Michelson, who headed the first permanent party publicity bureau, created by the Democratic national committee in 1929.[8] The Republican presidential nomination of Wendell Willkie in 1940 was attributable to the power of pretelevision mass media and the effectiveness of specialists in manipulating public opinion.

The media and political consultants became the two principal components in campaigning. Each of these will be taken up separately.

THE QUALITIES OF THE MEDIA

Skill in political advertising depends upon an understanding of the requirements and special advantages of the various mass media, which consist of print, electronic, billboards, and telephone banks. Newspapers, radio, and television are of special importance.

---

[7] Robert D. Marcus, *Grand Old Party: Political Structure in the Gilded Age 1880–1896* (New York: Oxford University Press, 1971) pp. 7–8.

[8] Jensen, "Armies, Admen, and Crusaders," pp. 43–44. Craig Lloyd, *Aggressive Introvert* (Columbus, Ohio: Ohio State University Press, 1972). Charles Michelson, *The Ghost Talks* (New York: G. P. Putnam's Sons, 1944). Kelley, *Professional Public Relations and Political Power*, pp. 30–35.

Media Before Television

Since candidates are dependent upon the reporting of news, they first learned how to take advantage of *newspaper publicity*. This involved making stories and headlines by timing statements and activities to conform to newspaper deadlines and learning what would likely warrant pictures as part of a news story. Newspapers, in turn, emphasized candidates' records and reputations by describing what they did. The printed word standing between the reader and the candidates created an image which is derivative and secondary.[9] When *radio* appeared, people in politics looked upon it as a powerful supplement to newspapers and generally greeted it with enthusiasm.

The qualities of radio were easy to grasp, and candidates adjusted to it quickly. By the mid-1920s, radio had become indispensable in campaigning. At last there was a medium which brought voices directly to voters and emphasized talk, which had always been the staple political commodity. Communicating over air waves presented the fabulous opportunity to reach an entire constituency instantaneously.

However, radio involved something more than just talking into a microphone. Although radio reached a large number of people at one time, the members of the audience listened in solitude or in small groups, not as part of a large gathering where crowd response could be a factor in the communication. Intimacy was one of the principal qualities of radio. Franklin Roosevelt recognized and successfully exploited it in his famous "fireside chats" from the White House. Radio created images through the dimension of sound, but the listener played a largely personal role in creating the images. At its height, radio was characterized as the "theater of the mind. People became their own art directors, their own costume designers and every set was a color set." [10] Radio listening makes it possible to concentrate upon words. As with print media, one is able to grasp ideas and follow a train of thought because there is no inherent distraction in radio communication itself.

Some political techniques, now associated with television, originated on radio; spot advertisements, for example, were used in Alfred Landon's 1936 presidential campaign.[11] The stampede to television was largely at the expense of radio, but television did not make radio obsolete in politics. Radio is so accessible and so intimate a part of daily life that it is taken for granted and often overlooked. It has a dependable audience, because listener

[9] Gene Wyckoff, *The Image Candidates: American Politics in the Age of Television* (New York: The Macmillan Company, 1968) pp. 11, 100–1.

[10] One-time radio star, Brett Morrison, quoted *St. Louis Globe-Democrat*, December 9, 1974, p. 2A.

[11] Edward W. Chester, *Radio, Television and American Politics* (New York: Sheed and Ward, 1969) pp. 8–64.

loyalty to a particular station is greater than in the case of television. Many radio stations appeal to special groups which have similar tastes in music and features. Thus, a candidate can "zero in" on a particular audience with some assurance that the message will be received. Compared with television, radio time is cheaper, can be purchased more quickly, and production is far simpler.[12]

Television

When the possibilities of television were recognized, the medium was acclaimed as the supreme instrument for communicating to a mass audience. At last it was possible to control what was seen as well as what was heard. Timeless problems could be solved once and for all.

Television has bequeathed us the word "image" because the medium conveys visual impressions. Image has been defined as "the conceptions of qualities that people associate with certain objects, products, or individuals." [13] The concept of image in politics, of course, is ancient. Political leaders have always built images but before television, the more likely term was "magnetic," "impression," or "effect," and image was not equated with any one medium. Perhaps the printed word and radio conveyed images more and ideas less than we have been inclined to think, but the impact of television upon politics has been more completely image.

The qualities of television make it a new kind of communication because it is important for techniques of presentation rather than substance. With television, it has been said, the medium itself is the message. Unlike all of the other media, television image is direct but there is a monumental difference between image and influence. Television influence is indirect rather than direct, covert rather than overt, and subtle rather than obvious.[14] Television supports the judgment that images of events and persons are synthetic and ambiguous because they are the likeness of something and, in turn, become "a likeness of the image. The image of a thing becomes more real than the thing itself." [15]

Some of these distinctive qualities were not immediately understood. The response of most candidates in the 1950s was to saturate television with time-tested techniques on the assumption that all the new medium did was to magnify the effects of visual exposure. As late as the 1960s, a

[12] Joseph Napolitan, *The Election Game and How to Win It* (New York: Doubleday and Company, Inc., 1972) pp. 88–92. Wyckoff, *The Image Candidates,* pp. 63–144.

[13] Dan Nimmo, *The Political Persuaders* (Englewood Cliffs, N.J.: Prentice-Hall, Inc., 1970) p. 144.

[14] Harold Mendelsohn and Irving Crespi, *Polls, Television, and the New Politics* (Scranton, Pa.: Chandler Publishing Company, 1970) p. 255.

[15] Boorstin, *The Image,* pp. 9–40.

campaign analyst could still write that "Too often the political candidate approaches TV as though it were radio with a picture." [16] Speakers also failed to realize that they were directly competing with entertainment shows. Viewers who did not relish a candidate's speech could easily change channels and escape.

Creating Television Personalities

Some specialists in the use of television conclude that viewers are influenced by the presentation of the overall situation. The audience is oriented toward the people they see without being consciously aware of their orientation. Thus, television has indirect, subtle, and covert influences. Crystallization of preexisting viewer orientations, rather than audience conversion, is the most common effect.

Television characterizes candidates directly but how they come through to an audience is determined by their *appearance, demeanor,* and *style* of presentation more than by the substance of what they say. The most difficult thing for candidates to learn is that talk is the smallest part of the message and, therefore, of the image. As Eugene McCarthy once observed, "You don't have to have anything to say to appear on television." [17] People invite a candidate into their living rooms for a visit, not to hear a speech, and they lose their feeling of involvement if the candidate seems to bombard the camera. Intimacy is not inherent in television although the setting may create the feeling of intimacy, especially with the use of close-up camera shots. The audience may not always distinguish between close-ups and intimacy.[18]

Television invites viewers to employ their stereotypes, those pictures we have in our minds which influence our thinking and our decisions. Consciously or not, viewers are likely to "match the images in their mental picture galleries against the images of candidates seen on television and derive an impression of the candidates' characters accordingly." To project a winning image, then, requires the awakening in the viewer of "elements of projection that reside in the viewer rather than in the person viewed." [19]

Candidates should appear to be fighters but not disturbingly aggressive. A particular illustration of this distinction occurred in 1962, during the

[16] Stephen C. Shadegg, *How to Win an Election* (New York: Taplinger Publishing Company, 1972) p. 168.

[17] Quoted in John Whale, *The Half-Shut Eye* (New York: St. Martin's Press, Inc., 1969) p. 173.

[18] Kurt Lang and Gladys Engel Lang, *Politics and Television* (Chicago: Quadrangle Books, 1968) p. 204.

[19] Wyckoff, *The Image Candidates*, p. 208. Lang and Lang, *Politics and Television*, p. 189.

first joint television appearance of Edward M. Kennedy and Edward J. McCormack, Jr., who were competing for the Democratic senatorial nomination in Massachusetts. McCormack closed his remarks with an attack reminiscent of hard-hitting, old-time politics: "If his name was Edward Moore, with your qualifications, Teddy, your candidacy would be a joke, but nobody's laughing because his name is Edward Moore Kennedy." Voter reaction made it clear that McCormack had committed a serious tactical error by arousing a defensive sympathy for Kennedy. The validity of what McCormack said apparently was not considered except by those who already opposed Kennedy.[20]

Familiarity. Television rewards techniques which project images and, within these limits, the medium presents great possibilities. Two, in particular, are of major importance. Television offers a candidate unique opportunities to become quickly *familiar to the public.* It is possible now for a stranger to become a distinct personality and even a star performer in the period of a few weeks. Familiarity does not always produce votes, but television provides the means for becoming familiar.

Audience Appeal. Candidates learned how to make use of the large audiences provided by television entertainment. With *spot-advertisements,* candidates can control the time and circumstances of their appearances, either for large audiences watching prime-time shows, or for specifically selected audiences watching such programs as sporting events or afternoon serials. Candidates can purchase these ads in time-segments up to five minutes to be used during commercial breaks or sandwiched in between programs. Audiences already conditioned to interruptions for commercials will not tune out. Television spots make "politicians happy, do not annoy audiences by interrupting their entertainment, and make money." [21]

Short spots are designed to project a personal image. By producing them in a studio, it is possible to rehearse until the film is satisfactory. As an alternative, a film-maker can shoot scenes of a candidate engaged in the question-and-answer format or campaigning out among the people. The film can be edited to be put in documentary form for longer showings or be chopped up into short segments for spots. The candidate can be advertised by testimonials either from a well-known figure or a nobody representing the average honest voter who is looking for a candidate who says things which make sense.

Leaving the candidate out of his advertisements can be a matter of the highest strategy. In Governor Nelson Rockefeller's reelection campaign in New York, in 1966, it became necessary to draw attention away from

[20] Murray B. Levin, *Kennedy Campaigning* (Boston: Beacon Press, 1966) pp. 187–232.

[21] Robert MacNeil, *The People Machine* (New York: Harper and Row, 1968) p. 195.

him personally because his popularity was at such a low point. Spots of graphic motion pictures concentrated on the Rockefeller record in office depicting his efforts to fight crime and improve highway safety, but Rockefeller himself was never shown. The productions were a fascinating supplement to the rule of personal advertising, and the strategy was apparently vindicated. In a four-man race, the Governor was reelected.[22]

CONSULTANTS

Public relations became an industry of advertising agencies, and because some of these agencies were located on Madison Avenue, in New York City, they all became known as "Madison Avenue agencies." The birthplace of "Madison Avenue" in politics was not in New York, however, but in California. There, the Progressive Movement took root early and was very successful in weakening party organizations and making elections revolve solely around individual candidates. One of the principle results, which Progressives generally had not foreseen, was the rise of professional political consultants to replace the parties. In 1936, Whitaker and Baxter became the first *political consultant firm* and soon built a national reputation by managing both candidates and referenda on the California ballot.[23]

The nomenclature applied to specialists in campaigns is far less exact than the services they render. For example, a candidate can hire an agency to manage a campaign, but there are hundreds of agencies of various kinds, offering a wide assortment of services. Some large advertising agencies, which handle commercial accounts, have taken on political campaigns as a sideline. Among agencies that handle only political campaigns, some provide various services and others are, actually, one person who hires out to a candidate and then makes contracts with other free-lance specialists. All of these agencies, large and small, are usually referred to as "consultants." Therefore, specialists become consultants whether they are generalists with the ability to manage a campaign or merely take polls, make films, or buy television time. Some consultants work only for candidates of one party or even of one particular ideology. Other consultants contract with candidates of either party and without regard to ideology.

Advertising candidates is a specialized application of the strategies of persuasion. Compared with other advertising programs, a political campaign is short, progressively intensive, and directed toward one final culmin-

[22] *Ibid.*, pp. 209–22. Wyckoff, *The Image Candidates*, pp. 229–30.

[23] Robert J. Pitchell, "The Influence of Professional Campaign Management Firms in Partisan Elections in California," *The Western Political Quarterly*, 11 (June 1958) 278–300. James M. Perry, *The New Politics* (New York: Clarkson N. Potter, Inc., 1968) pp. 7–16.

ation on election day. Within these limitations, consultants propose courses of action designed for a particular candidate in a particular campaign.

Research and Campaign Management

The so-called "Madison Avenue" political campaign is a plan to be executed by specialists. The intricacies of the plan and the number of specialists vary only with the level of the office sought and the amount of effort and money to be expended. Any service can be provided from raising money, to recruiting volunteers, to supplying computerized information. *Accounting and legal services* are now imperative for congressional and presidential candidates to keep them within the technical requirements of federal law.

Members of Congress are a special case, for they have a *permanent campaign staff* in their Washington offices as well as back home. Members of the House often use their field secretaries as managers, and some of these secretaries operate advertising agencies, so the candidates have their services at a lower cost. Some House candidates hire a manager who has experience in a service such as the media, advertising, party affairs, or local campaigns which is valuable in a particular congressional district.[24]

A campaign plan requires both data and judgment so as to win the maximum number of votes for the amount of energy expended. Research is the means for providing data about voters, obtained from them with or without their knowledge.

Polls and Surveys. Campaigns have always involved two-way communication as candidates sought out voters to listen as well as to talk. The impossibility of meeting all voters face-to-face gave rise to systems for encouraging voters to provide information for political assessments.

Throughout the nineteenth century, leaders used the network of party committees as a polling organization. In the summer of 1860, the chairman of the Pennsylvania Republican state committee correctly predicted the Republican victory based on an actual count and on a careful estimate made "by reliable men residing in the precincts." [25] Party leaders became experts in interpreting *trends* and in "sizing up" a political situation. Their accumulated wisdom, when fortified by reports from party associates and head counts of various kinds, was usually sufficient for managing a campaign. When the country became more diverse, fragmented, and independent of party, better sources of political information were needed.

[24] David Leuthold, *Electioneering in a Democracy* (New York: John Wiley & Sons, Inc., 1968) pp. 86–89.

[25] Michael Fitzgibbon Holt, *Forging a Majority: The Formation of the Republican Party in Pittsburgh, 1848–1860* (New Haven, Ct.: Yale University Press, 1969) pp. 264–66.

The public relations industry carried on *research* to produce reliable *data* which would satisfy dollar-conscious business executives. One important advantage of large, well-organized companies, as compared with individual business entrepreneurs, was the development of superior means for knowing how to merchandise their products. Political leaders, who relied upon hunches and impressionistic evidence of what voters were thinking, have been likened to those individual entrepreneurs and their more primitive ways of doing business. As the corner grocery store was no match for a supermarket chain, neither were political leaders a match for the new research specialists.[26]

Gathering political information, outside of political party polling, began with "straw polls," which were taken as far back as the presidential election of 1824.[27] These polls suffered from weak methodology because opinions were solicited indiscriminately without regard to demographic differences or political attitudes. It was not until the 1930s that attention was given to selecting representative samples and to the wording of questions.[28]

Simply asking a question of a sample of respondents and tabulating the answers is satisfactory for some limited purposes, but polling as a research technique is substantially more than a mere head count. It is possible to broaden and deepen the quality of data by investigating such areas as the relationship of attitudes to party identification and voting decisions; the identification of characteristics associated with voters and nonvoters; and the political significance of such demographic characteristics.

Private polling has become a regular service for candidates to help them assess their prospects before entering a campaign and to keep up with voters' reactions during the course of a campaign. From these polls, candidates can learn the public's images of them, the relative salience of issues, and where to concentrate their campaigns. Because information from private polls can strongly influence a campaign staff, creating either over-optimism or over-pessimism, only the candidate and a few of his closest associates may be given the data.

Through polling, candidates seek an audience with the people and, in the process, learn far more about them than they in turn are likely to learn about the candidates. Attempting to find out what people want and how they respond has always been an objective in politics, and polling has provided more refined ways to find out. Interpretations of research data

---

[26] Mendelsohn and Crespi, *Polls, Television, and the New Politics*, pp. 25–31, 166–67.

[27] Boorstin, *The Image*, p. 235. C. E. Robinson, *Straw Votes* (New York: Columbia University Press, 1932).

[28] On the techniques in polling, see Mendelsohn and Crespi, *Polls, Television, and the New Politics*, pp. 9–16. Nimmo, *The Political Persuaders*, pp. 85–110.

do not influence the public but directly influence the behavior of candidates who, to avoid being vulnerable themselves, must discover where voters are vulnerable.[29]

Data and Computers. Attempts to make campaign decision-making as scientific as possible have not been confined to polling. Candidates' staffs compile *lists of voters* from those who have written letters, contributed money, registered to vote, and answered questions either in door-to-door canvassing or in polls. These means can identify voters as being favorable, opposed, or capable of being persuaded by a candidate.

Much research, however, involves voters as anonymous individuals whose motivations can only be inferred, for example, from analyses of media markets, the areas served by specific media. Investigators give a great deal of attention to differences in age, sex, occupation, and residence, although it is risky to be carried away with assumptions about the relationship of demography and voting. In researching behavior and trends, voters should be examined in the smallest electoral boundaries which can be pinpointed.

Carrying out a campaign on the basis of such extensive data involves systems of collecting, indexing, processing, and retrieving information—from simple card-files to electronic data processing. *Computerized systems* are used for storing and handling voter lists and financial data. They allot television time and provide data banks of polling and election information. Computers match messages to a particular television audience and prepare personalized letters for direct mailings.[30] They have also been programmed to write pretested political speeches.

EFFECTS OF MEDIA AND CONSULTANTS

The principal components in campaigning can be examined separately, but they blend together to create a total result. The changes in campaigns brought about by political parties went beyond the simplicity of a candidate asking fellow-citizens for their votes, but the changes introduced by parties were modest compared with the technologies and services which have progressively appeared during the twentieth century. There is far more

[29] *The Political Image Merchants*, eds., Ray Hiebert, Robert Jones, Ernest Lotito, and John Lorenz (Washington, D.C.: Acropolis Books Ltd., 1971) pp. 63, 106, 134–36.

[30] Robert Agranoff, *The New Style in Election Campaigns* (Boston: Holbrook Press, Inc., 1972) pp. 123–205, 232–52. Robert P. Abelson, "Computers, Polls, and Public Opinion—Some Puzzles and Paradoxes," in *Politics/America, Transaction Society Reader*, ed., Walter Dean Burnham (New York: D. Van Nostrand Company, 1973) pp. 46–54. Joel D. Barkan and James E. Bruno, "Locating the Voter: Mathematical Models and the Analysis of Aggregate Data for Political Campaigns," *The Western Political Quarterly*, 27 (December 1974) 710–30.

involved than the survival of parties, for the effects have extended to candidates and beyond, to the integrity of the entire political process.

The Democratic Ideal

The political intrusion of the mass media has carried us further away from any aspirations for a simpler political system and the idealization of a citizen-politician democracy. This intrusion was so gradual that, for many years, it was not fully appreciated. Few apparently foresaw the impact of television but one who did, as early as the year 1925, commented that the prospects "should rouse the resentment of Mr. (William Jennings) Bryan, for the dangers seem greater on first glance than the teaching of evolution." [31]

The case against the mass media in general and television in particular is that the advertising industry has destroyed the *integrity* of the *democratic process* by developing the ability to sell us a candidate with the same deadly effectiveness as it sells us toothpaste. Neither as citizens nor as consumers are we equipped to see through the artistry and the sophistry. "Madison Avenue," with its legions of scientists and image-makers, can foist both synthetic commercial products and synthetic candidates upon us because we are automatons in front of our television sets, lacking either the moral fibre or the energy to turn them off and read a good book. All that is needed to make this process complete is the money to employ the brains to put the techniques to work.

One writer, who believed television had such effects upon the voters, developed a nostalgia for the "boss and the machine" in the "good old days," when even the passive, disinterested voter "was master of his own mind. Voting by instinct, by emotion, by prejudice, by bribery as he may have done; ignorant of the issues, unfamiliar with the candidates, putty in the hands of political bosses, perhaps, each voter still had the power, if he wished, to resist, and to make a decision in a private corner of his own thinking." [32] If the ghosts of Progressive reformers would writhe in agony at these words, contemporary mortals should at least be skeptical. The unquestioned belief in the power to manipulate is not only unflattering to voters but is also an exaggeration of the power of public relations and the media.

Candidates

Television brought changes both obvious and obscure. Its impact has been so great that a new word, "polivision," was coined to designate the phe-

---

[31] Quoted, *TV Guide*, September 29, 1973, p. 28.
[32] MacNeil, *The People Machine*, p. 227.

nomena of perceiving *politics inflenced by television.*[33] Even if it be true that the more things change, the more they are the same, it is difficult to see polivision as nothing more than the extension of old practices. The effects of television are more than political advertising in the traditional sense. By creating images through direct exposure, the effect goes far beyond conventional familiarity.

Superficiality. It is now possible to keep a public record of a candidate's every word, inflection, and facial expression, so the danger of saying or doing something which may stir up opposition is tremendously magnified. The requirements for projecting an acceptable image have put a premium upon the superficiality of blandness—the sugar-coated, cautious campaign style which has been referred to as "the bland leading the bland."

Unfortunately, speed in communication has encouraged artificiality and pretense, not depth and substance. There was a time when candidates could communicate without having a stop-watch held on them. Now, to be articulate is often equated with the ability to explain the state of the nation or the world in a few well-chosen words. Even five-minute spot-ads do not allow much opportunity for getting down to really substantive matters, so television has been blamed for short, snappy, facile statements.

Length of communication does not necessarily determine the calibre of communication as anyone can find out by reading samples of pretelevision speeches. Being forced to come to the point, because of space or time limitations, can make a presentation more concrete as well as more compact. Many candidates would be glad to purchase longer segments of television time to explain their positions if only the audience response was more encouraging. Thirty-minute television speeches have usually proved to be worth the cost only when candidates knew there was an audience out there that could be moved to send in contributions in response to the appeal for money at the close of the speech.

The mass communications industry is not responsible for candidates being selective in what they emphasize; they never were prone to give their opponents' arguments. Nor were simplification and distortions in campaigns unknown before the appearance of television and consultants. The use of effective slogans began at least in 1840 with "Tippecanoe and Tyler, too." Ambiguous meanings become attached to words and are then exploited for emotional political effect, such as "the missile gap" in 1960. Politics is a peripheral concern for many, and the first problem is to secure attention. Without the bombardments through the media, how much general public interest would there be?

Manipulation. Because candidates have the potential to become television personalities or "stars," it is easy to conclude that cynical statements

[33] Bernard Rubin, *Political Television* (Belmont, Calif.: Wadsworth Publishing Co., Inc., 1967) p. 1.

about the power of slick image-advertising are statements of absolute fact. John F. Kennedy's father, Joseph Kennedy, told his friends that "we're going to sell Jack like soap flakes." [34] The consultants seldom talk this way. As one facetiously put it: "We can sell candidates, it's almost impossible to sell soap." [35] Despite the frequent comparisons, candidates are not commercial products. Audiences do not make simple transfers from commercial advertising to candidate advertising. They perceive the two differently, so they feel differently about them. For example, people are more likely to be suspicious of a candidate than of a commercial product.[36]

The effectiveness of a skillful political performance has always been acclaimed as being a sure vote-getter, and candidates' successes have often been attributed to the most apparent and shallow causes. The assumption that a good "sales pitch" will inevitably succeed may be irresistible, but it is erroneous, even naive, to assume that attempts to persuade are necessarily successful. Activity should not be confused with effectiveness, and using television effectively is not the same thing as winning an election. If candidates always created the desired response, most candidates would win and there would be few losers.

If sincerity is an essential part of an image, as many consultants insist it is, then a successful image really cannot be synthesized. A sow's ear is never going to be seen as a silk purse, and a phony will come through very much like a phony. When there is little personal contrast between the images of opposing candidates, or when they differ sharply on issues, newspapers may have more influence than television. Controversy is unlikely to center on personalities alone unless there is otherwise a fundamental consensus.[37]

Even those candidates who are not heavily dependent upon television must learn how to use it as part of their stock-in-trade if they have political ambitions. It is no more insincere or cynical to learn how to use television with the aid of consultants than learning how to cope with other media. The only difference, which is monumental, is that candidates must learn television techniques in running for all major offices.

Investigations of the effectiveness of television spots in 1970 discovered that respondents saw more of those candidates who were the most heavily advertised but gave more attention to those spots which they found enter-

[34] Quoted in Richard J. Whalen, *The Founding Father* (New York: The New American Library of World Literature, Inc., 1964) p. 446.

[35] Jim Callaway, "Let's Cut the Baloney About Political Advertising," *Politeia*, 1 (Summer 1972) 36.

[36] Lloyd G. Whitebrook, "Madison Avenue Techniques in Political Campaigns," Paper delivered at American Political Science Association, September 6, 1958. *New York Times*, October 27, 1958, p. 15.

[37] Wyckoff, *The Image Candidates*, p. 108. Napolitan, *The Election Game and How to Win It*, p. 203. Mendelsohn and Crespi, *Polls, Television, and the New Politics*, p. 297. Lang and Lang, *Politics and Television*, pp. 190–203, 207–210.

taining or informative. Respondents tended to learn more about candidates they already favored than about their opponents. Only about one-third of the sample said that the spots of the candidates they already favored strengthened their intentions to vote for them. About one-third reported that the opposing candidate's spots had a negative effect upon them. When researchers in 1970 asked a sample of Michigan voters to rate the factors which influenced their decisions, the twelve they rated highest did not include any television political advertising. Instead, the Michigan sample gave higher ratings to media news, documentaries, editorials, educational programs, talk shows, and conversations with family and friends. Among a panel of 1972 respondents, only 16 percent were reported as clearly influenced by Nixon or McGovern spot-ads.[38]

There is still no evidence that short-term media impact has changed the outcome of a national election. It even remains to be shown that television alone was responsible for the election of any candidate for high office.[39] That such proof is lacking does not mean the case cannot be proved sometime. Perhaps a convincing case can be made that television was largely responsible for the success of Jimmy Carter in 1976. There is little doubt that "small incremental changes" among people who watch television may have had a cumulative effect although the connection "between what people see on television and how they decide to vote is at best obscure. All that can be safely said is that television is a prime provider of the information which helps people decide."[40]

Candidates and Uncontrolled Media Exposure

When candidates purchase space in print media or time on the air, they have control over what is said and shown. Candidates do not control coverage through news reports, features, and editorials because they do not pay for the advertising.

The distinction between *controlled and uncontrolled exposure* is most important in television where the cost of buying time is high. Uncontrolled coverage is doubly welcome: It is free and it attracts a large audience on news shows. Candidates for presidential nominations are under increased

[38] Congressional Quarterly, *Weekly Report*, July 31, 1971, pp. 1622–23. Walter DeVries and Lance Tarrance, Jr., *The Ticket-Splitter: A New Force in American Politics* (Grand Rapids, Mich.: William B. Eerdmans Publishing Company, 1972) pp. 75–78. Thomas E. Patterson and Robert D. McClure, *The Unseeing Eye: The Myth of Television Power in National Politics* (New York: G. P. Putnam's Sons, 1976) p. 135. Gary C. Jacobson, "The Impact of Broadcast Campaigning on Electoral Outcomes," *The Journal of Politics*, 37 (August 1975) 769–93.

[39] Whale, *The Half-Shut Eye*, p. 199.

[40] *Ibid.*, p. 157; in general, pp. 151–58. Lang and Lang, *Politics and Television*, pp. 209–10, quotation, p. 10.

pressures to find gimmicks to get themselves on television because their total spending is limited by law.[41]

Even if candidates could afford to campaign exclusively on television, they would not because a television camera is no substitute for a crowd.[42] Personal campaigning out among the voters, even though it does not reach many people, serves at least two purposes for candidates. There is the stimulation of personal contact and the opportunity for creating news which will be covered by the media, hopefully television. The television networks assign reporters and camera crews to cover presidential candidates. Campaigns for other offices are more dependent upon local stations and must adapt to their requirements. Candidates schedule their public appearances between the hours of 10:00 A.M. and 2:30 P.M. on weekdays when local television crews will be available and there will be time to process the films for showing in the evening.[43]

Candidate Involvement in News. Just because publicity is uncontrolled does not mean candidates or public officials cannot manage it to their advantage on occasions. Presidents obviously have the best opportunities for getting media attention and influencing both what is reported and how it is reported. Consequently, presidents and even presidential candidates may use strategies in making news more successfully simply because of their prominence. For example, television network newsmen often depend upon such newspapers as the *New York Times* and the *Washington Post* for news stories so, if a story is "leaked" to one of these newspapers and is printed, television is likely to report the story also.[44]

News reports are not the only form of uncontrolled exposure. *Feature articles* and *interviews* are especially valuable for establishing identity. Even when several people are interviewed together on local or network television, a candidate has an opportunity to make an image directly. Despite relatively small audiences for the network shows—*Meet the Press, Issues and Answers,* and *Face the Nation*—they are symbolic of national recognition, and what is said in the course of the questioning may be disseminated as news.

One of the characteristics of television news reporting which deeply affects candidates is the need for a *theme* which can be presented succinctly and clearly. The theme contained within each news story is structured and complete within itself. Stories usually involve conflict through rising and falling action with a beginning, a middle, and an end. The unity of the story also becomes personalized by the appearance and voice of the reporter.

[41] Neil Hickey, "Only $10 Million—Including Sandwiches," *TV Guide*, March 27, 1976, pp. 4–7.

[42] Henry Fairlie, *The Kennedy Promise: The Politics of Expectation* (New York: Doubleday and Company, Inc., 1973) p. 65.

[43] Rick Neustadt and Richard Paisner, "How to Run on TV," *New York Times Magazine*, December 15, 1974, p. 20.

[44] William Barry Furlong, "Manipulating the News," *TV Guide*, June 11, 1977, pp. 4–10 and June 18, 1977, pp. 4–8.

Facts and events are used to illustrate the theme. Yet, the report is most likely to be interpretative since it passes over the surface events in order to explain what is really going on, to expose the "real substance" of the news.[45]

In 1976, Jimmy Carter succeeded in creating his own themes which could be easily projected on television: his roots in farming, his firm moral principles, and his religious conversion.[46] Normally, candidates are not able to choose their own themes. In the 1972 presidential campaign, the television networks selected the theme of "frontrunner" for Edmund Muskie, and the reporters decided what percentage of the vote he should receive. When he received 46 percent of the vote in New Hampshire and McGovern received 37 percent, McGovern became the "winner" and Muskie became a "slipping" candidate. Nevertheless, according to polling results, Muskie appeared to be the only Democrat who could defeat Nixon.[47] Many people probably believed that Eugene McCarthy defeated Lyndon Johnson in New Hampshire in 1968 because of the way the news was reported. Actually, Johnson won 49.6 percent as a write-in candidate and McCarthy received 41.9 percent.

Not only are candidates seldom able to choose their themes, but themes may be overtly unflattering as was much of the television publicity showered upon George Wallace in the 1960s. Nevertheless, both his level of support, and Nixon's level as well, rose in 1968 among those who watched television the most and were most upset with pictures of violence and rioting.[48]

Media News Reporting.   The public is far more dependent upon *uncontrolled media exposure* than the candidates are. Politically speaking, we perceive events and define reality as conveyed to us through the media. What is communicated, we can know; what is not communicated, we have no way of knowing.

No news medium can possibly make all current news stories available to the public, so news reporting involves editorial judgments of what to include and exclude. As the late CBS star newscaster Edward R. Murrow frankly admitted, "It's news because I say it is." Television news, compared

[45] *Report on Network News' Treatment of the 1972 Democratic Presidential Candidates*, The Alternative Educational Foundation, Inc. (Bloomington, Indiana, 1972) pp. 7–8. Edward Jay Epstein, *News from Nowhere* (New York: Random House, 1973) pp. 4–5, 39, 263. Michael J. Robinson, "American Political Legitimacy in an Era of Electronic Journalism: Reflections on the Evening News," in *Television as a Social Force*, ed., Richard Adler (New York: Praeger/Aspen, 1975) pp. 112–14.

[46] Kevin Phillips, "TV's Decisive Impact on Primary Results," *TV Guide*, July 3, 1976, pp. A–3–A–4. John P. Roche, "How TV's Erratic Coverage Helped Carter's Campaign," *TV Guide*, July 17, 1976.

[47] *Report on Network News' Treatment*, pp. 11–12. Lanny J. Davis, *The Emerging Democratic Majority* (New York: Stein and Day, 1974) p. 145.

[48] Michael J. Robinson and Clifford Zukin, "TV and the Wallace Vote," *Journal of Communication*, 26 (Spring, 1976) 79–83; and Robinson, "Public Affairs Television and the Growth of Political Malaise: The Case of 'The Selling of the Pentagon,'" *The American Political Science Review*, 70 (June 1976) 421–25.

with print media, is more nearly a headline service with pictures because of the tight limits upon time and the need for action and involvement as part of any television news story. These restrictions are especially serious because a large portion of the public receives most or all of its news from local and network newcasts, and more people report they trust television news than those who say they trust newspapers. Will Rogers made famous the statement, "All I know is what I read in the newspapers." A majority now may be saying all they know is what they see on television. Rogers, presumably, was better informed.

Although the audience for the network evening news is representative of the public in age, education, race, and economic status, those who are higher in education, economic status, and levels of political participation use more media and are less dependent upon television. People rely on different media for information on different subjects but for all political information except local politics, there is greater reliance upon television than the press among the public as a whole. There is also some evidence that dependence upon television increases one's sense of inefficacy and cynicism.[49]

By deciding what is news, the media have much to do with deciding what the issues are and, therefore, with setting the public agenda. This role is especially true in television because of its dominance and pervasiveness.[50] A CBS official in 1976 noted that, instead of continuing to let the candidates pick the issues, "we took some of this out of their hands by defining the issues ourselves." [51] The Washington press corps, through which the country gets much of its understanding of national and international events, has long been an unofficial fourth branch of government. It has, in fact, a privileged status because of its tremendous power at the seat of government to determine what the news is and how to report it. It has increasingly reflected the views of liberals within the Democratic party and has become more and more estranged from the general public.[52]

[49] Michael Parenti, *Democracy for the Few* (New York: St. Martin's Press, 1974) p. 167. Nimmo, *The Political Persuaders*, pp. 114–17. Mendelsohn and Crespi, *Polls, Television, and the New Politics*, pp. 264–65. Gary L. Wamsley and Richard A. Pride, "Television Network News: Re-Thinking the Iceberg Problem," *The Western Political Quarterly*, 25 (September 1972) 436–38. W. Phillips Davison, James Boylan, and Frederick T. C. Yu, *Mass Media: Systems and Effects* (New York: Praeger Publishers, 1976) pp. 116–18. Edward M. Glick, "The Credibility Gap," *Politeia*, 1 (Summer 1972) 28–30. Robinson, "Public Affairs Television and the Growth of Political Malaise," pp. 409–32, especially 418–20. In general, Epstein, *News from Nowhere*.

[50] Davison and others, *Mass Media*, pp. 92, 181–82. Herbert B. Asher, *Presidential Elections and American Politics: Voters, Candidates, and Campaigns since 1952* (Homewood, Ill.: The Dorsey Press, 1976) pp. 237–38.

[51] Quoted in Frank Sean Swertlow, "Images and Issues," *TV Guide*, April 24, 1976, p. 5.

[52] Douglass Cater, *The Fourth Branch of Government* (New York: Vintage Books, A Division of Random House, 1959) p. 13. Robert D. Novak, "The New Journalism," in *The Mass Media and Modern Democracy*, ed., Harry M. Clor (Chicago: Rand McNally College Publishing Company, 1974) pp. 2–3.

It seems that most people are aware of, and some are fearful of, the significant alterations in the way candidates conduct their election campaigns. Particularly, there has been concern with candidates creating images through their controlled exposure on television. There seems to be much less appreciation of the media potential, in their day-by-day reporting of public affairs, to determine, not just our images of candidates and the political system, but our conceptions of political reality and, therefore, our reactions to this reality.

PARTIES AND THE WINNING OF THE VOTES

Political parties have access to the media and to consultants. They can pay for special services and, like the Republican party in 1975–1976, can buy television spots to refurbish the party image. What all of this means is that parties themselves are, at most, only one component in elections and can no longer mobilize voters entirely on their own, except at the local level.

Television, in particular, has usurped the role of parties by becoming essential for candidates. It is also a crystallizing force in its presentation of public affairs. Television, along with the other mass media, has reciprocated in part by reinforcing the legitimacy of the two major parties. When the media gave attention to Wallace in 1968, they seemed to be forcing him to prove that his American Independent party was not really alien to the political system. Eugene McCarthy attacked the press in 1976 as a self-appointed protector of the public in refusing to report his campaign for fear it would affect the outcome of the election.[53]

The parties cannot do much about the media, any more than candidates can, but party leaders can do something about taking back the management function in campaigns. If the mass media had made this function obsolete, there would have been no consultants and the role of party would have dwindled even faster. On the contrary, what the media did was to make campaign management more crucial to candidates and more specialized. The alternatives presented to party leaders are either to become specialists themselves or to employ consultants for party purposes.

Objectivity in Campaigns

Public relations marked a new frontier in the development of the arts of persuasion by adopting more objective methods for the gathering, interpreting, and application of data. In time political campaign management

---

[53] Nimmo, *The Political Persuaders*, p. 191. *St. Louis Globe-Democrat*, October 11, 1976.

reflected these changes, but consultants are not miracle workers nor are they scientists peering through microscopes in a laboratory.

All of the skill in planning and execution has not changed the frantic haste and confusion of campaigns. The account manager for the agency working on the Kennedy presidential campaign in 1960, noted later, "For all the talk about the Kennedy machine, it seemed very much a myth when you were in the middle of it. Its basic characteristic was chaos." [54] A campaign staff is caught up in a mass of responsibilities, and few have the opportunity to see beyond their own efforts and take stock of the campaign as a whole. The greatest perfectionists cannot control, much less foresee, the twists and turns of events. Campaigns can be the result of a comedy of errors and misjudgments along with the applications of consultants' campaign textbooks.

Consultants as Usurpers

If, initially, their assistance was required as technical aides to candidates, there came a point when consultants began to write speeches and advise on policy because policy is inseparable from the creation of images. As a case in point, Joseph Napolitan, Director of Advertising for Hubert Humphrey's presidential campaign in 1968, became so concerned about the prospects of defeat that he wrote a memorandum to Lawrence O'Brien, Chairman of the Democratic national committee, strongly urging specific policy positions for Humphrey on Vietnam and on law-and-order. [55] Humphrey did not take the advice in either policy area, but Napolitan could see no distinction between directing advertising and advising on what should be done to produce better advertising. And, of course, he was correct.

Most specialized services cannot be kept in airtight compartments. Everything that is done in the course of a campaign affects the candidate directly or indirectly so everyone connected with the campaign is concerned with everything which is being done. A volunteer, making telephone calls, is not responsible for advertising, but the kind of advertising can influence the responses to telephone solicitations.

Once consultants are immersed in a candidate's campaign, it is not always easy to distinguish them from the so-called party professionals who either came up through the party ranks or learned about politics from their experience on the staffs of public officials. These professionals also provide a variety of specialized services. As long as their own positions are not threatened they can appreciate the value of those services which they lack the time or expertise to perform. The one area, apparently, where consultants have not yet systematically injected themselves is in the recruitment

---

[54] Agranoff, *The New Style in Election Campaigns*, p. 92.
[55] Napolitan, *The Election Game and How to Win It*, pp. 45–47, 288–92.

of candidates. It has been party committee leaders who have talked about finding "photogenic" candidates.

Because they have worked in candidate-centered campaigns, consultants have magnified candidates as individuals, have contributed little to party regularity, and have generally ignored party organization. Perhaps consultants find a greater satisfaction, or sense of power, working for a candidate than for an "institutionalized organization." [56] This sense of power is accentuated for those employed by presidential candidates and, especially, by presidents. In 1978, for the first time, a consultant became a member of the White House staff when Carter made Gerald Rafshoon a presidential assistant with considerable authority over personnel and strategies, hoping to refurbish the President's sagging public image. Nevertheless, candidates are not the only employers of consultants.

Party Campaign Management

Party leaders should be among the most realistic about methods for planning and executing campaigns. These leaders are too much aware of political affairs to join the chorus which acclaims or the chorus which fears the consultants. It is pointless to argue that the services themselves should not be available; the only point is the *effective use of services*.

The Republican and Democratic national committees have computerized systems, media services with taping facilities, systems for allocating radio and television time, television consultants, and information manuals. The committees have also prepared television spots for use on local channels. There are, however, limitations. The committees do not provide individual consultant services, and they are mostly available only in Washington, D.C., so they primarily benefit incumbents who are less in need of the help. Members of both houses already have media services at cost through the facilities provided by Congress.

Party organizations are most useful when they provide services where the candidates are. In 1972, about two-thirds of state party committees did some polling to help candidates plan strategy, develop issues, and determine their standing in their races. Some state committees employ automatic data processing and raise money for the state tickets. The two parties' state committees in Minnesota have been especially active in providing a large range of services for legislative and House candidates.[57]

As the state parties develop their potential for campaign leadership, they also create possibilities for more centralization. Candidates will turn to

[56] Perry, *The New Politics*, p. 219.

[57] Robert J. Huckshorn, *Party Leadership in the States* (Amherst, Mass.: University of Massachusetts Press, 1976) pp. 132–33, 150, 265–66. Agranoff, *The New Style in Election Campaigns*, pp. 98–114.

those who can offer help, and local party organizations are not likely to have the resources to provide specialized services except for precinct work—the oldest and still most basic service of all. No greater compliment was ever paid to the party organization than the discovery of house-to-house canvassing by a new generation of campaign workers in the 1960s. This national phenomenon of returning to the grass-roots to win elections was a return to traditional party methods. The new campaign workers were simply doing what active party organizations had always done.

A requiem for parties still seems premature. Party leaders are capable of adapting to new styles in the winning of the votes just as they have survived the various reforms. Nevertheless, these challenges are real, and they raise serious questions about the continuity of the party system, the subject to be considered in Section III.

SECTION THREE

THE PROSPECTS

From its beginning, the party system operated on the basis of giving individuals incentives to work through party organizations. After all, the winning party distributed the rewards of government. The election of government officials became a contest in catering to popular pressures, and winning elections was accepted as an end in itself. This was the essence of practicality for a two-party system that consists of two large coalitions composed of a variety of interests often at odds with one another.

The party system became dominant during the nineteenth century. Voters formed strong and enduring loyalties to their respective parties and generally voted their partisanship. Each party, as it governed, influenced public policy, but election victories were a triumph for a party rather than a mandate to carry out a specific set of party commitments. This bears out Anthony Downs' hypothesis that "parties formulate policies in order to win elections, rather than win elections in order to formulate policies." [1]

By the 1890s, the party system started to deteriorate as a result of the maturing industrial system and the consequent symptoms of withdrawal from parties. The Progressive Movement and the Communications Revolution in the twentieth century contributed further to this decline. Most people continue to think in party terms when voting and when deciding who they are, politically. Even Independents, who deny a party attachment, have meaning only because there is a party system. Parties have survived but progressively fewer people rely upon them.

With the passing years, institutions either strengthen their roots or begin to wither, but the party system seemed to defy this logic. It appeared to be continuous despite its ups and downs. Perhaps the party system could become venerable and still remain about the same. By the middle of the twentieth century, however, it could be asked

---

[1] Anthony Downs, *An Economic Theory of Democracy* (New York: Harper & Row Publishers, 1957) p. 28.

if, at some point in the aging process, a distinction should be made between maturity and senility, if the party system is really perpetual or is evolving into a state of decadence.

The prospects for the continuity of the party system will be investigated in the four chapters of this Section of the book: in realignment (Chapter 7), in relative party strength in voting (Chapter 8), and in the possibilities for issue and ideological party differences (Chapters 9 and 10). The concluding chapter is reserved for speculations about a political system without political parties.

7

Continuity and Discontinuity

The political party system has been many things which are real. It is not just an apparition emerging from the ectoplasm of political systems past. The most important evidence of parties is the way people have divided themselves when they voted. Coalitions in presidential elections can be found as far back as the fragmentary election returns from the 1790s and early 1800s. The continuity of the party system can be traced through presidential elections because they are both the most complete record we have and the best barometer of what was occurring simultaneously among all the voters of the country.

STABILITY IN VOTING

The most impressive single tendency discovered in election returns is the stability of voting. This may seem a natural tendency in local or even state elections, but it would not necessarily be expected in choosing presidents, when the whole nation's stresses and strains are brought into focus at one time. It is all the more remarkable, therefore, that patterns have been found and that *presidential elections* can be classified according to their degree of *stability*.

Classifications of Presidential Elections

The largest proportion of presidential elections, by far, has been *maintaining* elections in which voters attested to their party attachments by voting for their respective parties' candidates. The basic partisan distribution throughout the country remained undisturbed even though maintaining elections were not, and could not be, exact reproductions of one another. The appearance of stability, in fact, was somewhat illusory because the coming and going between the parties and the variations in turnout usually canceled one another out.[1] If these factors did not cancel out, an election became *deviating* because of the effects of *short-term forces*. Even though the basic division of party strength within the country was not seriously disturbed, temporary influences led to the defeat of the majority party, for example, the election of Woodrow Wilson in 1912 and 1916. However, when voting became unstable as a result of *long-term forces*, as in the 1850s, the 1890s, and the 1930s, *realigning* elections occurred.[2]

Maintaining, deviating, and realigning elections can be differentiated and their characteristics can be summarized (Table 7.1). There is one fact, however, which is frustrating. There is no sure way to spot realignments until they have occurred. Political forces are somewhat inscrutable to those experiencing them. Afterwards, it is possible to point out what happened and to explain why, at least in part. Based on extensive examination, we can say that realignments did not break the continuity of the party system but did occur periodically over the years.

Continuity in Realignments

Each of the three types of presidential elections has been intrinsic to the party system. Even though realignments were sharp breaks in voting continuity, the historical turning points marking the beginning of each new party system, the thread of continuity of the system persisted.

Like maintaining elections, realignments were not carbon copies of one another. Each realignment mirrored a particular national crisis and created its own distinctive party division.[3] There were also other variations. The Republican party had a very slight national majority in presidential elections before 1896 and a much stronger majority thereafter. This *realignment*, which did not reverse the majority position of the two parties, has been called a *converting election*.[4] However, this is a distinction in gross changes in party balance resulting from a realignment. It is not a

[1] Richard M. Merelman, "Electoral Instability and the American Party System," *The Journal of Politics*, 32 (February 1970) 115–39. Edward C. Dreyer, "Change and Stability in Party Identification," *Ibid.*, 35 (August 1973) 712–22. V. O. Key, Jr., *The Responsible Electorate: Rationality in Presidential Voting 1936–1960* (New York: Vintage Books, A Division of Random House, 1966) pp. 16–22, 34–39.

[2] This terminology is taken from Angus Campbell, "A Classification of Presidential Elections, in *Elections and the Political Order*, eds., Angus Campbell, Philip E. Converse, Warren E. Miller, and Donald E. Stokes (New York: John Wiley & Sons, Inc., 1966) Chapter 4.

[3] Thomas P. Jahinge, "Critical Elections and Social Change: Toward a Dynamic Explanation of National Party Competition," *Polity*, 3 (Summer 1971) 465–500. Douglas Price, "Critical Elections and Party History: A Critical View," *Polity*, 4 (Winter 1971) 240. If realignments were all alike in that they changed the structure of the party system, then realignments represented discontinuity, not continuity. John E. Chubb, "Systems Analysis and Partisan Realignment," *Social Science History*, 2 (Winter 1978) 146.

[4] Gerald Pomper, "Classification of Presidential Elections," *The Journal of Politics*, 29 (August 1967) 537–38.

TABLE 7.1 Differentiating the Three Types of Presidential Elections.

Types of Elections

	Maintaining	Deviating	Realigning
General Political Situation	Nothing occurs to affect the usual voter reactions.	Temporary situation affecting voter reactions	Crisis situation: basic social and economic changes affecting voter reactions.
Party Identification	Stable distribution between the two parties	Stable distribution between the two parties	Unstable: shifting distribution between the two parties
Duration	32–40 years	One or two elections	Usually one presidential election.
Winning Party	The one with the majority of voter identification	The one with the minority of voter identification	The one benefitting from the new distribution of party identification.
Result in Electoral Party Strength	No basic change	No basic change, but temporary repudiation of majority party.	Basic change in party identification and in relative strength of the two parties. (Note: sometimes classed as *converting* if the existing majority party becomes stronger.)

fourth category of presidential elections. The realignment of the 1890s, like the others, was a transitional period of unstable voting caused by *changes in party identification*. Once these changes became stabilized, there was a corresponding change in the *relative strength of the two parties*.

What realignments had in common was a set of signals from both the electorate and party leaders. *First, familiar voting patterns* were disrupted during a relatively short period of critical elections. *Second, new issues* cut across existing coalitions and could not be contained by the typical reactions of temporizng or making gradual adjustments. *Third*, there was an abnormally high *intensity of electoral involvement* as ideological polarization increased.[5] The fact that changing party loyalties did not disturb the continuity of the party system raises the question if the magnitude of the shift can be fully explained by groups moving from one party to the other.

Changes in the composition of both parties' coalitions, brought about by realignments, may have occurred simply because of the passage of time. A generation, no longer concerned about the issues of a previous generation, would more likely be attracted by a set of new issues and adopt new party attachments.[6] In the realignment of the 1930s, there was some conversion of Republicans to Democrats.[7] But much of the growth in Democratic strength appears to have come from the entry into the electorate of new groups: youth, women, urban workers, and immigrants. Many of these people had either been too young to vote in the 1920s or had been voluntary nonvoters.[8]

The realignment of the 1890s may have been comparable to the 1930s, but the realignment in the 1850s leaves little doubt that party conversion is a very slow process. This realignment was different because the Whig party disappeared, and its members had to disperse. Many Whigs, both in the North and in the South, were reluctant to adopt a new party and temporized with minor parties in 1856 and 1860. As late as the 1870s, there was still a body of southern Whigs who were not firmly committed to the Democratic party.[9]

For generations, election returns demonstrate the stability of party voting despite social and economic changes and new mixtures of social characteristics within the population. Sometimes the past recurs: The

[5] James L. Sundquist, *Dynamics of the Party System: Alignment and Realignment of Political Parties in the United States* (Washington, D.C.: The Brookings Institution, 1973) pp. 275–98. Walter Dean Burnham, *Critical Elections and the Mainsprings of American Politics* (New York: W. W. Norton and Company, 1970) pp. 6–10. Paul Kleppner, *The Cross of Culture: A Social Analysis of Midwestern Politics 1850–1900* (New York: The Free Press, 1970) p. 271. Increased ideology was also reflected in more polarized congressional voting. W. Wayne Shannon, *Party, Constituency and Congressional Voting: A Study of Legislative Behavior in the United States House of Representatives* (Baton Rouge, La.: Louisiana State University Press, 1968) pp. 175–76, 180–81. Barbara Deckard Sinclair, "Party Realignment and the Transformation of the Political Agenda: The House of Representatives, 1925–1938," *The American Political Science Review*, 71 (September 1977) 940–53.

[6] Herbert B. Asher, *Presidential Elections and American Politics: Voters, Candidates, and Campaigns since 1952* (Homewood, Ill.: The Dorsey Press, 1976) pp. 301–3.

[7] Sundquist, *Dynamics of the Party System*, pp. 335–36.

[8] Norman H. Nie, Sidney Verba, and John R. Petrocik, *The Changing American Voter* (Cambridge, Mass.: Harvard University Press, 1976) Chapter 5. Philip E. Converse, "Public Opinion and Voting Behavior," in *Handbook of Political Science*, eds., Fred Greenstein and Nelson Polsby (Reading, Mass.: Addison-Wesley, 1975) 4, 136–57. Angus Campbell, Philip E. Converse, Warren E. Miller, and Donald E. Stokes, *The American Voter* (New York: John Wiley & Sons, Inc., 1960) pp. 153–56. This was found to be true of realignment in the City of Hartford, Connecticut, see Edmond J. True and Fred W. Grupp, "The Growth of the Democratic Party in a Period of Political Change," Paper presented at the Southern Political Science Association, Atlanta, Georgia, November 4, 1976.

[9] C. Vann Woodward, *Reunion and Reaction* (Boston: Little Brown and Company, 1951).

Democrats' 1932 victory in Ohio restored the voting pattern which had existed from the time of Jackson to Wilson.[10] Other times, the past simply seems to linger on: Party divisions in Michigan in the 1830s and 1850s persisted one hundred years later. A "curious timelessness" was found in the 1964 presidential voting.[11]

There are movements of partisans away from their parties during realignments, but the *holding power of a party* has usually been strong enough to bring some dissidents back after one or two elections. Although coalitions change by those leaving and entering, they have maintained continuity because of the large numbers who neither leave nor enter but stay where they are.

Cycles of Realignment and Equilibrium

Presidential years are used as convenient dates of realignments, but the signs of disruptive voting first appeared in midterm congressional elections. The new voting pattern then continued through the succeeding presidential election and for an election or two thereafter. Realignments have been a series of "critical elections." [12] Gradually, a new pattern of voting became established and a new series of maintaining elections began interspersed, from time to time, with deviating elections until the next realignment.

The time element in realignments became reasonably regular for an event in human affairs. Abnormal sectional conflict cut short the second party system, and it ran its course in approximately twenty years. Thereafter, making allowances for differences in computations, realignments occurred every thirty-two to forty years between the 1850s and the 1930s. These periods have been too regular to have occurred simply at random. Even granting that the length of time between realignments varies, making the periods irregular, electoral change through critical elections has been periodic.[13]

[10] Thomas A. Flinn, "Continuity and Change in Ohio Politics," *The Journal of Politics*, 24 (August 1962) 541, 544.

[11] Ronald P. Formisano, *The Birth of Mass Political Parties: Michigan, 1827–1861* (Princeton, N.J.: Princeton University Press, 1971) p. 4. Walter Dean Burnham, "American Voting Behavior and the 1964 Election," *Midwest Journal of Political Science*, 12 (February 1968) 1–40. Also, V. O. Key, Jr. and Frank Munger, "Social Determinism and Electoral Decision: The Case of Indiana," in *Voters, Parties, and Elections: Quantitative Essays in the History of American Popular Voting Behavior*, eds. Joel H. Silbey and Samuel T. McSeveney (Lexington, Mass.: Xerox College Publishing, 1972) pp. 29–45. William R. Shaffer and David A. Caputo, "Political Continuity in Indiana Presidential Elections: An Analysis Based on the Key-Munger Paradigm," *Midwest Journal of Political Science*, 16 (November 1972) 700–11.

[12] V. O. Key, Jr., "A Theory of Critical Elections," *The Journal of Politics*, 17 (February 1955) 3–18. James F. Ward, "Toward a Sixth Party System? Partisanship and Political Development," *The Western Political Quarterly*, 26 (September 1973) 406–7. Sundquist, *Dynamics of the Party System*, pp. 294–95. Kleppner, *The Cross of Culture*, p. 271. Burnham, *Critical Elections*, p. 6.

[13] Pomper, "Classification of Presidential Elections," p. 561. William L. Shade, *Social Change and the Election Process* (Gainesville, Fl.: University of Florida Press, 1973) p. 60.

The cyclical nature of realignments means that over a period of time party identification was subject to cyclical changes which, in turn, changed the relative strength of the two parties. Thus, if we look at the lifetime of the party system, we see that unequal distribution of party identification created a "competitive disequilibrium," or imbalance favoring one party.[14] By the realigning process, the competitive advantage resulting from this unequal distribution of party identification has shifted from party to party so that alternating tides of disequilibrium created a long-term condition of equilibrium.

Through the election of 1960, this equilibrium occurred in two different ways. The party vote oscillated during the unstable voting phase of realignment when the majorities for one party rose and fell, not randomly, but in "regular, graded steps." Then the majorities stabilized in maintaining elections in which the differential between the two parties was approximately 5 percent of the total vote in presidential elections and approximately 15 percent of the seats in the House of Representatives. The two parties maintained their equilibrium share of the vote between realignments except, temporarily, when deviating elections occurred. This tendency toward equilibrium appeared to be built into the party system and it, too, could not have occurred by chance.[15]

A similar voting cycle was found in individual states during the nineteenth century as their county percentages became polarized during realignments and then subsequently tended to become similar. Even though this tendency toward equilibrium did not apply equally to all counties within a state, there was a cycle because of "some degree of repetition in the sequence of events."[16]

WHY REALIGNMENT?

The alternation between long-term stability and short-term instability strongly implies that these periods were the result of forces indigenous to American society. While broad social and economic changes occurred frequently, realignments occurred periodically. Political forces followed a

[14] John D. May, *Sources of Competitive Disequilibrium between Competing Political Parties* (Morristown, N.J.: General Learning Press, 1973) pp. 2–5.

[15] Charles Sellers, "The Equilibrium Cycle in Two-Party Politics," in *Electoral Change and Stability in American Political History*, eds. Jerome M. Clubb and Howard W. Allen (New York: The Free Press, 1971) pp. 149–69. Donald E. Stokes and Gudmund R. Iversen, "On the Existence of Forces Restoring Party Competition," in *Elections and the Political Order*, p. 191. Duff Spafford, "A Note on the 'Equilibrium' Division of the Vote," *The American Political Science Review*, 65 (March 1971) 180–83.

[16] Lee Benson, *The Concept of Jacksonian Democracy: New York as a Test Case* (Princeton, N.J.: Princeton University Press, 1961) p. 127; italics in original; in general, see pp. 126–31. Kleppner, *The Cross of Culture*, pp. 9–14.

course of their own by building up gradually and then creating an explosion every thirty-two to forty years.

Consensus and Change

The contrast in the rhythms of social and political change reminds us of the distinction between the "new society" and the "old state," noted in Chapter 4. Maintaining the stability of the old state required political processes geared to make adjustments based upon areas of general agreement. Thus, consensus appeared to set *limits* upon political conflicts. Whenever the political system was called upon to introduce changes which were sudden and far-reaching, this consensus would be challenged. Consequently, there was an understandable tendency to ignore or put off the painful task of facing up to situations where no consensual basis for a solution could be found.[17] Whenever the problems did not go away, however, they were likely to be intensified by the tactics of evasion, and the country would be put through the traumatic experience of a realignment.

Economic development was an important factor in undermining political stability. Economic self-interest motivated individuals but realignments, in their broad effects, were not solely the result of a rising new class. They also reflected an interdependent class culture and ethnic culture.[18] Even the demands for taking from some groups and giving to others were accompanied by strident arguments over what was morally right and wrong. Both economic discontents and ideological differences disturbed consensus, but the middle-class society manipulated the symbolism of realignments so as to incorporate the changes into its value structure.[19] Realignments may have been substitutes for economic revolution, but except for the Civil War following the realignment of the 1850s, the society managed to pass through them with its values generally intact.

Party Continuity and Change

Realignments could not be avoided when arrangements became outdated, then new accommodations and shifts in the center of political gravity had to be accepted.[20] To know that some people opposed change because of

---

[17] Robert A. Dahl, *Pluralistic Democracy in the United States* (New York: Rand McNally and Company, 1967) pp. 282–98.

[18] Thomas P. Jahinge, "Critical Elections and Social Change: Towards a Dynamic Explanation of National Party Competition," *Polity*, 3 (Summer 1971) 479, 500.

[19] Carl D. Tubbesing, "Predicting the Present: Realigning Elections & Redistributive Policies," *Polity*, 7 (Summer 1975) 383–89. Sundquist, *Dynamics of the Party System*, p. 30.

[20] E. E. Schattschneider, *The Semi-Sovereign People* (New York: Holt, Rinehart and Winston, 1960) p. 75.

their vested interests is considerably less illuminating than the realization that the party system survived because it provided Americans what they wanted.

The willingness to tolerate patchwork arrangements for so long a time can be attributed, at least in part, to Americans' low tolerance for omens of unresolved strife. We usually pay tribute to those who are able to give to a cold-blooded settlement the appearance of a happy ending by their ability to deal with brutish confrontations among strong-willed spokesmen for grasping private interests. Only when gradualism ceased to work, when something more than a patchwork agreement was needed, have leaders from outside of the consensual society and its major party leadership been able to gain a hearing.

If voters want changes which do not appear to be extreme, this is what political leaders will try to give them. By so doing they will avoid basic conflicts. Political parties were designed for the purposes of winning elections and enjoying the fruits of victory, not for the purpose of starting arguments party leaders could not settle. George Washington Plunkitt, the early twentieth-century Tammany leader who has become a legend in political lore, agreed it was all right for the two parties to argue over the tariff or the currency but they should not argue about something really important like patronage.[21] Issues were all right as long as they did not cramp your style.

It is a modest understatement to point out that our "two-party system has usually been strongest when contesting for power, weakest when engaging in ideological dispute." Even the Jeffersonian-Republicans after winning their great victory in 1800, paid a price "that later successful parties also paid," by their "avoidance of potentially divisive policy changes for so long that the system, relying on outmoded agreements, failed to promote the general welfare and encouraged violent reactions against its continued existence." [22]

The parties became too broadly based to bear the brunt of real crises without shattering their lines, but once they went through the crucible of realignment, they hastened to reform their lines and gradually began to function "normally" again. It is as though the party system has been a game in which voters were periodically required to choose up sides all over again. This perpetual motion helps to explain why the American party system has been nondevelopmental, why it is cyclical rather than cumulative.[23]

[21] *Plunkitt of Tammany Hall*, Recorded by William L. Riordan (New York: E. P. Dutton and Company, Inc., 1963) pp. 38–40.

[22] Rudolph M. Bell, *Party and Faction in American Politics: The House of Representatives, 1789–1801* (Westport, Ct.: Greenwood Press, 1973) pp. 6, 192.

[23] Walter Dean Burnham, "American Voting Behavior and the 1964 Election," *Midwest Journal of Political Science*, 12 (February 1968) 39–40.

WHY NOT REALIGNMENT?

Accepting the year 1932 as the beginning of the fifth party system, a realignment should have occurred between 1964 and 1972, on the basis of cycles varying between thirty-two and forty years. There were tantalizing bits of evidence suggestive of the threads of continuity but when they were followed, they became enmeshed and knotted in contradictions. The evidence appeared and then either disappeared or assumed a new guise. Two developments in the 1960s were particularly good examples: the appearance of a serious minor party and new centers of power in national nominating conventions.

The American Independent Party

One of the first serious signs of realignment has been widespread *protest movements* which found immediate outlets in minor parties: the Antimasonic party in the 1820s–1830s, the Free-Soil and American parties in the 1850s, the Populist party in the 1890s, and the Progressive party in 1924. Each of these parties provided a "way-station" for some voters by making it easier for them either to change or to acquire a new party identification.[24]

In 1968, the American Independent party, led by George Wallace, appeared to be the "way-station" to the Republican party. Wallace's greatest support was in the South, but the issues he pressed had nation-wide appeal. Half of the Survey Research Center respondents who voted for Wallace had voted for Johnson in 1964. In the South, as many as one-third of Wallace voters had voted for Goldwater in 1964 and thus repudiated the Democratic presidential candidate for the second consecutive election. Although Nixon's victory over Humphrey was only a difference of .7 percent in 1968, 40 percent of the Nixon voters had voted for Johnson in 1964, many of them Republicans returning to the party fold.[25]

Republicans could take further encouragement from the evidence that Nixon would probably still have won if Wallace had not been running

---

[24] Sundquist, *Dynamics of the Party System*, pp. 289–90. Burnham, *Critical Elections*, pp. 27–31. Duncan MacRae Jr., and James A. Meldrum, "Critical Elections in Illinois: 1888–1958," *The American Political Science Review*, 54 (September 1960) 669–83. John M. Allswang, *A House for All Peoples* (Lexington, Ky.: The University Press of Kentucky, 1971) pp. 51–52. Bruce M. Stave, "The 'LaFollette Revolution' and the Pittsburgh Vote, 1932," in *Voters, Parties, and Elections*, eds. Joel H. Silbey and Samuel T. McSeveney (Lexington, Mass.: Xerox College Publishing, 1972) pp. 307–12.

[25] Philip E. Converse, Warren E. Miller, Jerrold G. Rusk, and Arthur C. Wolfe, "Continuity and Change in American Politics: Parties and Issues in the 1968 Election," *The American Political Science Review*, 63 (December 1969) 1084, 1091, 1101.

and that a majority of 1968 Wallace voters voted for Nixon in 1972.[26] However, that was about the extent of encouragement. The power of Democratic party identification kept most of its partisans from becoming Republican identifiers. Of greater significance was the failure of chronic nonvoters or new voters to become Republicans.

National Convention Voting

The discontent which had produced new minor parties in periods of realignment had also divided one or both major parties. The signs of this internal struggle appeared in the national conventions.[27] In both major parties' conventions between 1940 and 1964, whenever there was a contest for either the presidential or vice presidential nominations, the delegates were found to be, not random or ad hoc alliances, but representative of distinct factions within their parties.[28] In 1968, this consistency ended. In the Republican convention, Nixon's support was more dispersed than either Taft's in 1952 or Goldwater's in 1964. In the Democratic convention, Humphrey's support was completely different from the faction which had dominated since the time of Franklin Roosevelt. These shifting factional patterns were not interpreted as realigning, but as a decline of recognizably coherent factions and a sign of party decay.[29]

The break in continuity was extended for the Democrats in 1972 when their convention was captured by the counterculture faction espousing the new politics. There had been a small, quiet bolt from the nominee in 1968. In 1972, it was large and boisterous. Yet, forecasts of a Democratic party breakup proved to be conspicuously premature. Carter had the nomination before the delegates assembled for the 1976 convention and had a united party when the convention adjourned. It was the Republicans in 1976 who had an abrasive factional division, but the convention voting revived the Republican factional divisions of 1940–1964.

Thus, this sign of realignment also faded away.

Adaptation, not Realignment

In the past, when divisive issues arose and party leaders tried to straddle them, the situation grew worse. Polarizing forces formed more rapidly and

---

[26] *Ibid.*, p. 1092. Richard A. Brody, "Communications," *The American Political Science Review*, 70 (September 1976) 924–26. Harris computer analysis for NBC, cited in *U.S. News & World Report*, October 27, 1969, pp. 74–75. Theodore H. White, *The Making of the President, 1972* (New York: Bantam Books, 1973) p. 462.

[27] Burnham, *Critical Elections*, pp. 6–7.

[28] Frank Munger and James Blackhurst, "Factionalism in the National Conventions, 1940–1964: An Analysis of Ideological Consistency in State Delegation Voting," *The Journal of Politics*, 27 (May 1965) 375–94.

[29] Gerald Pomper, "Factionalism in the 1968 National Conventions: An Extension of Research Findings," *The Journal of Politics*, 33 (August 1971) 826–30.

brought on a cycle of realigning elections. In the late 1960s and early 1970s, party leaders rode out the issues by accommodating them and defusing the threat of realignment.[30] The whole process became stillborn because political moderates kept control of both parties. In the early twentieth century the situation was reversed. Realignment was avoided then because moderates of both parties lost control to the Progressive reformers.[31]

Nevertheless, the assumption that realignment will occur has been irrepressible, and speculations have probably had the effect of heightening anticipation. The result is a strange mixture of reactions. There is "a kind of thirst for the event" along with fears that the failure of the event to materialize threatens the continuity of the party system.[32] Were the Republican and Democratic parties victims of their own success? Did they achieve too well in forestalling a basic shift in their relative strengths?

To answer "yes" to these questions is irresistible but in a real sense, the answer does not matter because these are the wrong questions. They assume a situation which did not exist. When the parties were able to come through the 1960s and enter the 1970s apparently unscathed by the tumultuous events, the *continuity of the party system had already been broken*. Otherwise, all of the classic signs of realignment which appeared right on schedule would have had their traditional effects. Party realignment, by definition, did not take place, but there was a realignment of forces.[33]

We have the anomalous situation of both continuity and discontinuity. As the country went through a major trauma, fewer people professed a party identification and their voting became unstable. This was not a phase of a cycle, but an exhibition of popular disregard for the institutional party system. Now, the choice does not lie between continuity with realignment and discontinuity without it. The choice lies between coherent coalitional voting and unpredictable voting by ad hoc groupings for each office on the ballot.

To examine the record of what happened, we will begin with the most obvious, if not most basic, explanation for the discontinuity of the party system, the change in individual attachments to parties.

[30] Sundquist, *Dynamics of the Party System*, pp. 283–89. David Knoke, *Change and Continuity in American Politics* (Baltimore, Md.: The Johns Hopkins University Press, 1976) pp. 147–48. Kevin P. Phillips, *Mediacracy: American Parties and Politics in the Communications Age* (Garden City, N.Y.: Doubleday & Company, Inc., 1975) pp. 146–47. Jerrold G. Rusk and Herbert F. Weisberg, "Perceptions of Presidential Candidates: Implications for Electoral Change," *Midwest Journal of Political Science*, 16 (August 1972) 408–9.

[31] Sundquist, *Dynamics of the Party System*, pp. 290–92, 296.

[32] Walter Dean Burnham, "Revitalization and Decay: Looking Toward the Third Century of American Electoral Politics," *The Journal of Politics*, 38 (August 1976) 147, 149. Everett Ladd, Jr., Charles Hadley, and Lauriston King, "A New Political Realignment?" *The Public Interest*, 4 (Spring 1971) 47–48.

[33] Nie and others, *The Changing American Voter*, pp. 212–13.

THE NATURE OF PARTY ATTACHMENTS

What is remarkable about discussions of realignment in the 1960s–1970s is the expectation that a shift in relative party strength would make the Republicans the majority party.[34] Actually, a shift in the relative voting strength of the parties had occurred, but in favor of the Democrats.[35] It was hazardous to assert that realignment had taken place when the other half of the definition, a commensurate shift in party identification, was missing. Democratic party identification, instead of increasing, had decreased although it remained much higher than Republican identification which also decreased. The important change in identification was the increase in Independents. In addition, analysis was complicated by concentrating upon presidential elections, where the parties were competitive after 1964, instead of taking account of increased Democratic strength in other voting.

The Meaning of Party Identification

The immediate significance of party identification is its relationship to voting behavior. From the record in those states where voters make a declaration of party when they register, it has long been known that these registration figures could not be relied upon in predicting election outcomes. As early as 1952, using survey results, the explanatory power of party identification in elections declined. This led to the bracketing of identification, as a long-term voting influence, with candidates and issues as short-term influences.[36] Combined, they have become analogous to a three-legged stool. One leg or the other may be stronger in explaining any one election, but all three have to be taken into account in a total explanation. Even if party identification is usually the most important determinant of the vote, it can no longer stand alone.[37]

Partisans, generally, are more dependable in voting for their party than other groups, but Table 7.2 shows a contrary trend for the Democrats. In five of the seven presidential elections covered by the Table, the percentage of nonwhites voting Democratic exceeded the percentage of Democrats. It was the Republican identifiers who voted for their party's candidates in greater proportions than any other group.

The analyst's justification for measuring identification and voting separately is to learn something about the motivational force of identification.

[34] A notable example was Kevin P. Phillips, *The Emerging Republican Majority* (Garden City, N.Y.: Anchor Books, Doubleday & Company, Inc., 1970).

[35] Ladd and others, "A New Political Realignment?" 46–63.

[36] Angus Campbell, Gerald Gurin, Warren E. Miller, *The Voter Decides* (Evanston, Ill.: Row, Peterson and Company, 1954) Part Two.

[37] Nie and others, *The Changing American Voter*, pp. 53–55.

TABLE 7.2   Reported Votes by Selected Groups, Presidential
Elections, 1952–1976.*

Voting Democrat	1952	1956	1960	1964	1968	1972	1976
Democrats	77%	85%	84%	87%	74%	67%	82%
Nonwhites	79	61	68	94	85	87	85
Catholics	56	51	78	76	59	48	57
Manual Workers	55	50	60	71	50	43	58
Voting Republican							
Republicans	92	96	95	80	86	95	91
College	66	69	61	48	54	63	55
Protestants	63	63	62	45	49	70	53
Professional, Business	64	68	58	46	56	69	56

* Taken from Gallup Poll Index, December, 1976, Report No. 137.

This kind of investigation is probably of little concern to most voters, who may see no distinction, much less inconsistency, between what they say they are and what they do. There is not much doubt that for those who have a party identification, it is a cue in evaluating candidates and issues, but exactly what a voter has in mind when reporting an identification can only be inferred from the data.

The Survey Research Center in each of its election studies since 1952 has measured the intensity of party identification by letting respondents distribute themselves along a seven-point scale consisting of strong Democrats, weak Democrats, Independents leaning to the Democrats, pure Independents, then Independents leaning to the Republicans, weak Republicans, and strong Republicans. Individual respondents, however they defined these categories in their own minds, have regularly spread themselves across the whole range of the scale. This distribution makes it clear that whatever meaning an identification has, the meaning is not the same for everyone who identifies.

Constant changes in the degree of partisan intensity can be termed a "psychological safety valve" used by voters to adjust their perception, such as a negative reaction to their party's candidates, while still voting for their party.[38] Party identification has been called "a purely nominal attachment of slight motivational significance", and it has also been conceived as a

[38] Douglas Dobson and Douglas St. Angelo, "Party Identification and the Floating Vote: Some Dynamics," *The American Political Science Review*, 69 (June 1975) 484–85. Also Kenneth J. Meier, "Party Identification and Vote Choice: The Causal Relationship," *The Western Political Quarterly*, 28 (September 1975) 496–505.

"running balance sheet on the two parties" and a mechanism in itself for changing identification.[39]

In realignments of the past there was probably a time-lag in bringing one's party loyalty into conformance with one's voting behavior.[40] Now, voting behavior can change from one presidential election to the next, but the effect appears to be fleeting and leaves no residue of a new party attachment.

New Voters and Party Identification

Continuity in party identification has depended upon its transmission from generation to generation, most particularly through the family. Beginning about 1968, the proportion of young people maintaining the identity of their parents began to fall. Compared with previous groups, fewer new voters in the 1960s held a strong party identification, but those who did have an identification maintained it. Therefore, those coming of voting age have increasingly contributed to the decline in party identification. This trend became more conspicuous when the minimum age was lowered to 18, in 1971. Among voters under 25 years of age, Independents increased 30 percent between 1952 and 1974, compared with increases of 5 percent for ages 25–34, 12 percent for 35–64, and 3 percent for those 65 and older. Only in 1976 was a change observed when 47 percent of new voters were Independents compared with 50 percent in 1968 and 52 percent in 1972.[41]

Because the strength of *party identification* had been found to increase with age, it had been explained as a *life-cycle process*. As people grew older, their partisanship became stronger because of the length of time they had held it.[42] Research in the 1960s and 1970s contradicted this interpretation in the case of white voters. For each generation coming into the electorate since 1914, there was an almost uniform decline in strong identifiers after 1964, and the number of Independents did not diminish as the generations grew older. For there to have been a life-cycle process, political conditions should have reinforced party identification, but conditions were no longer doing so.

Instead, other research explained party identification as a *generational*

[39] Donald E. Stokes, "Party Loyalty and the Likelihood of Deviating Elections," *The Journal of Politics*, 24 (November 1962) 702. Morris P. Fiorina, "An Outline for a Model of Party Choice," *American Journal of Political Science*, 21 (August 1977) 618.

[40] Everett Carll Ladd, Jr. and Charles D. Hadley, "Party Definition and Party Differentiation," *Public Opinion Quarterly*, 37 (Spring 1973–1974) 32.

[41] Nie and others, *The Changing American Voter*, pp. 28–29, 59–65, 70–73. Knoke, *Change and Continuity in American Politics*, p. 135. Warren E. Miller and Teresa Levitin, *Leadership and Change: Presidential Elections from 1952 to 1976* (Cambridge, Mass.: Winthrop Publishers, Inc., 1976) pp. 244–51.

[42] Campbell and others, *The American Voter*, pp. 161–65. Philip E. Converse, *The Dynamics of Party Support: Cohort-Analyzing Party Identification* (Beverly Hills, Ca.: Sage Publications, 1976).

process whereby each generation went through a formative period when it developed attitudes. Subsequently people acquired and maintained either a strong or weak identification. The formative period following World War II had featured weak party leadership, notably periods of Republican presidents with Democratic congresses. Candidates had often played down their parties, and television had become the leading medium of political communication. It was not surprising that party loyalties did not develop when there was so little political stimuli to encourage them.

Blacks, on the contrary, were influenced by events irrespective of generation and to a greater degree than whites although even among blacks, the number of strong Democrats had declined and the number of Independents had grown.[43]

Identifiers v. Independents

Unless voters entering the electorate begin acquiring a party identification, whether by the life-cycle or generational process, Independents will eventually submerge the total number of party identifiers. Consequently, it is important to have an idea of how many Independents there are and what, in general, their growth implies for the party system.

How Many Independents? There is inevitable confusion about the number of Independents. Many measurements of party identification divide all identifiers into Democrats, Republicans, and Independents. The seven-point scale of partisan intensity has the advantage of capturing shifts in degree, as shown in Table 7.3.

The percentage of pure Independents in 7.3A quadrupled between 1952 and 1974, but declined in 1976 to just triple the 1952 figure, the same pattern is found in 7.3B where all Independents are combined. Comparing 1952 with 1976, pure Independents increased 9 percent, all Independents 14 percent, and strong identifiers fell 11 percent (7.3C). Between 1964 and 1966, years not shown in the Table, strong Democrats suffered a loss from which they had not recovered by 1976. Both strong Democrats and Republicans declined in the 14-year period, but weak identifiers remained about the same and Independent "leaners" increased a little. Since 1972, pure Independents equalled or exceeded each category of Republicans. The sharp increase in pure Independents and a Republican decrease, especially among strong and Independent Republicans in 1974, may be attributed in large part to Watergate.

The threat to each party is the clear trend toward weaker partisan

---

[43] Knoke, *Change and Continuity in American Politics*, pp. 134–35. Paul R. Abramson, "Generational Change and the Decline of Party Identification in America: 1952–1974," *The American Political Science Review*, 70 (June 1976) 469–78; and Abramson, *Generational Change in American Politics* (Lexington, Mass.: Lexington Books, 1975) Chapter 4.

TABLE 7.3   Comparative Trends in Partisanship,
Selected Years, 1952–1976.*

A

	1952	1972	1974	1976
Democrats				
Strong	22%	15%	18%	15%
Weak	25	25	23	25
Independents, leaning	10	11	13	12
Total Democrats:	57%	51%	54%	52%
Pure Independents	5	13	20	14
Republicans				
Strong	13	10	6	9
Weak	14	13	12	14
Independents, leaning	7	11	8	10
Total Republicans:	34%	34%	26%	33%

B

Democrats (Strong, Weak)	47	40	41	40
All Independents	22	35	41	36
Republicans (Strong, Weak)	27	23	18	23

C

All Identifiers				
Strong (D, R)	35	25	24	24
Weak (D, R)	39	38	35	39

* Data taken from Warren E. Miller and Teresa E. Levitin,
Leadership and Change: Presidential Elections from 1952 to 1976
(Cambridge, Mass.: Winthrop Publishers, Inc., 1976) p. 36.
Note: Columns do not add to 100% because of respondents who
did not know their identification.

intensity although the total Democratic and Republican identifiers have not
changed much, except for Republicans in 1974 (7.3A). The only other ray
of light for the parties is that, for the time being anyway, the growth of
pure Independents has come to a halt.[44]

Independents as Partisans.   For a long time there was more interest in
describing party identifiers than Independents, but as Independents have increased in number, interest in them has increased. Not surprisingly, the
characteristics of Independents have changed as they have grown both
in absolute and in relative numbers.

[44] Miller and Levitin, *Leadership and Change*, pp. 189, 211.

A distinction must be made between the categories of Independents. Independent "leaners," compared with weak identifiers, have been found generally to be more attentive to campaigns and more concerned with the outcome of elections. They have the higher socioeconomic status which is associated with greater political involvement. During the 1970s, they were also more consistent in supporting their party. Many of these Independent "leaners" were both young and issue-oriented and took their cues from parties.[45] Although pure Independents have a lower voting rate than identifiers, in 1972 all Independents together cast a higher proportion of the presidential vote than strong identifiers because the relative proportion of Independents within the total electorate was larger.[46]

With the *rising level of education* and *economic status*, it is likely there will be a continued *increase in Independents*.[47] The result promises to be continued ambiguity. On the one hand, Independents give no indication of being a vanguard for destroying the party system. On the other hand, they are contributing to the prolonged unstable voting behavior. To the extent Independents are issue-oriented, they can conceivably become more firm partisans if the parties more clearly represent issues, but Independents are increasingly the kinds of people who seem least inclined to identify strongly with a party. Their increased political interest and activity will more likely take the form of a positive response to those candidates with whose images and whose positions on issues the Independents can identify.

Declining Party Status

Critics of the party system have usually been optimists. They have advocated changes which they thought would strengthen the system. It was once foreseen that as political sectionalism ended and as issues became national in scope, the parties would become more unified. Party differences would become clearer, and parties would become more competitive and more popular with the people.[48] To the extent that issues of national scope have dominated campaigns, parties as a whole have remained as tweedledum-tweedledee as ever, while becoming more ideologically factionalized, less competitive, and more unpopular.

The weakened intensity of partisanship has been accompanied by

---

[45] John Petrocik, "An Analysis of Intransitivities in the Index of Party Identification," *Political Methodology* 1 (Summer 1974) 31–47. Miller and Levitin, *Leadership and Change*, pp. 209–10, 251–52.

[46] Asher, *Presidential Elections and American Politics*, p. 81.

[47] Knoke, *Change and Continuity in American Politics*, pp. 136–37.

[48] E. E. Schattschneider, "The Functional Approach to Party Government," in *Modern Political Parties*, ed., Sigmund Neumann (Chicago: University of Chicago Press, 1956) p. 215.

negative opinions of parties as such. Over the years, fewer than 10 percent of respondents had a positive evaluation of both parties, but the negative evaluation of both parties rose from 29 percent in 1960 to 51 percent in 1972. As many as 63 percent had a positive evaluation of their own party up to 1960; then the figure dropped to 45 percent by 1972.[49]

The withdrawal from parties at the turn of the twentieth century is accounted for by a growing lack of interest. There is no doubt now, with the data available, that withdrawal is tinged with active hostility and even an urge to withdraw from organized politics. Expressions of extreme reactions are probably misleading, but no one has produced much of any evidence to disprove the conclusion that attitudes toward parties are far more negative than positive.

SHIFTING COALITIONS

The indeterminate status of parties seems to be the easiest conclusion anyone can reach about the party system. Millions of Americans profess a party identification, but we are not quite sure what it means to them because of its declining motivational force in voting. Independents, whether leaning toward one of the parties or not, have sprouted up like weeds in an untended garden. People both pull and are pulled in different political directions, and many of them appear to be making an effort to express something with their votes.

That the composition of the two major parties has changed, both sectionally and by demographic groups, may reflect attempts to nudge each party in the direction of realignment. At best, though, the changes have been qualified by the decline in partisan intensity and by a mercurial and disconnected pattern of voting which will be pointed out in Chapter 8. Though obscured by inconsistencies, these signs of change still have a certain clarity.

The North: Decline of Status Differences

The last majority party coalition, created by the Democrats in the 1930s, became known as the New Deal coalition. Although it attempted to appeal to the maximum number of people by dispensing benefits to almost every identifiable group, it emphasized social class distinctions and gave the Democrats the image of a "have-not" party. By this definition, there was no longer a New Deal coalition by the 1950s. In the course of twenty years, many of the poor, or at least their offspring, had become middle class and

---

[49] Nie and others, *The Changing American Voter*, pp. 49, 57–59, 68–70.

were numbered among the "haves," whether by moving into professional ranks or remaining blue-collar at middle-class wage rates.[50]

The class distinctions which became associated with the Democratic party in the 1930s were mainly a northern phenomena, but measured by socioeconomic status in the 1970s the New Deal coalition was disappearing in the North. Attitudes toward federal government policies on behalf of the poor were no longer associated with social class distinctions. Among white Protestants, those of lower and middle status became more unfriendly toward this government activism and those of higher status became more nearly polarized in favor or in opposition. In fact, the higher their status the more people favored government social welfare policies. Concurrently, Republican identification declined among all northern white Protestants, especially those of higher status; the Democrats made small gains; and Independents made larger gains. Catholics, irrespective of status, became more polarized on government policies. Overall, there were fewer Catholic Democrats and more Catholic Independents. Republican voting increased among higher status Catholics, and Democratic voting increased among those of lower status. Blacks were nearly unanimous in both Democratic voting and identification.[51]

The South: Rise of Status Differences

The eleven states which formed the Confederacy during the Civil War had been the bedrock of the Democratic party beginning with the last quarter of the nineteenth century, particularly after the realignment of the 1890s. When the Democrats became the majority party in the 1930s, no realignment could take place in these Solid South states beyond a few percentage points increase in the overwhelming Democratic majorities. The New Deal made the Democratic party dominant at the polls in northern cities, but the South dominated the Congress because of the seniority system. Gradually, the Solid South lost its preeminence within the party. The abolition of the two-thirds rule in Democratic national conventions broke the South's control over presidential nominations after 1936. By the late 1930s, southern Democratic leaders were contesting for control over federal policies, and by the 1940s, parts of the South were voting against the national party.

Figure 7.1 shows that the Democratic percentage of the presidential vote in the South fell from nearly 80 percent in 1940 to about 50 percent in 1948, when the South was barely above the Democratic percentage for the whole country. During the Eisenhower elections, the South was more

[50] Ladd and others, "A New Political Realignment?" p. 55.
[51] Nie and others, *The Changing American Voter*, pp. 223–32, 253–62.

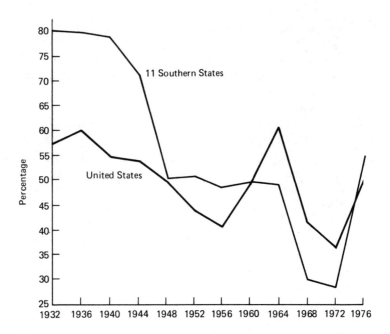

FIGURE 7.1 Democratic Percentage of Total Presidential Vote, the United States, and Eleven Southern States, since 1932.

strongly Democratic than the nation, but in 1960 the percentages were virtually identical. Thereafter, the South was more Republican than the nation until 1976.

The Solid South could not have continued to exist once it ceased to be insulated from the rest of the country. Following World War II, northern migrants were attracted by the climate and by the rapid industrialization and growth of defense installations. For these reasons, southern status distinctions between the parties began to increase at the time they were decreasing in the North.[52] A new Republican vote began showing up in the metropolitan South in contrast with Democratic voting in the traditionally rural, small-town, and status quo South. Migrants, at first, tended to be more Republican than native southerners, but the association of white Republican voting with status and ideology began to break down the distinction between migrants and natives.[53]

Ideology soon proved to be *stronger* than *socioeconomic status*. By the 1970s, both native and migrant white southerners had become more

[52] *Ibid.*, pp. 221–23.

[53] Bernard Cosman, "Presidential Republicanism in the South, 1960," *The Journal of Politics*, 24 (May 1962) 303–22. Anthony M. Orum and Edward W. McCranie, "Class, Tradition, and Partisan Alignments in a Southern Urban Electorate," *The Journal of Politics*, 32 (February 1970) 156–76. Jerry Perkins, "Bases of Partisan Cleavage in a Southern Urban County," *The Journal of Politics*, 36 (February 1974) 208–14.

conservative on nonracial as well as racial issues. Native southerners of middle and upper economic status were far more anticommunist in foreign policy. Those of lower economic status, who had not been particularly conservative in the 1950s, revealed a sharp increase in opposition to government economic-welfare policies.[54]

Commitment of northern blacks to the Democratic party dates from the 1930s. In the South, monolithic support among blacks of all ages occurred with the civil rights issue in 1964. In contrast, weakening Democratic support among southern whites was not the result of a single issue but a gradual movement, with the youngest age groups showing somewhat more Republican identification than the middle-aged and older whites.[55]

The one-party system in southern politics had been directly related to the voting rate. Turnout in the South had been depressed by the exclusion of blacks from the ballot following the 1870s, and especially beginning in the 1890s, when legal provisions, notably poll taxes, were adopted to keep blacks from voting. Both legal exclusions and other devices, such as intimidation, directed against blacks gradually disappeared, and the Civil Rights Act of 1965 marked the end of this form of discrimination.

As black voting increased in the South, the racial balance at the polls became more proportional, increasing status differences in voting. In five large southern cities, for example, the same percentage of blacks and whites were registered and the white voting rate was only slightly higher. Actually, comparing whites with blacks in lower socioeconomic precincts, blacks had a higher rate of turnout.[56] This difference in racial voting rates conforms with the general finding that overall, blacks vote at a lower rate but, class by class, vote about as heavily as whites.[57]

Even as voting behavior more nearly coincided with ideology and economic status in the South, Republican identification still lagged behind the Republican vote. *Changes in identification* were a negative reaction to

---

[54] Nie and others, *The Changing American Voter*, pp. 247–50. Southern Democrats in the House, who had supported social welfare programs during the 1930s, thereafter became the least supportive compared with other sections of the country. Barbara Deckard Sinclair, "The Policy Consequences of Party Realignment—Social Welfare Legislation in the House of Representatives, 1933–1954," *American Journal of Political Science*, 22 (February 1978) 83–105.

[55] Bruce A. Campbell, "Patterns of Change in the Partisan Loyalties of Native Southerners: 1952–1972," *The Journal of Politics*, 39 (August 1977) 730–61; and Campbell, "Change in the Southern Electorate," *American Journal of Political Science*, 21 (February 1977) 37–64. For a more specialized study, Bernard Cosman, *Five States for Goldwater: Continuity and Change in Southern Presidential Voting Patterns* (University, Ala.: University of Alabama Press, 1966).

[56] Richard Murray and Arnold Vedlitz, "Race, Socioeconomic Status, and Voting Participation in Large Southern Cities," *The Journal of Politics*, 39 (November 1977) 1064–72. For a similar earlier report, Harry Holloway and David M. Olson, "Electoral Participation by White and Negro in a Southern City," *Midwest Journal of Political Science*, 10 (February 1966) 99–122.

[57] Lester W. Milbrath and M. L. Goel, *Political Participation: How and Why Do People Get Involved in Politics?* 2nd ed. (Chicago: Rand McNally College Publishing Company, 1977) pp. 119, 120.

the national Democratic party rather than a positive reaction to the Republican party. In a twenty-year period, Democratic identification among white Protestant southerners fell from 78 percent to 47 percent, but Republican identification grew only from 9 percent to 18 percent. Independents increased from 13 percent to 35 percent.[58]

The South appears more likely to vote as a unit in presidential elections, but nonpresidential elections reflect state differences. Republicans have elected governors, senators, state legislators, and from 25 to 30 percent of the southern seats in the House of Representatives. A sign of increased party competition is the sharp decline, since 1960, in the southern House seats uncontested by one major party, although the number is still

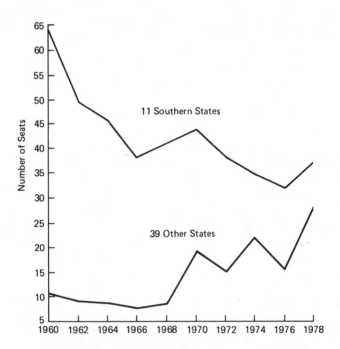

FIGURE 7.2   Number of Seats With Only One Major Party
Candidate, House of Representatives, since 1960.

Note: Since 1978, Louisiana law requires House candidates of both parties in each district to compete against one another in the primary. A candidate who receives over 50% of the vote in a district is, in fact, then elected. If no candidate receives a majority, the two highest candidates, irrespective of their party, run against each other in the general election. The total uncontested seats in the South, beginning in 1978, include those Democrats and Republicans in Louisiana who received over 50% of the vote in the primary.

[58] Nie and others, *The Changing American Voter*, pp. 218–21. Glenn F. Abney, "Partisan Realignment in a One-Party System: The Case of Mississippi," *The Journal of Politics*, 31 (November 1969) 1102–6. Bruce A. Campbell, "Patterns of Change in the Partisan Loyalties of Native Southerners: 1952–1972," *The Journal of Politics*, 39 (August 1977) 730–61.

much larger than in the other thirty-nine states (Figure 7.2). Adding to Republican difficulties, a new breed of Democratic candidates dimmed prospects for a genuine party realignment on the state level. By adopting a moderate position on the race issue and by not projecting a rural, fundamentalist background, they made inroads into the Republican white-collar support.[59]

All along, too much may have been made of issue voting in the South and too little of *candidate appeal*, even in presidential elections, judging from Carter's carrying all of these states except Virginia in 1976. Although Republicans have built state and local parties, the traditional weakness of organized competition in the South has not changed much except that it now involves two parties instead of one.[60]

In retrospect, the data bearing upon the nature of party attachments and shifting voting coalitions display some tendencies toward realignment. However, there still remains the failure to bring identification into line with new voting behavior and then to stabilize that behavior. There is evidence which both documents changes in attitudes toward the two parties and confirms the weak prospects for continuity through genuine realignment. This apparently strange combination of two bodies of data results from the growth of Independents at the expense of party identifiers, and from groups shifting their party voting without a commensurate shift in party identification.

This incongruity should be reflected in the general pattern of party competition, and we shall see in the next chapter that this expectation is borne out.

[59] Louis M. Seagull, *Southern Republicanism* (New York: John Wiley and Sons, 1975) pp. 109–10, 143–52. As Seagull notes, this development was unforeseen in the forecast of realignment by Phillips, *The Emerging Republican Majority* (Garden City, N.Y.: Doubleday & Company, Inc., Anchor Books, 1970). But Phillips was aware when he wrote *Mediacracy* (Garden City, N.Y.: Doubleday & Company, Inc., 1975), see pp. vi–ix.

[60] Eugene R. Declercq, Thomas L. Hurley and Norman R. Luttbeg, "Presidential Voting Change in the South: 1956–1972," *The Journal of Politics*, 39 (May 1977) 480–92. Daniel J. Elazar, *American Federalism: A View from the States*, 2nd ed. (New York: Thomas Y. Crowell Company, 1972) pp. 135–37. For a general survey, Jack Bass and Walter DeVries, *The Transformation of Southern Politics* (New York: Basic Books, Inc., 1976).

8

Party Competition and the Party Vote

The discussion of realignment in the previous chapter concentrated upon competition in presidential elections because realignment involves the whole country, but presidential elections are only a part of party competition. There is no body of comprehensive data covering party competition for all offices on all levels of government, so this Chapter will be limited to elections of executive and legislative officials on the federal and state levels.

WHAT IS COMPETITION?

The term "party competition" is constantly bandied about as though competition were some absolute condition like heat or cold rather than the degrees of variation on a thermometer. No longer can we take the easy way out by talking about party competition, without specifying what it is. Unfortunately, when we have to decide what it is, we encounter difficulties because there is no universal agreement on the definition of party competition.

Measurements and Criteria

By measuring competition, we are able to distinguish among *party systems*, whether they are dominant one-party, two-party, or multiparty.[1] Competition in the American two-party system has been measured by the vote cast for numerous offices over varying periods of time in federal and/or state elections. Analysts use the percentage of the party vote, the percentage of the time a party wins an office, and cyclical periods of party dominance. Some writers then classify the states according to their degree of competition: one-party, modified one-party, and two-party competitive.[2]

Others have expressed the variability of competition from state to state

---

[1] David J. Elkins, "The Measurement of Party Competition," *The American Political Science Review*, 68 (June 1974) 685.

[2] Austin Ranney and Willmoore Kendall, "The American Party Systems," *The American Political Science Review*, 48 (June 1954) 477–85. Joseph A. Schlesinger, "A

by use of numbers: One example is the "Index of Competitiveness" computed by averaging the percentage of the vote in gubernatorial and state legislative elections and the percentage of terms won by each party in these elections. Another example is the use of *index numbers*, derived from averaging data for presidential, gubernatorial, and congressional elections, in order to measure changes in party strength over a period of time.[3] Criteria for competition within an individual state are: the relative party strength in the electorate and/or in legislative seats, the relative percentage of the time the two parties control an office, and the percentage of the time the two parties divide control of offices.[4]

Percentages, by themselves, are not necessarily indicative of competition. One party can hold an office for twenty years consecutively with margins varying from 53 to 58 percent, or a party can win an office five times out of eight with over 60 percent. A rule of thumb that the competitive range for a winner is less than 55 percent is not a definition of competition if the same party always wins.

Irrespective of the measurement used, competition has to mean that officeholders are not self-perpetuating, that elections can lead to a party turnover, and that there is party alternation over a period of time. To the extent there are variations in the ability of the two parties to win a given office, there is variation in competition. Finally, competition is not only a quantitative measure, but also a *psychological* factor that one can sense in conversations, public statements, and political maneuvers. This factor is *uncertainty* about who will win a given election.[5]

Competition and One-Party Voting

Defined as alternation between parties, competition is more likely to be found over a period of time than in individual elections. The most common

Two-Dimensional Scheme for Classifying the States According to Degree of Inter-Party Competition," *The American Political Science Review*, 49 (December 1955) 1120–28. Robert T. Golembiewski, "A Taxonomic Approach to State Political Party Strength," *The Western Political Quarterly*, 11 (September 1958) 494–513. William H. Standing and James A. Robinson, "Inter-Party Competition and Primary Contesting: The Case of Indiana," *The American Political Science Review*, 52 (December 1958) 1068–69. Richard I. Hofferbert, "Classification of American State Party Systems, *The Journal of Politics*, 26 (August 1964) 550–67. David G. Pfeiffer, "The Measurement of Inter-Party Competition and Systematic Stability," *The American Political Science Review*, 61 (June 1967) 457–67.

[3] Austin Ranney, "Parties in State Politics," in *Politics in the American States: A Comparative Analysis*, 2nd ed., eds. Herbert Jacob and Kenneth N. Vines (Boston: Little, Brown and Company, 1971) pp. 84–91. Paul T. David, *Party Strength in the United States, 1872–1970* (Charlottesville, Va.: University Press of Virginia, 1972) and subsequent updating in *The Journal of Politics*, 36 (August 1974) 785–96; 37 (May 1975) 641–42; 38 (May 1976) 416–25; 40 (August 1978) 770–80.

[4] Richard E. Dawson and James A. Robinson, "Inter-Party Competition, Economic Variables, and Welfare Politics in the American States," *Ibid.*, 25 (May 1963) 274.

[5] Elkins, "The Measurement of Party Competition," pp. 682–84, 686, 700.

pattern of competition is periods of alternating *one-party domination*, not equal strength of the two parties all of the time. Even where competition has been strongest, there is a basic one-party voting behavior underlying the competition. This was the situation in presidential elections following the middle of the nineteenth century as more states became dominated by one party, and campaigns were concentrated in a few large competitive states. Even in the most competitive states, there are counties which are consistently one-party Democrat or Republican. States are competitive, not because the parties are closely competitive throughout the states, but because of the balance between one-party sections. This balance makes election outcomes depend upon the response in those counties which are competitive and upon temporary influences affecting turnout and party percentages in the one-party counties.[6]

DETERIORATION OF COMPETITION

The failure of the parties to realign in the 1960s–1970s is the major evidence of discontinuity in the system, but there had already been a deterioration of party competition at least by the 1950s. Therefore, discontinuity in the party system produced two results. Not only has party realignment eluded us but party equilibrium in competition has been disappearing as well.

Competitiveness of Offices

There is now such a well established pattern of variability in voting for different offices that it has become the norm. This pattern is a sharp contrast, not between federal and state offices, but between executive and legislative offices.

Executives. Presidential and gubernatorial elections have been relatively competitive, measured by party alternation but not necessarily when measured by percentages.

Volatility best describes *presidential voting* in the twentieth century. In the seventeen elections between 1832 and 1896, the winning presidential candidate had a majority of the popular vote in eight elections and a plurality in nine elections. Since 1900, presidents have won with only a plurality in five out of twenty elections. Defining a landslide as 55 percent or more of the vote received by the winner, only two elections (12 percent) were landslides before 1900 but nine (45 percent) have been since 1900. In

[6] Raymond E. Wolfinger and Fred I. Greenstein, "Comparing Political Regions: The Case of California," *The American Political Science Review*, 58 (March 1969) 74–85. James Walter Lindeen, "Intra-State Sectionalism: Nebraska Presidential Election Behavior, 1916–1968," *The Western Political Quarterly*, 24 (September 1971) 540–48.

Table 8.1 the percentage-point differences between winning and losing candidates show that all of those 20 percent and above occurred in this century. Nearly half of the elections since 1900 have been 15 percent or above, but over half were below 5 percent before 1900.

Now, there seems to be no pattern in presidential elections. Each one appears to be separate from all of the others. We cannot call them deviating because there is no longer the norm of maintaining elections to use as a standard for identifying deviations.

Party alternations in *gubernatorial elections* are more likely in those states that limit the number of consecutive terms a governor can serve. In some states with no such limitations, governors have sometimes served several consecutive terms. About one-fourth of incumbent governors have been defeated either in primaries or general elections since the 1960s, and the percentage of party turnovers averaged about 38 percent in the 1960s and 1970s.

Only thirteen states elect governors in presidential years, so the office is more likely to develop its own distinctive patterns of competition in the other 37 states. This insulation of gubernatorial elections from presidential elections may have helped to increase the visibility of governors even if they have not become more vulnerable. The declining role of partisanship in elections is not strong enough to indicate party decomposition, but it does contribute to short-term fluctuations that can affect incumbent governors. Otherwise, the advantage of incumbency has grown independently of party trends.[7]

TABLE 8.1   Percentage Differences in Total Vote Between Winning and Losing Major Party Candidates, Presidential Elections, since 1832.

Number of Elections

Percentage Difference	Nineteenth Century	Twentieth Century	Total
20% and above	0	5	5
15% to 19.9%	1	4	5
10% to 14.9%	4	2	6
5% to 9.9%	3	4	7
below 5%	9	5	14
	17	20	37

[7] Stephen J. Turett, "The Vulnerability of American Governors, 1900–1969," *Midwest Journal of Political Science*, 15 (February 1971) 108–32. James E. Piereson "Sources of Candidate Success in Gubernatorial Elections, 1910–1970," *The Journal of Politics*, 39 (November 1977) 939–58.

Legislators.   *Legislative elections* are far *less competitive* than *executive elections* because of the high reelection rate of legislators.

In elections for the House of Representatives there has been an average of 15 percent of the 435 seats uncontested by one of the major parties since 1952 (See Figure 7.2 in Chapter 7). The percentage of candidates winning by less than 55 percent has been declining and the number winning by 60 percent or more is increasing. Measuring competition by party turnover, between 20 to 25 percent of the seats have been competitive since 1940 compared with 50 percent competitive between 1890 and 1900.[8] The turnover rate increased somewhat because of the widespread redrawing of congressional district lines in the 1960s. Two contradictory facts about the House are that incumbents are seldom defeated for reelection but there has been a high rate of turnover because of retirements.

Some older members in both houses of Congress are, from time to time, beaten by young challengers. A notable exception, however, was S. I. Hayakawa who, at age 70, ousted 42-year-old John V. Tunney from the Senate in California in 1976. *Senate elections,* of course, are far *more competitive* than *House elections.* Both parties generally run candidates, and from five to ten senators have been defeated every two years since 1960. In the most competitive party states, there is some evidence that senators are more likely to be defeated for reelection after serving three terms.[9]

Incumbent state legislators are generally reelected although turnover for all of the states is high because of retirements. Actually, the turnover rate varies considerably so that in some states the membership is quite stable. Every two years, between 1963 and 1971, the number of new members of state senates ranged from 16.8 to 50.2 percent or an average of 30.4 percent for all states. In lower houses, the range was from 22.8 to 53.6 percent, a 36.1 percent average. As compensation for members has risen, the rate of voluntary retirement has declined, and the percentage of incumbents reelected has increased.[10]

Party Equilibrium

Improved Republican fortunes in *presidential elections* could be a sign of realignment if there were a corresponding shift in party identification, but Republicans have merely benefited from a volatility in voting unrelated to

[8] David W. Brady, "A Research Note on the Impact of Interparty Competition on Congressional Voting in a Competitive Era," *The American Political Science Review,* 67 (March 1973) 153–55.

[9] Warren Kostroski, "The Effect of Number of Terms on the Re-election of Senators 1920–1970," *The Journal of Politics,* 40 (May 1978) 488–97.

[10] Alan Rosenthal, "Turnover in State Legislatures," *American Journal of Political Science,* 18 (August 1974) 609–16. Ray David, "Voluntary Retirement and Electoral Defeat in Eight State Legislatures," *The Journal of Politics,* 38 (May 1976) 426–33.

identification. There is no longer an equilibrium in party competition in general because of the weakness of the Republican party.

During the 1960s, Republicans gradually elected more governors until they stood at thirty-one after the election of 1968. During the 1970s, the number of Republican governors fell to twelve in 1976, then rose to eighteen by 1978, while the Democrats won from 58 to 76 percent of the governors elected every two years.

In the House of Representatives, the Republicans have failed to run a candidate in forty to sixty districts in each election since 1962. After losing their control of the House in 1953–1954, the proportion of Republican seats has fallen to about one-third. The only section of the country where Republicans have increased their House membership is the South where they now elect more than four times the number they elected in 1960. There are about half as many Republican state legislators in the Northeast and three-fourths as many in the Midwest since 1960 while changes in the west and border states have been small (Figure 8.1). The Republicans have also been the minority party in the Senate since 1954. They elected a majority of the senators running only in 1966, 1972, and 1978.

Republican *weakness* in state legislatures can be illustrated in two ways: *control of legislative houses* and the total *number of members*. Republicans controlled nearly half of all legislative houses at the beginning of the 1970s but only one-third by the end of the decade. Since 1960, the highest proportion of Republican legislators in all states has been 43 percent, about as much as Republicans can achieve because of the one-party southern and border states.

There is probably not a state where Republicans can win an election solely by the votes of Republican identifiers. The rapid decline of the party seems to validate the conclusion that defeat eventually begets defeat.[11]

Sources of Competition

The variation in competition for different offices and the overall decline of party competition make one wonder what *party competition* depends upon in the first place, and if the nation has reached the point where party competition has become outmoded.

Size and Diversity. It would appear that the circumstances associated with the rise of political parties, pointed out in Chapter 1, should continue to contribute to party competition. Parties arose when there were conflicts among a more heterogeneous and concentrated population at a time of improved means of communicating. Party competition throughout American

[11] John D. May, *Sources of Competitive Disequilibrium between Competing Political Parties* (Morristown, N.J.: General Learning Press, 1973) pp. 6–14.

Midwest: Illinois, Indiana, Iowa, Kansas, Michigan, Minnesota, Nebraska, North Dakota, Ohio,
   South Dakota, Wisconsin.
Northeast: Connecticut, Delaware, Maine, Massachusetts, New Hampshire, New Jersey, New York,
   Pennsylvania, Rhode Island, Vermont.
West: Alaska, Arizona, California, Colorado, Hawaii, Idaho, Montana, Nevada, New Mexico,
   Oregon, Utah, Washington, Wyoming.
South: Alabama, Arkansas, Florida, Georgia, Louisiana, Mississipppi, North Carolina,
   South Carolina, Tennessee, Texas, Virginia.
Border: Kentucky, Maryland, Missouri, Oklahoma, West Virginia.

FIGURE 8.1   Number of Republicans Elected to House of
            Representatives, by Sections, since 1960.

political history has been more prevalent in states and their subdivisions
which developed these preconditions for parties.

As one would expect, *equilibrium* in party competition was found in
large geographical units, the nation more so than states, and states more
so than counties. Diverse interests are more likely to be found in larger areas
and lead to party competition while smaller, more *homogeneous areas* are
likely to be *one-party*.[12] This finding is further borne out by individual states.
California, Illinois, Indiana, Ohio, and New York are highly competitive

[12] Charles Sellers, "The Equilibrium Cycle in Two-Party Politics," in *Electoral
Change and Stability in American Political History*, eds., Jerome M. Clubb and
Howard W. Allen (New York: The Free Press, 1971) pp. 166–67.

compared with Mississippi and Vermont. Even in North Carolina, as it began to shake off its traditional one-party past, party competition was associated with areas of greater socioeconomic diversity within the state.[13] Yet, party competition, is not confined to relatively large states for nearly all of the mountain states have been classified as two-party, but Texas remains one-party Democratic in the *Index of Competitiveness*.[14]

Equating party competition with size of geographical units would mean, logically, that urban states are more competitive than rural states. Investigations to verify this conclusion led to conflicting findings, in part, because the investigators used different methodologies and definitions.[15] When the urban-rural distinction was approached the other way around in the Index of Competitiveness, *two-party states* were found to be more *urbanized* and to reflect more socioeconomic diversities than either one-party or modified one-party states.[16] *Two-party competition* is associated with *diversity* but diversity by itself does not necessarily create two-party competition.

Below the state level, the urban-rural distinction becomes more dubious. In the 1960 presidential election, no relationship was found between party competition and county urbanization.[17] The strength of the Democratic party in legislative districts has been associated with the percentage urban and nonwhite, with greater population density, and with fewer owner-occupied dwellings.[18] The end of any real party competition since the 1930s in most of the largest cities refutes the rule that diversity of interests and size of population encourage party competition. It is significant that large congested populations have turned to the Democratic party and have fought out their differences as intraparty factions on the local level. The heterogeneity of large cities has produced one-party homogeneity.[19]

It is still true that party competition depends upon divisions among voters which can be organized by opposing groups of leaders, but the characteristics identified as preconditions of parties no longer insure party competition in the twentieth century. Instead, the widespread factionalism in the

[13] Douglas S. Gatlin, "Toward a Functionalist Theory of Political Parties: Inter-Party Competition in North Carolina," in *Approaches to the Study of Party Organization*, ed., William J. Crotty (Boston: Allyn and Bacon, Inc., 1968) pp. 217–45.

[14] Ranney, "Parties in State Politics," p. 88.

[15] For a review and critique of the studies, Philip Coulter and Glen Gordon, "Urbanization and Party Competition," *The Western Political Quarterly*, 21 (June 1968) 274–88.

[16] Ranney, "Parties in State Politics," pp. 90–91.

[17] Charles M. Bonjean and Robert L. Lineberry, "The Urbanization-Party Competition Hypothesis: A Comparison of all United States Counties," *The Journal of Politics*, 32 (May 1970) 305–21.

[18] Lewis A. Froman, Jr., *Congressmen and Their Constituencies* (Chicago: Rand McNally & Co., 1963) pp. 118–19.

[19] Charles E. Gilbert and Christopher Clague, "Electoral Competition and Electoral Systems in Large Cities," *The Journal of Politics*, 24 (August 1962) 326.

Democratic party, whether in large cities or in southern states, demonstrates that the *sources of political competition need not create party competition.*[20]

Institutional Effects.   The importance of legal provisions upon turnout and ticket-splitting was discussed in Chapter 4. In the case of *party competition,* however, it has influenced the laws instead of the laws accounting for competition.

The most obvious illustration of this relationship can be found in the South where Democrats are required by state laws to hold a direct primary because of the number of voters the party receives in general elections. Traditionally, the Republican vote was so small, the party was permitted by law to make nominations in conventions or by committee designations. The laws were not responsible for the weakness of the Republican party. They merely recognized the weakness. As the Republicans became stronger in some of these states, they began to nominate candidates in direct primaries.

The same cause-and-effect relationship between state laws and party competition is found in *cross-filing legislation* which permits candidates to seek the nomination of more than one party by entering their names in each of the parties' primaries. California adopted cross-filing in 1913 at the height of the Progressive Movement. It was sometimes blamed for discouraging party competition when actually, the lack of party competition was a principal reason for adopting the law in the first place.[21] If cross-filing was meant to discourage party competition, it ultimately failed in its purpose and was repealed when party competition finally developed in California. New York, the only state still using cross-filing, adapted it to the state's multiparty system. However, it protected the parties by requiring a candidate to have the permission of a party committee to cross-file in the party's primary.

Party competition has deteriorated, no matter how it is measured, regardless of circumstances which should encourage competition. Equilibrium between the parties ebbs away with the growing weakness of the Republican party even as it holds some of its enclaves and continues to compete in executive and some legislative elections.

TICKET-SPLITTING

Ticket-splitting accounts for the increasing lack of party relationship in voting for different offices. Although this practice now dominates elections, there has always been some degree of ticket-splitting throughout the course of the party system.

[20] Edward T. Jennings, "Some Policy Consequences of the Long Revolution and Bifactional Rivalry in Louisiana," *American Journal of Political Science,* 21 (May 1977) 225–46.

[21] Stanley D. Hopper, "The Institutional Context of Cross-filing," *Social Science History,* 1 (Fall 1976) 1–18.

Parties v. Groups of Candidates

A curious contrast was found in the first half of the twentieth century in the election of state officials. In one-party states, elected officials generally failed to cooperate with one another. In two-party states, each party had stronger bonds holding its elected officials together, but neither party was likely to elect its entire state ticket. Candidates for governor and senator, whether they assumed or encouraged ticket-splitting, were inclined to run their campaigns separately from their parties.[22]

Failure to elect all of a party's candidates may be expected when the parties are highly competitive, and there is moderate ticket-splitting. Now, *ticket-splitting* has become the *source* for some *party competition*. Along with this change has gone some rethinking about parties and voting.

Conceiving of the party system as an institution makes each party appear to be a collective whose candidates are to be accepted or rejected in their entirety. As many voters appear to be thinking, *a party is not a single entity*. Instead, an election offers groups of candidates at different geographical levels for different branches of government. Perhaps voters see candidates as being of different kinds with different policy consequences but whatever they see, they are certainly organizing themselves differently for different groups of candidates.[23] It is one electorate that goes to the polls, but it votes as different coalitions for different offices.

This disregard for parties in elections is shown in simultaneous elections of governors and senators in Table 8.2. The averages for presidential and midterm elections show different tendencies in the first two time periods. It was between 1940 and 1956, when the momentum of ticket-splitting in-

TABLE 8.2   Average Percentage of Governors and Senators of Different Parties Elected Simultaneously, since 1914.*

Periods	Midterm Years	Periods	Presidential Years
1914–1934	17.6%	1916–1936	10.4%
1938–1958	16.2	1940–1956	21.7
1962–1978	47.8	1960–1976	47.2
Overall:			
1914–1978	26.0	1916–1976	26.8

* Based on author's computations.

[22] V. O. Key, Jr., *American State Politics: An Introduction* (New York: Alfred A. Knopf, 1956) pp. 201–2.
[23] Robert Warren and James J. Best, "The 1968 Election in Washington," *The Western Political Quarterly*, 22 (September 1969) 536–45. Barbara Hinckley, "Incumbency and the Presidential Vote in Senate Elections: Defining Parameters of Subpresidential Voting," *The American Political Science Review*, 64 (September 1970) 842.

creased in presidential years. The big jump for each group of election years began in the 1960s when the averages in both columns approach one-half of all elections. For the entire period since 1914, the average is just over one-fourth of elections in midterm and presidential years.

Party Identification and Ticket-Splitting

Ticket-splitting cannot be attributed entirely to pure Independents. Over one-fourth of those respondents professing some degree of party identification reported defecting from their party in presidential elections between 1952 and 1972. Identifiers voting split tickets in Senate and House elections approximately doubled between 1956 and 1974 and, in state and local elections, the proportions rose from 26 percent in 1958 to 56 percent in 1974. In twenty years, 1952–1972, the number of both identifiers and Independents reporting they had voted a split ticket, increased from one-third to over one-half and, for party identifiers only, the increase was from 25 to 46 percent.[24]

Independents' voting is increasingly associated with their *evaluations* of presidents, for Independents are likely to vote a straight ticket both in presidential and in midterm elections if they approve of the President.[25] Presidential approval-disapproval scores are closely associated with midterm voting both in turnout and in direction of the vote. Except for those who identify with the President's party, *disapproval* is associated with *higher turnout*, and since 1960, pure Independents have reported voting at midterm in about the same proportion they voted in presidential elections. Both Independents and identifiers who disapprove of the President are more likely to vote for the opposition party at midterm than in presidential years.[26]

These are the general findings from survey research, and there is no way to take account of the fact that we cannot always be sure if Independents are what they say they are or if they have a partisan preference which they choose to conceal.

Motivations in Ticket-Splitting

Ticket-splitting is a fact of political life even though its extent is difficult to measure. Respondents in surveys report if they split their tickets, and elec-

---

[24] Norman H. Nie, Sidney Verba, and John R. Petrocik, *The Changing American Voter* (Cambridge, Mass.: Harvard University Press, 1976) pp. 50–55.

[25] David Knoke, *Change and Continuity in American Politics: The Social Bases of Political Parties* (Baltimore, Md.: The Johns Hopkins University Press, 1976) pp. 141, 145. James E. Piereson, "Presidential Popularity and Midterm Voting at Different Electoral Levels," *American Journal of Political Science*, 19 (November 1975) 683–94.

[26] Samuel Kernel, "Presidential Popularity and Negative Voting; An Alternative Explanation of the Midterm Congressional Decline of the President's Party," *The American Political Science Review*, 71 (March 1977) 46, 60–62.

tion returns show candidates of both parties winning offices. Still, we do not know exactly how many voters mark their ballots for just one party or for both parties. What is more important, the motivations behind ticket-splitting are open to interpretation.

Realistically, we cannot judge the health of the party system today by the standards of nineteenth-century straight-ticket voting. Ticket-splitting, like the increase in Independents, has posed no threat to the *two-party system* as such, but ambiguity now infects voting just as it does party identification. What voters seem to be saying is that their motives in voting are not as important for distinguishing party identifiers from Independents as for distinguishing straight- from split-ticket voters.

Widespread and continuous ticket-splitting is normally considered a sign of party decomposition. To prescribe decomposition as a means of party system revival seems comparable to breaking an arm in preparation for body building. Nevertheless, there is a school of thought that glorifies ticket-splitters. They have been found to be politically *involved* and *discriminating*, to be what Independents were supposed to be, and to offer the best hope for revitalizing American democracy. They were also found to be candidate-oriented, dependent upon the media for information, and representing a large part of the undecided vote.[27] Even this description of the motives of ticket-splitters is incomplete.

Ticket-splitting may be a purposeful attempt to preserve *checks and balances* by voting Republican for President and Democratic for Congress, or it may be simply a reflection of *candidate-orientation*. It appears to result from political influences unrelated to generational differences, for the proportion of split-ticket voting has been similar for each of the various age groups since 1952. To cast a split ticket at least infers that the voter is more candidate- or issue-motivated than party-motivated, but the voter would not necessarily agree. A split vote may represent to the voter a consistency of response or a compromise whereby he deserts his party only on one office.[28]

Motives can also be less purposeful. The record of split-ticket voting seems to be about the same whether a state uses a party-column or office-block ballot, but the form of the ballot can still encourage or discourage individual ticket-splitting as it did at the turn of the twentieth century. Voting either straight or split can be the result of a special motivation or of indifference.[29]

[27] Walter DeVries and Lance Tarrance, Jr., *The Ticket-Splitter: A New Force in American Politics* (Grand Rapids, Michigan: William B. Eerdmans Publishing Company, 1972) pp. 115, 122.

[28] Warren E. Miller and Teresa E. Levitin, *Leadership and Change: Presidential Elections from 1952 to 1976* (Cambridge, Mass.: Winthrop Publishers, Inc., 1976) pp. 253–54. Nie and others, *The Changing American Voter*, pp. 67–68.

[29] See Chapter 4; see also Angus Campbell and Warren E. Miller, "The Motivational Basis of Straight and Split Ticket Voting," *The American Political Science Review*, 51 (June 1957) 293–312.

THE PARTY VOTE

The more nearly voting is determined by party identification, the more nearly it is a party vote or, what is designated, a "normal vote."[30] It is not possible to have a completely "normal vote," in this sense. For everyone with a party identification to vote that identification in every election would be too much to expect under any circumstances. Compared with the decline in straight-ticket voting, identification has remained relatively stable, allowing for variations in degrees of intensity. What party voting requires is that voters with a party identification use it as the major criterion for their voting decision. The evidence indicates this test is being met by identifiers as a whole, although there is no way of knowing if party identification will weaken among those who continue to vote contrary to their identification.[31]

Which Is the Party Vote?

The growing body of voting-behavior research leads to conflicting conclusions about the extent and location of a party vote:

1. The reliability of party identification in voting has not changed as much as it would appear. Deviations from the "normal vote" concept have been erratic in presidential elections—as high as 16 percent in 1972—but averaging only 2.5 percent between 1952 and 1976 in House elections (a discouraging omen for realignment which has traditionally begun in House voting at midterm). The overall rate of party defection, which is a different statistical concept than the deviation from the "normal vote," was only 17 percent in 1976 compared with 27 percent in 1972.[32]

2. Presidential elections involve the least amount of party voting, not only because of the extent of defection by identifiers but also because those Independents and weak identifiers, who are stimulated to vote, are influenced more by publicity and personalities than by party. According to this conclusion, party is no longer relevant to presidential elections, so the party vote is found in House elections.[33] Party identification

[30] Philip E. Converse, "The Concept of a Normal Vote," in *Elections and the Political Order*, eds., Angus Campbell, Philip E. Converse, Warren E. Miller, and Donald E. Stokes (New York: John Wiley and Sons, Inc., 1966) pp. 9–39.

[31] James F. Ward, "Toward a Sixth Party System? Partisanship and Political Development," *The Western Political Quarterly*, 26 (September 1973) 402–3, 412. William G. Vanderbok, "Cohorts, Aggregation Problems and Cross-Level Theorizing: The Case of Partisan Stability," *The Western Political Quarterly*, 30 (March 1977) 110–11. Nie and others, *The Changing American Voter*, pp. 67–68, 156–57. Knoke, *Change and Continuity in American Politics*, p. 139.

[32] Miller and Levitin, *Leadership and Change*, pp. 35–41, 228–30.

[33] Gerald M. Pomper, *Voters' Choice: Varieties of American Electoral Behavior* (New York: Dodd, Mead & Company, 1975) pp. 215–16. Richard P. Y. Li, "A Dynamic Comparative Analysis of Presidential and House Elections," *American Journal of Political Science*, 20 (November 1976) 671–91.

proved to be a better predictor of congressional than presidential voting in 1952–1972 surveys, although the association fell in both elections because of an increased Republican vote for Democratic congressional candidates.[34]

3. Throughout the country, the parties are no longer competitive either in most measurements of voting or in any measurement of party identification. The party system, as reflected in party voting, has retreated downward within the federal governmental structure. There is greater importance attached to party on the state and local levels, as seen by the relatively high degree of one-party dominance.[35]

4. Occasionally, it has been argued that the decreased importance of party identification in presidential elections cannot be confirmed. The hypothesis was advanced, instead, that voters feel personal qualifications of governors and senators are more important than party. Also, in case of differences between national and state issue cleavages, there is more reliance upon candidate images in state-level elections.[36]

About the only common finding among these four conclusions is that *presidential voting is distinctive from all other voting.* Except for the first conclusion, they all find a declining party vote, more or less. Three of them do contrast presidential and House voting, but the implications of this contrast especially in numbers 2 and 3 are devastating for the party system.

We find ourselves in this general situation. Presidential elections have been unstable but competitive because of the decline of party voting. Stable voting for the House is party voting, but there is relatively little competition. The most competition occurs in elections where party identification is the least important in influencing the vote. The least party competition occurs where party identification is a far more important influence on the vote. In other words, where there is a party vote, there is weak party competition and where there is competition, there is weak party voting.

Whatever the meaning of these election data, at least it is sure that voting behavior now stands in sharp contrast to the period from 1872 to 1896, when the party system was at its height. Figure 8.2 compares the Democratic vote in both presidential and House elections for that period of the nineteenth century with the period since 1960. Between 1872 and 1896, presidential elections were closely competitive, but there were wild swings in congressional party strength as shown by the vertical zigzag lines in the lower left hand segment of Figure 8.2. Since 1960, support for Democratic presidential candidates has been unstable, varying from a landslide in 1964 to

[34] Knoke, *Change and Continuity in American Politics*, pp. 142–45.

[35] V. O. Key, Jr., "Partisanship and County Office: The Case of Ohio," *The American Political Science Review*, 48 (June 1953) 525–32. Kevin P. Phillips, *Mediacracy: American Parties and Politics in the Communications Age* (Garden City, N.Y.: Doubleday & Company, Inc., 1975) pp. 146–47. DeVries and Tarrance, *The Ticket-Splitter*, p. 37.

[36] Gerald C. Wright, Jr., *Electoral Choice in America*, Institute for Research in Social Science (Chapel Hill, N.C.: University of North Carolina, 1974) pp. 113–43.

Percentage of Total Presidential Vote

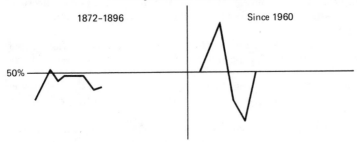

1872–1896   Since 1960

50%

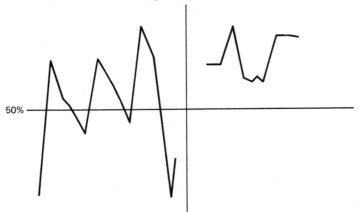

Percentage of Total House Seats

50%

FIGURE 8.2   Democratic Percentage of Total Presidential Vote and
of House Seats, 1872–1896 Compared with
Elections since 1960.

a Republican landslide in 1972. At the same time, Democratic control of the
House of Representatives was never challenged although it fluctuated considerably, from 68 percent of the seats in 1964 to 56 percent in 1968 and
1972. If the last quarter of the nineteenth century was the model of party
competition, the model has been turned upside down since 1960.

Of course, voting behavior can take on a different appearance with the
passage of even short periods of time. For example, the Republican presidential victories in 1952 and 1956 were generally interpreted as deviating
elections, for they did not basically disturb party attachments. Democrats
voted for Eisenhower because they were attracted to him personally.[37] By
the late 1970s, it was possible to interpret these elections differently. Instead

[37] This is the interpretation in Angus Campbell, "Voters and Elections: Past and
Present," *The Journal of Politics*, 26 (November 1964) 752–54.

of being deviating, they could have been the sign of something new in American politics. Since 1952, presidential elections have followed an alternating eight-year party cycle.[38] They appear to have moved into their own separate orbit, leaving Congress to move in another orbit, independent of the influences of presidential elections, as Figure 8.2 makes clear.

Party Voting and Coattail Voting

Historically, the relationship between presidential and congressional voting followed a general pattern: The party holding the White House lost seats at the following midterm election, but if it lost a majority of the seats, the other party would win the presidency two years later. Both of these patterns have disappeared.

Party Voting. The rhythm of alternating party voting has been broken. Since winning a majority of Congress in 1930, the Democrats have only been dislodged twice, in 1946 and 1952. Party shifts in the presidency are no longer foretold at midterm, and Republican presidents have not brought in a Republican congressional majority except in 1952. Since the 1960s, there has been no consistent pattern of a party winning the presidential election and also increasing its strength in the House.

Midterm Elections. The Democrats increased their congressional majority in 1934, seemingly as a continuation of their landslide in 1932. Since World War II, Democrats have gained House seats in three midterm years with increases of 8 percent of the seats in 1954 and 20 percent in both 1958 and 1974. The voting rate in each of these three years was below the average turnout for all midterm elections from 1950 to 1974. They may be explained by a generalization applied, not to the number of seats won or lost, but to the national vote in House elections. As *turnout declines*, the majority party receives a larger percentage of the vote cast in House elections throughout the country unless the vote is distorted by short-term forces.[39] In 1954, 1958, and 1974, the Democrats benefited both from low turnout and from short-term forces which normally benefit the opposition party.

Coattail Voting. Changes have occurred in the so-called coattail vote, which is measured by the *loss of House seats at midterm by the White House party*. The explanation of the coattail vote has been either that a popular presidential candidate attracts straight-ticket voters who usually do not vote at midterm;[40] or that a presidential candidate stimulates straight-

[38] Phillips, *Mediacracy*, pp. 146–47, also ix and 12.

[39] Harvey M. Kabaker, "Estimating the Normal Vote in Congressional Elections," *American Journal of Political Science*, 13 (February 1969) 58–83.

[40] Campbell, "Voters and Elections," pp. 749–51.

ticket voting in close districts. As the number of these districts increases, the greater the party's loss will be two years later.[41]

Coattail voting would lead one to expect that presidential and House candidates of the same party would either win or lose a congressional district together rather than have a split result, with one of them winning and the other losing. Early in the twentieth century, presidential and congressional candidates of the same party generally ran consistently in individual districts, except for the disruptive election in 1912. The proportion of split districts increased, beginning in 1928, but was less than 20 percent through 1952, then rose to one-third in 1964 and to 44 percent in 1972. Nearly all Democratic incumbents were reelected in 1968 and 1972—even where Nixon carried their districts with very large majorities. Some of these districts, of course, were in the South. Presidential coattails have become much weaker against incumbents but appear to help in districts where neither candidate is an incumbent.[42]

Coattail voting is deduced from voting returns and from survey data, but it is obviously *subjective*, not objective. If you vote for a House candidate *because* of your *presidential choice*, it is a coattail response. If you vote for the same party's candidates for both offices *because* of your own *party identification*, it is a party response. Only you can say if you cast a coattail or a party vote—or an unrelated vote.

The distinction becomes more concrete by contrasting the influence of the presidential vote cast for Franklin Roosevelt with that cast for Dwight Eisenhower. When Roosevelt was running, it was often said he had broad coattails because so many other Democrats were elected along with him. The Democrats, however, were the dominant party, and the higher turnout in presidential years was the result of Roosevelt's stimulating more Democrats to vote. Thus, Roosevelt's coattails were really a party vote. When Eisenhower was running, the Republicans were the minority party, and the higher turnout was not accounted for by chronic nonvoting Republicans. No doubt, some Republicans were elected on Eisenhower's coattails, but Eisenhower did not win with a Republican vote.[43]

---

[41] Charles Press, "Presidential Coattails and Party Cohesion," *Midwest Journal of Political Science*, 7 (November 1963) 328–29. Barbara Hinckley, "Interpreting House Midterm Elections: Toward a Measurement of the In-Party's 'Expected' Loss of Seats," *The American Political Science Review*, 61 (September 1967) 694–700.

[42] Charles M. Tidmarch and Douglas Carpenter, "Congressmen and the Electorate, 1968 and 1972," *The Journal of Politics*, 40 (May 1978) 479–87. Milton C. Cummings, Jr., *Congressmen and the Electorate: Elections for the U.S. House and the President, 1920–1964* (New York: The Free Press, 1966) especially pp. 10, 32. Walter Dean Burnham, "Insulation and Responsiveness in Congressional Elections," *Political Science Quarterly*, 90 (Fall 1975) 424–30.

[43] John W. Meyer, "A Reformulation of the 'Coattails' Problem," in *Public Opinion and Congressional Elections*, eds., William N. McPhee and William A. Glaser (Glencoe: The Free Press, 1962) pp. 53–54, 63–64.

INCUMBENCY

Defining party competition as either alternation in office over time or uncertainty of the outcome of elections, legislative offices are generally at the bottom of the scale of competition because of the remarkable rate of return of incumbents to office. Since World War II, over 80 percent of Senate incumbents and over 90 percent of House incumbents have won. Even the extensive redrawing of congressional districts within the states during the 1960s did not result in much turnover either by defeat or retirement although what turnover there was appeared to stop the trend toward less competition.[44]

Why are incumbents so difficult to defeat?

Some Explanations

Members of *Congress*, regardless of their party or their senority, have the advantages of resources typical of all incumbents, but their resources appear to be more advantageous than those of *incumbent governors*. A congressional district is not cordoned off by boundaries in the way a state is. A district is a temporary creation for the purpose of electing a member of the House. It is more difficult, therefore for a congressional challenger to gain the attention comparable to that of a candidate for governor. But a member of Congress does gain attention and identification within his or her own district because of the continuing publicity which incumbents can command.

It is not certain that *House incumbents* benefit so much from name recognition, but they may have an advantage in reputation because of their exposure. Moreover, voters do not have to remember names in order to have an opinion about a candidate. These intangible resources are incalculable and are reinforced by incumbents generally spending more money on radio and television advertising. Incumbency, it has been estimated, is worth 5 percent or more of the vote in a House election.[45]

The money spent by a House incumbent on franking, staff salaries, and other perquisites, such as toll-free telephones, may amount to as much as $1.3 million a year in political money. Some members have kept up with the times by spending out of their allowances (that is, out of public funds) for

[44] Charles S. Bullock III, "Redistricting and Congressional Stability, 1962–1972," *The Journal of Politics*, 37 (May 1975) 569–75.

[45] Alan I. Abramowitz, "Name Familiarity, Reputation, and the Incumbency Effect in a Congressional Election," *The Western Political Quarterly*, 28 (December 1975) 668–84. Gary C. Jacobson, "The Effects of Campaign Spending in Congressional Elections," *The American Political Science Review*, 72 (June 1978) 469–91; and Jacobson, "The Impact of Broadcast Campaigning on Electoral Outcomes," *The Journal of Politics*, 37 (August 1975) 785–88. David R. Mayhew, *Congress: The Electoral Connection* (New Haven, Ct.: Yale University Press, 1974) p. 36, note 53, in general 49–52.

computerized mailing lists to give themselves a headstart against challengers during a campaign. Although this practice has officially been banned, it may prove to be a practical impossibility to distinguish between its legitimate use for carrying out official duties and its illegitimate use in winning votes.

Incumbents usually are at an advantage in raising campaign funds because so many contributors favor incumbents. In 1978, for instance, the Federal Election Commission reported that business corporations' political action committees contributed $2.4 million to incumbents of both parties but only $370,873 to challengers of both parties. Other contributors, who stress party and ideology more heavily, may give relatively more to challengers.[46]

Candidates who challenge incumbents need more money to achieve parity in recognition, but usually have more difficulty raising money because of the odds against them. Nevertheless, considering the value of all of the resources available to House incumbents, restrictions on campaign spending, especially through exclusive government financing, would benefit them even more. The only way challengers have a chance to overcome their inherent disadvantages is the opportunity to raise money to advertise themselves. If they were prohibited from raising more than a given amount of money, they would have few additional resources to fall back upon.

Political parties themselves may be a declining resource, for House elections are less and less dependent upon a party vote. Even strong Republicans have been found more likely to vote for Democratic incumbents than for Republican challengers. Incumbents, not their parties, are becoming the cue in many congressional districts, but it is not an issue-oriented cue because the public is not well informed about incumbents' voting records. People, therefore, do not just defect from their own party to vote for incumbents, they sometimes contradict their own issue positions with their vote. Perhaps, part of the difficulty in interpreting House voting is the inclination to overestimate the effects of national issues, and overlook the importance of local interests and perspectives.

Those who have no issue positions and those who do not see differences between the parties are likely to cast a party vote in presidential elections and vote for the incumbent in congressional elections.[47] This attraction

---

[46] *The Miami Herald*, November 6, 1978, p. 7A. Washington Post Service, *Ibid.*, November 3, 1978, p. 17A.

[47] Stanley Kelley, Jr. and Thad W. Mirer, "The Simple Act of Voting," *The American Political Science Review*, 67 (June 1974) 572–91. John E. Jackson, "Issue, Party Choices and Presidential Votes," *American Journal of Political Science*, 19 (May 1975) 161–86. Kendall L. Baker and Oliver Walter, "Voter Rationality: A Comparison of Presidential and Congressional Voting in Wyoming," *The Western Political Quarterly*, 28 (June 1975) 316–29. Nie and others, *The Changing American Voter*, p. 349. If there were no incumbents in marginal districts, issues would be decisive; in safe districts with incumbents, issues do not matter; see John L. Sullivan and Eric M. Uslaner, "Congressional Behavior and Electoral Marginality," *American Journal of Political Science*, 22 (August 1978) 548, in general 548–52.

to incumbents is not only a triumph of fact over the theory of what competition should be, but also a challenge to democratic theory.[48]

Whatever voters think they are doing when they persist in returning incumbents to office, the logic of their behavior puts them in a seemingly untenable position. As they become too discriminating to vote party identification blindly, they blindly vote for incumbents. At one and the same time, voters have become both "smarter" and "dumber." [49] It may help to save the integrity of voters' thought processes, if not the validity of political theory, to point out that congressional incumbents are insulated from controversy by their being relatively inconspicuous, a development they are not entirely responsible for.

Voters' information about executives and legislators is different. Executives are more likely to be seen as responsible for what government does, more likely to stand out before the public as individual candidates.[50] If an executive leads a more precarious existence in office, he also attracts the voters by his personality because he stands alone. This distinction may account for the greater vulnerability of United States senators who also stand out because they run alone. A candidate for the state legislature or the House of Representatives has the advantage of anonymity by running as a member of a crowd.

The final explanation for the invincibility of incumbent legislators is the nature of the legislature itself which is best illustrated by the Congress.

Insulation of the Congressional Institution

Members of the House of Representatives have insulated themselves, for collective political protection, by transforming an elective office into a professional career service. The institutionalization of the House has helped members escape party organization and, as a result, both intraparty and interparty competition.

In the years between the Civil War and World War I, membership in

[48] John A. Ferejohn, "On the Decline of Competition in Congressional Elections," *The American Political Science Review*, 71 (March 1977) 173–74. Andrew T. Cowart, "Electoral Choice in the American States: Incumbency Effects, Partisan Forces and Divergent Partisan Majorities," *The American Political Science Review*, 67 (September 1973) 852–53. Warren Lee Kostroski, "Party and Incumbency in Postwar Senate Elections: Trends, Patterns, and Models," *The American Political Science Review*, 67 (December 1973) 1223–24. Albert D. Cover, "One Good Term Deserves Another: The Advantage of Incumbency in Congressional Elections," *American Journal of Political Science*, 21 (August 1977) 523-42.

[49] Morris P. Fiorina, "The Case of the Vanishing Marginals: The Bureaucracy Did It," *The American Political Science Review*, 71 (March 1977) 177; and Fiorina, "An Outline for a Model of Party Choice," *American Journal of Political Science*, 21 (August 1977) 620–21.

[50] Wright, *Electoral Choice in America*, pp. 79–81, 111. Joseph A. Schlesinger, *Ambition and Politics: Political Careers in the United States* (Chicago: Rand McNally and Company, 1966) p. 69.

the House came to be a career in itself instead of a means for moving to another career. As the congressional parties weakened, and the role of the federal government expanded, the prestige of public life became greater. The growing complexity of governing required a longer period of apprenticeship because of the need for greater specialization in the legislative process and a more professional leadership.

The demand for longer tenure led to a more stable membership. In some congressional districts, counties had taken turns electing the member, but these rotational agreements ended by the twentieth century. Adoption of the direct primary also made it easier for incumbents to be renominated. Whereas 60 percent of incumbents were renominated in the 1850s, 80 percent were renominated by the 1900s. Even in the nineteenth century, there was less likelihood of a party turnover if an incumbent was running. After 1896, there were fewer party turnovers even when incumbents were not running.

The dramatic public turning point in the institutionalization of the House was the so-called "revolution of 1910–1911," when the Speaker was stripped of some of his powers, including the appointment of committee chairmen. In actuality, this event was part of the long-term development of the House as a stable social system resting on seniority and decentralization of power.[51]

Specialization and professionalism in Congress have subsequently given members prestige while they avoid dangerous issues, in part, by taking on "errand-boy" tasks for their constituents. The errand-boy role, when it is examined, is not entirely as onerous as it may appear. In fact, it is largely a self-created role. Congress constantly creates new federal programs to win favor back home. Then, constituents, who need help in order to take advantage of the new benefits, call upon members of Congress. They, in turn, must intercede with the bureaucracy on behalf of deserving citizens. Not only do constituents make increasing demands for these services of an intermediary, but are encouraged to see their representatives as "servants" for this purpose.[52]

To help keep pace with the demands, both houses of Congress have continued to increase appropriations for individual members to hire more staff. These employees, sometimes referred to as the "hidden government," attend directly to constituents' problems, write speeches, and provide a

---

[51] Samuel Kernell, "Toward Understanding 19th Century Congressional Careers: Ambition, Competition, and Rotation," *American Journal of Political Science*, 21 (November 1977) 669–93. Richard Born, "House Incumbents and Inter-Election Vote Change," *The Journal of Politics*, 39 (November 1977) 1008–34. Nelson W. Polsby, "The Institutionalization of the U.S. House of Representatives," *The American Political Science Review*, 62 (March 1968) 144–68. Nelson W. Polsby, Miriam Gallaher, and Barry Spencer Rundquist, "The Growth of the Seniority System in the U.S. House of Representatives," *The American Political Science Review*, 63 (September 1969) 787–807.

[52] Morris P. Fiorina, *Congress—Keystone of the Washington Establishment* (New Haven, Ct.: Yale University Press, 1977).

range of expertise on legislative matters including advice to members on how to vote on specific bills. Marginal districts have been turned into safe districts by incumbents spending much of their time at home, and by maintaining a large staff in their local offices to service constituents directly and immediately. Instead of concentrating upon national policy in Washington, D.C., House members specialize in providing nonpartisan services for constituents dealing with the federal bureaucracy. This change in representational roles permits the members to protect their careers by responding to individual and group pressures. They are able to take on an institutional gloss by running for reelection as professionals rather than as members of parties dealing with divisive issues.[53]

Competition in presidential elections, as we have seen, has become associated with a weak party vote in contrast with House elections. Now, even this distinction is disappearing. Presidential competition and lack of House competition are both the result of a weak party vote. Party identification is not a true test of presidential voting and is also increasingly irrelevant in congressional voting because voters prefer incumbents. Even when House elections are competitive, they take on, more and more, a nonpartisan aura.

This attraction to legislative incumbents may actually be a cultural preference for unity and consensus. It has been traced to a nonpartisanism in adults' political environment as well as childhood socialization favoring positive evaluations and agreement with others.[54] But the conciliatory theme of nonpartisanism is widespread among all elected officials. The Governor of Illinois, in 1977, noted in his inaugural address that the job of government "has little to do with parties or ideologies or labels. It has everything to do with earning your trust." [55]

As the party vote disappears, party competition becomes more and more meaningless. At best, party competition is only one objective to be balanced against others in the pantheon of American values.

WHAT DIFFERENCE DOES PARTY COMPETITION MAKE?

Given the state of party competition, it is worth asking what it accomplishes anyway, particularly in legislative elections. In some individual elec-

[53] Mayhew, *Congress: The Electoral Connection*, pp. 84, 108–10. Fiorina, "The Case of the Vanishing Marginals," 178–79, 181. Richard F. Fenno, Jr., "U.S. House Members in Their Constituencies: An Explanation," *The American Political Science Review*, 71 (September 1977) 883–917.

[54] David O. Sears and Richard E. Whitney, *Political Persuasion* (Morristown, N.J.: General Learning Press, 1973) p. 21.

[55] Governor James R. Thompson, quoted in *St. Louis Globe-Democrat*, January 11, 1977.

tions for the House of Representatives, researchers found that candidates offered voters a choice and that winners voted consistently with their promises on specific issues.[56]

Yet, in 1966, when the policy orientations of all incumbents and their challengers were compared, it would have made no difference on major issues if every incumbent had been defeated. If only a selected 100 incumbents had been defeated, however, it would have made a great deal of difference.[57] These artificial projections attest to the power of members from safe districts who have reached positions of strategic influence. When it comes to counting votes in the House, do members from safe districts vote differently than members who win by small majorities and are worried about reelection?

Competitive Districts and Legislative Voting

A political party's legislative program is likely to be opposed by a majority of constituents in some of the districts represented by legislators who are members of that party. These members supposedly face the choice, from time to time, of voting with their party or voting with their constituents. Conversely, if a party represents a particular interest, a district where that interest predominates will be compatible with the party, and the legislator does not have the problem of choosing between constituents and party. The very high levels of party support in the House of Representatives at the turn of the twentieth century can be accounted for by the relatively greater homogeneity of congressional districts then than now.[58]

The greater variety of interests within districts now means that many legislative constituencies, congressional and state, are less likely to coincide with either party's position on a given bill. Therefore, members who are elected by a small majority should be less likely to vote with their parties than members from safe districts. Nevertheless, efforts to prove these conclusions have had mixed results. There is no consistent evidence that party support on legislative roll calls is different for members from competitive districts compared with members from safe districts, although findings vary with different periods of time and for the two parties. In addition, there is

[56] John L. Sullivan and Robert E. O'Connor, "Electoral Choice and Popular Control of Public Policy: The Case of the 1966 House Elections," *The American Political Science Review*, 66 (December 1972) 1256–68. Jeff Fishel, "Party, Ideology, and the Congressional Challenger," *The American Political Science Review*, 63 (December 1969) 1213–32.

[57] Jeff Fishel, *Party and Opposition: Congressional Challengers in American Politics* (New York: David McKay Company, Inc., 1973) p. 196.

[58] David W. Brady, "Congressional Leadership and Party Voting in the McKinley Era: A Comparison to the Modern House," *Midwest Journal of Political Science*, 16 (August 1972) 439–59; and Brady and Phillip Althoff, "Party Voting in the U.S. House of Representatives, 1890–1910: Elements of a Responsible Party System," *The Journal of Politics*, 36 (August 1974) 753–75.

no assurance that the margin of electoral victory is the motivation for legislative voting, or that a vote contrary to party necessarily reflects constituents' interests.[59]

Party Competition and State Policies

Attempts to demonstrate that party competition results in higher state welfare expenditures have had some dismal results. There have been strong disagreements on the methodologies used to measure the association of the two variables, with resulting confusion about what is being correlated. The most competitive states are generally the most affluent, and it may be the affluence itself, measured by per capita income, that explains policies, especially those for the benefit of the poor.[60]

Party differences may not show up even in states with party competition. Comparing the distribution of benefits to the poor in 34 northern states between 1951 and 1967, it made little difference which party controlled the state government. First, there is the "bidding effect," whereby each party promised approximately what the other promised. Second, the state budgets are too large and complex for either party to make quick changes in them. Third, drastic changes are unlikely because of the effects of federal grants.[61] Even if the parties alternate in passing through the government structure, programs appear to go on much the same.

There are, of course, other state issues besides welfare where party competition may make a difference.[62] Even at that, we still must look to the

[59] Lewis A. Froman, Jr., *Congressmen and Their Constituencies* (Chicago: Rand McNally & Co., 1963) pp. 111–16. W. Wayne Shannon, *Party, Constituency and Congressional Voting* (Baton Rouge, La.: Louisiana State University Press, 1968) pp. 158–63. Duncan MacRae, Jr., "The Relation between Roll Call Votes and Constituencies in the Massachusetts House of Representatives," *The American Political Science Review*, 46 (December 1952) 1046–55. David W. Brady, "A Research Note on the Impact of Interparty Competition on Congressional Voting in a Competitive Era," *The American Political Science Review*, 67 (March 1973) 153–56. Pertti Pesonen, "Close and Safe State Elections in Massachusetts," *Midwest Journal of Political Science*, 7 (February 1963) 54–70. Bryan D. Jones, "Competitiveness, Role Orientations, and Legislative Responsiveness," *The Journal of Politics*, 35 (November 1973) 924–47. James H. Kuklinski, "District Competitiveness and Legislative Roll-Call Behavior: A Reassessment of the Marginality Hypothesis," *American Journal of Political Science*, 21 (August 1977) 627–38. Barbara Sinclair Deckard, "Electoral Marginality and Party Loyalty in House Roll Call Voting," *American Journal of Political Science*, 20 (August 1976) 469–81.

[60] Dawson and Robinson, "Inter-Party Competition, Economic Variables, and Welfare Policies in the American States," 281–89. Duane Lockard, "State Party Systems and Policy Outputs," in *Political Research and Political Theory*, ed., Oliver Garceau (Cambridge, Mass.: Harvard University Press, 1968) 198–210. Dennis D. Riley, "Party Competition and State Policy Making: The Need for a Reexamination," *The Western Political Quarterly*, 24 (September 1971) 510–13.

[61] Richard Winters, "Party Control and Policy Change," *American Journal of Political Science*, 20 (November 1976) 597–636.

[62] Charles F. Cnudde and Donald J. McCrone, "Party Competition and Welfare Policies in the American States," *The American Political Science Review*, 63 (September 1969) 858–66.

whole country to find major trends in the party system, for national issues are more than a mere aggregation of state issues. No matter how wide the range of state issues may be, national party competition is different from party competition in individual states.

Competition and Survival

In each period of realignment, elections were issue-oriented and party competition was intense. Thereafter, competition continued even though the parties' issue differences became less extreme. It was the long intervals between realignments that gave the party system its reputation for moderation because of the similarity of party positions. Perhaps the time has come when people reject parties because party competition no longer seems to make much difference. The evidence of realignment in group voting since the 1960s suggests new responses to issues, and party leaders may have to respond to these hints in order to save the party system.

The possibilities for *party continuity* through realignment will be further explored in the next two chapters to see if the decline of parties is an irreversible trend or if the party system is merely in the doldrums, a period of calm before a gathering storm.

9

Issues and Party Differences

It appeared that the continuity of the traditional party system was broken when no realignment occurred in the period of the 1960s–1970s. The social and economic conditions associated with realignments did appear, and there were shifts in sectional and demographic voting patterns. Neither changes in party identification nor subsequent changes in the relative strength of the parties, the two requirements of realignment, materialized. Significant changes in identification increased the ranks of Independents. A change in the relative strength of the two parties favored the Republicans in presidential elections and the Democrats in most other elections.

Persistent disconnections in voting marked a deterioration in the party system. Where there has been party competition for President, there has been a weak party vote. Increasingly, in congressional elections, competition is weak, and the party vote is also weakening. Disconnections have become more prominent in all elections because of ticket-splitting and voter attraction to incumbents, particularly in legislative races.

The period when realignment should have occurred, according to the historical schedule, was filled with traumatic events. The fact that these events did not produce party realignment may confirm the belief that parties have become irrelevant and that a new kind of political system is in the making. Issues of the past have given way to issues of the future, but these issues are not necessarily associated with either party. Instead, they roam the political landscape outside of the party system.

Just because realignment is late, however, does not necessarily mean it is not coming. Its time schedule was only recognized comparatively recently, and it has not functioned with clock-like regularity. It is the continuity of the party system, not a calendar, with which we are concerned. In this chapter, we will examine the relevance of issues in elections and the clustering of issues into ideological divisions as the basis for another party realignment.

THE HERITAGE OF MODERATION

How much and what kinds of differences should exist between parties depends upon the concept of what a party system should be. Alexis de Tocqueville thought parties could only be great if they clung "to principles more than to their consequences; to general, and not to special cases; to ideas, and not to men." [1] Well over one hundred years later, a keynote speaker said a party was not a vehicle for individual candidates, but was formed by people sharing a common philosophy of government and that the main things to keep in mind about a party were its principles and platform. [2]

These statements are likely to find favor, for there has been much sentiment in this country extolling parties based on principles. But on what principles do we want the parties to differ? There has been a singular inability to agree on how much the parties should differ about anything. The difficulty may be the result, in part, of an apparently contradictory pattern in our popular evaluations. We believe, or at least often say, that there should be party differences but at the same time, we claim to be a generally nonideological nation. We insist that there should be vigorous political debate on the issues during an election campaign and demand unity after the election.

American political leaders have been quick to claim a philosophy, but their operational grounding has been pragmatic. They have agreed that a party should stand for something but also have cautioned that philosophical roots are of little value if a party does not win elections. The guiding principle of parties, normally, has been negative: Avoid the appearance of extremism. The whole point was concisely put by James A. Farley, one of the great strategists of American politics, "To the technical politician, extremism is not only a crime, but a blunder." [3]

The negative principle of avoiding the appearance of extremism has become the positive principle of moderation or, of what is often called, *centrist politics*. Moderation already had an ancient lineage when it began receiving powerful reinforcement from polling results. People's answers to simple issue questions tended to convey a message of average or median opinions. Both polls and elections thus became mandates for seemingly middle-of-the-road programs and a reaffirmation of the political wisdom of keeping out of trouble by not appearing to be extreme. At its worst, neutrality, in avoiding any semblance of provocation, can also make dead-center ambivalence appear to be the essence of moderation and reasonableness.

[1] Alexis de Tocqueville, *Democracy in America* (New York: The Colonial Press, 1900) I, 175.

[2] Representative Walter H. Judd, *Official Report of the Proceedings of the Twenty-Fifth Republican National Convention*, 1952, p. 213.

[3] Quoted *New York Times*, December 12, 1956.

Still, being viewed as taking moderate positions is not always indicative of other evaluations of a political leader. In September, 1977, the Gallup Poll found that 62 percent believed Carter evidenced strong leadership qualities, but this percentage fell to 36 percent in August, 1978. In the same period of time, however, those seeing Carter as moderate rose from 67 to 73 percent.[4]

Spatial Concept of the Center

Centrist politics becomes more concrete when voters and parties are visualized on a continuum where the positions of the voters determine the positions of the parties (Figure 9.1). If voters are polarized on the extremes, each party will cater to a particular group of voters, making the parties

The distribution of voters determines if two parties are similar or polarized in their ideological positions.

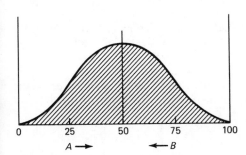

In this conception of the distribution of the voters at the center of the political spectrum, two parties, represented as *A* and *B*, will be drawn toward each other at the center where the bulk of the votes are and will ignore the relatively few voters at the extremes. Thus, parties will be similar.

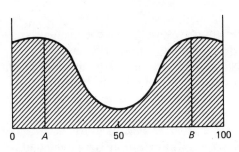

In this conception of the distribution of the voters at the extremes of the political spectrum, two parties will remain at the positions *A* and *B* because there are more voters there than in the center. Thus, parties will be polarized.

FIGURE 9.1   Spatial Concept of the Center *

* Figures 2 & 3 (pp. 118, 119) in AN ECONOMIC THEORY OF DEMOCRACY by Anthony Downs. Copyright © 1957 by Harper & Row, Publishers, Inc. By permission of the publisher.

[4] *The Miami Herald*, August 20, 1978, p. 14A. It has been suggested that candidates do not receive their strongest support from centrist voters. Rather, support depends upon the direction of a candidate's policy and "there is little advantage to being either relatively central or relatively extreme," George Rabinowitz, "On the Nature of Political Issues: Insights from a Spatial Analysis," *American Journal of Political Science*, 22 (November 1978) 816, in general 793–817.

equally polarized. If voters are bunched at the center, parties will be located near the center pursuing relatively similar policies. *Centrist voters* in America encourage a two-party system, for both parties are inclined to appeal to a majority view even though no one view has majority support.[5] The illusion of a majority position in a two-party system leads to a desirable situation: Both parties are responsive to voters, and the nation's stability is assured.

Even if all is well at the center, all is not well on the continuum.

1. Granting that a party's position is a weighted average of all of its individual positions, voters do not make choices on just one dimension.
2. Voters and party leaders do not necessarily share the same perceptions. Where parties think they have positioned themselves may not be the place where voters think they are positioned.[6]
3. In some instances, candidates have been found to be more alike where there was greater polarization and where there were more Independents.[7]
4. The majority of issues, like law-and-order and war-and-peace, do not conform to points along a scale. These have been called *style* issues because there is general agreement on objectives but controversy over how to attain the objectives. Other issues, like race, have been called *position* issues because they can involve different kinds of objectives, leading to polarization and even realignment.[8]

Rather than jostling each other at the same place in the center of the political spectrum, each party should be found at the center of its own coalition, but the coalitions overlap and intermingle.

Moderation and Party Differences

Political leaders making an effort to appear reasonable and conciliatory, convey moderation through rhetoric and posturing. Moderation is not a compass directing leaders to take one particular course in every situation which arises. It is really not a principle but a byproduct. The party system projects an image of moderation because of the composition of the parties and the necessity for dealing with day-to-day conflicts.

When considered in toto, *what is an American political party?* Its vertical social composition creates intraparty pluralism. It is a compound of

[5] Anthony Downs, *An Economic Theory of Democracy* (New York: Harper & Row Publishers, 1957) pp. 117–37.

[6] Donald E. Stokes, "Spatial Models of Party Competition," *The American Political Science Review*, 57 (June 1963) 368–77.

[7] John L. Sullivan and Daniel Richard Minns, "Ideological Distance between Candidates: An Empirical Examination," *American Journal of Political Science*, 20 (August 1976) 439–68.

[8] Jerrold G. Rusk and Herbert F. Weisberg, "Perceptions of Presidential Candidates: Implications for Electoral Change," *Midwest Journal of Political Science*, 16 (August 1972) 407.

fifty state parties and any number of issue factions. A party is not monolithic either in structure or in attitudes. People's perceptions of their own party vis-à-vis the other party, may produce emotional responses and even occasional tensions, but Americans who share similar beliefs springing from a common heritage do not generally convert their party differences into personal antagonisms.

Instead of portraying party antagonism, public officials deal day-by-day with conflicting group interests, and this pluralism gives the *appearance* of enforcing minimal party differences. In some cases, recalling the discussion in Chapter 8, it has been found in legislative bodies that Republicans were less conservative and Democrats less liberal if they were elected by a small majority. Also, Republicans and Democrats from safe districts were somewhat more likely to display party differences on roll call votes. As guarded as these generalizations are, they are further qualified by the variety of constituent interests. For example, there may be a division within a legislative district along liberal-conservative lines, but no division on tax questions.[9]

Since the 1930s, there has been a *party difference* not only in the groups more closely attached to one party or the other, but also in general approaches to group politics. Republicans have often talked about their revival by emphasizing a search for issues which will unify, not divide, the country.[10] Democratic leaders more explicitly exemplify the fact that American parties are not ideologically cohesive or even coherent.

Democrats have managed to have wide support simply because the party has not been unified internally except in its collective desire to win elections. The party offers such an assortment of positions as to span the spectrum of issues. Its candidates have sided with blacks in the ghettos and with segregationists in the South. They can be for or against budget deficits, détente, or forced busing. They are for the working man and the intellectual elite; and in each ethnic community, they favor that ethnic group. They had been the party favoring high spending but, in the late 1970s, became the party for cutting taxes and spending. A Democratic leader, when asked if his party had been repudiated at the polls, answered, "You tell me what my party stands for, and I'll try to answer your question."

[9] W. Wayne Shannon, *Party Constituency and Congressional Voting: A Study of Legislative Behavior in the United States House of Representatives* (Baton Rouge, La.: Louisiana State University Press, 1968) pp. 166–70. Wayne Shannon, "Electoral Margins and Voting Behavior in the House of Representatives: The Case of the Eighty-Sixth and Eighty-Seventh Congresses," *The Journal of Politics*, 20 (November 1968) 1028–45. Duncan MacRae, Jr., "The Relation between Roll Call Votes and Constituencies in the Massachusetts House of Representatives," *The American Political Science Review*, 46 (December 1952) 1046–55. James H. Kuklinski, "District Competitiveness and Legislative Roll-Call Behavior: A Reassessment of the Marginality Hypothesis," *American Journal of Political Science*, 21 (August 1977) 627–38.

[10] For example, the remarks of one-time Attorney General Elliott Richardson at a University of Pittsburgh seminar, excerpted in *First Monday*, publication of Republican National Committee, July 1974, pp. 11–12.

Democrats, by their very contradictions, can claim for themselves an all-American character in appealing to the nation and its many diversities. There is more than a grain of truth in the observation that *moderation* or middle-of-the-road *is a Republican, not a Democratic, campaign position*.[11]

There is also more to governing than presiding over group conflicts. The *party system* can sometimes be seen most clearly through *extraordinary*, rather than ordinary, *events*. Presidents occasionally take dramatic actions which are not judged by standards of moderation but tell us more about party differences than we can learn from any formal description.

It was the Democrat, John F. Kennedy, who "got away" with the Cuban missile crisis in 1962, and the Republican, Richard M. Nixon, who "got away" with the first official overtures to mainland China in 1972. If Nixon had confronted the Soviet Union in Cuba and Kennedy had made the first trip to Peking, Democrats and Republicans would instantly have been at each others' throats. In the actual instances, positive public reactions stifled protests from those Democrats who feared and loathed a confrontation with the U.S.S.R. and from those Republicans who dreaded and detested the government of Communist China.

In the world of party conflict, there is an element of unreality because "politics is often little concerned with reality. Rather, it deals with symbols and images which may indeed be called another kind of reality."[12] It is no wonder that party differences are sometimes so subtle that many Americans have difficulty detecting them.

Effects of the New Issues

Realignments have shattered the moderate image projected by the party system. New issues arose which were powerful enough to cut across existing issues and then either redivided the electorate or coincided with existing party differences, pushing the parties further apart. In either case, the new issues became the focus of attention because older issues were weakening in their importance to the public.[13]

During the 1960s–1970s, efforts to seal off and protect the political center from assault were not always successful. In 1964, Goldwater's nomination routed the liberals in the Republican party. Wallace mounted his third-party campaign in 1968, charging there was not "a dime's worth of difference" between the major parties. New Hampshire voters in the 1968

---

[11] Arthur Krock, "In the Nation," *New York Times*, November 22, 1955.

[12] Ray Nichols, *The Invention of the American Political Parties* (New York: The Macmillan Company, 1967) p. 330.

[13] James L. Sundquist, *Dynamics of the Party System: Alignment and Realignment of Political Parties in the United States* (Washington, D.C.: The Brookings Institution, 1973) pp. 76–77, 280–81, 297.

Democratic presidential primary repudiated moderation in the conduct of the Vietnam war by insisting that we win or get out.[14] When Muskie sought the 1972 Democratic presidential nomination by appealing to the various factions, Ramsey Clark among others publicly criticized him for being moderate.[15] And the forces of extremism won the day in 1972 when the counter-culture faction which nominated McGovern captured the Democratic party.

Nevertheless, the appeal of centrist politics insured there would be no immediate sixth party system. Two authors, peering through the maze of such disrupting issues as racism, poverty, abortion, law and order, consumerism, and the environment, made the unqualified statement: "The major thesis of this book is that the center is the only position of political power." [16] Except for Wallace, the new issues had not created a serious minor party challenge. There was the same cast of candidates on the national scene and elections were more akin to stalemates than a collapse in the face of an aroused electorate. By the time the clouds of smoke had cleared away, it appeared that the parties, in the words of Goldwater's 1964 campaign, were still offering the people echoes, not choices.

There were simply too many issues for any one of them to create a focus of attention. Whether the controversies were over different objectives or over alternate means for achieving an objective, the total effect was to divide people, to intensify factionalism, and to encourage intraparty discord. After devoting a whole book to the examination of policy problems, two authors concluded in 1972 that "there is no widespread consensus as to what constitutes a problem worthy of public attention; there is no version of a 'public interest' equally self-evident to all." [17]

The party system is no longer able to perform the role of sorting out issues so as to concentrate on a few at a time. As a result, the parties cannot be on opposite sides of all of the issues because each issue creates different divisions within the public. Neither party can position itself so as to benefit from all of these divisions. To make matters worse, there are more and more single-issue groups of people who vote on the basis of one issue alone whether it be abortion, the equal-rights amendment, gun control, or something else. Without a clear conflict between groups capable of being organized, discontent has grown as party ties have weakened.[18]

[14] Philip E. Converse, Warren E. Miller, Jerrold G. Rusk, and Arthur C. Wolfe, "Continuity and Change in American Politics: Parties and Issues in the 1968 Election," *The American Political Science Review*, 63 (December 1969) 1092–93.

[15] Congressional Quarterly, *Weekly Report*, December 4, 1971, p. 2514.

[16] Richard M. Scammon and Ben J. Wattenberg, *The Real Majority* (New York: Coward, McCann & Geoghegan, Inc., Capricorn Books, 1971) p. 200.

[17] John A. Strayer and Robert D. Wrinkle, *American Government: Policy and Non-Decisions* (Columbus, Ohio: Charles E. Merrill Publishing Company, 1972) p. 223.

[18] Norman H. Nie, Sidney Verba, and John R. Petrocik, *The Changing American Voter* (Cambridge, Mass.: Harvard University Press, 1976) pp. 104–6.

Effects of the Old Issues

New issues in the 1960s–1970s also failed to weaken or replace the old issue of personal economic security. Since the Great Depression, people's concerns with the economy have become an established fact of political life. Media reporting of the latest outpourings of statistics from governmental and private sources constantly brings home to us the marriage of economics and politics with dramatic flair. No matter what the current news may be, sooner or later, the *economy* intrudes upon our consciousness.

Issues involving the economy do not lend themselves to sharp party differences. No matter how significant economic problems are, people must see them in relation to their own interests. National economic issues tend to be either too complicated for effective use or too obvious for party differences. Balance of payments and rediscount rates do not stimulate widespread, informed discussion. Balanced budgets and fiscal integrity sound more like shibboleths and are less likely to arouse attention than *inflation and unemployment* which both parties resolutely oppose.

Political discourse emphasizes subsidies and grants to groups and individuals, the sum total of which on every level of government has been called the "social pork barrel." Candidates find it hard to differ about these welfare-state issues except for the extent and amount of benefits to be provided. A defeated candidate for Congress complained that his constituents had "all they want, all the way from surplus commodities to gilt-edged securities." [19] In a contest between a challenger and an incumbent, the incumbent either will out-promise the challenger or the challenger's promises will not be taken seriously. Some challengers have little to offer beyond a youthful new face in contrast to an aging incumbent.

To create party differences requires some new perspective, some new source of voter response such as discontent with taxes. Otherwise, in elections, like tennis matches, *you win by your opponents' mistakes.* This is a disturbing situation if one's conception of a party system is issue-competition between parties. The failure of issues, old and new, to sharpen party differences raises the question of how closely issues are related to the party system.

THE ISSUE OVER ISSUES

When party was the only, or the principal, cue which voters needed to decide how to vote, their political world was really quite simple. The burden upon voters becomes much greater when party is, at best, only one

[19] Quoted *U.S. News & World Report*, November 23, 1964.

cue. If candidate image is substituted for party, the decision-making process is still easily managed. If the cue for voting is the parties' and candidates' positions on issues, voters can perform well only when they know what the issues are and can evaluate the choices offered. There is considerable doubt that most voters make any effort to perform these tasks.

An Overemphasis upon Issues?

The conclusion that issues are of limited importance in voting and in party choice may be somewhat accidental. A great deal of the supporting documentation has been based upon findings of the Survey Research Center in the 1950s, when issue-consciousness was reported to be low.

In the period of the Eisenhower presidency, voters did not do well on the minimum criteria for voting on issues: knowledge and concern about issues, awareness of the parties' positions, and government policies affecting issues. About one-third of the respondents had enough familiarity to state an attitude on 14 of 16 issues included in the questionnaire, and about the same proportion had no knowledge of government policies on any of the issues. Although familiarity with issues increased with education, intensity of opinion depended upon the relevance of the issues to the respondents personally. Only 40 to 60 percent of those with an opinion (that is, one-third of the sample) were aware of party differences. On no issue did more than 36 percent have an opinion, perceive party differences, and know about government policies.

Those expressing opinions on the issues revealed that Democrats tended to favor and Republicans tended to oppose extensions of government activity in the economy. Yet, their pattern of response could best be understood in terms of self-interest, not ideology. There was no significant correlation between conservatism and party identification. Ideology, defined as a "far-ranging structure of attitudes" involving a "high order of abstraction," could be applied to only 2.5 percent of the whole sample although it was 10 percent for those with college training. So ideology characterized elites, not the rank-and-file citizen.[20]

The theme of these and other findings was that the "average voter is far more readily mobilized by criticism of the way the government is being run than by an ideological description of how it ought to be run." [21]

News of the *low state* of *public issue-consciousness* was greeted with unhappy surprise, but it may have reflected a misunderstanding of the American electorate. The impressions of elections long ago, when party communications were full of references to the issues of the day, may have

[20] Angus Campbell, Philip E. Converse, Warren E. Miller, and Donald E. Stokes, *The American Voter* (New York: John Wiley & Sons, Inc., 1960) Chapters 8–10.

[21] Angus Campbell, "Book Reviews," *The American Political Science Review*, 60 (December 1966) 1007.

created an image of philosophical man in the voting booth. When the results of elections during those same years were analyzed, the search for significant policy differences often appeared to be fruitless. There were, in effect, two presentations of the past: One, parties presented issues and voters responded accordingly; two, nothing much ever seemed to come of it all. Both could not be true.

Judging from the results of the party battles, only a small part of the electorate react to issues in general, except in periods of realignment. The majority of voters were, at most, concerned with only those few issues which affected them personally. Perhaps the best generalization is that, *between realignments*, issues are more important in some elections than in others and that no single election merits one conclusion.[22]

The Case Against Issues

According to the conventional wisdom, elections should be decided by the issues. If voters are not issue-oriented, it is necessary to find out why. There are at least three different explanations.

The Priority of Candidates. A mistake sometimes made in discussing the role of issues is to assume they exist in a water-tight compartment, separate from both parties and candidates. Politics is seldom so impersonal. A candidate who draws attention by advocating lower taxes, or larger welfare spending, or fewer guns, or more wilderness trails, is still being advertised by name. *Issues* are often *personalized*, and voters are encouraged to understand them in terms of some popular or unpopular *person or group*.[23]

Mass communications have reinforced this association. News reporting during election campaigns emphasizes the *personality of candidates* rather than issues.[24] Furthermore, some consultants look upon issues as simple projections of images; "as a rule the issue serves purely as a device for a performance." [25] In presidential campaigns, issues are "not really as

[22] Paul Kleppner, *The Cross of Culture: A Social Analysis of Midwestern Politics 1850–1900* (New York: The Free Press, 1970) pp. 147–48. Nelson W. Polsby and Aaron Wildavsky, *Presidential Elections: Strategies of American Electoral Politics* 4th ed. (New York: Charles Scribner's Sons, 1976) p. 27. Mark A. Shulman and Gerald Pomper, "Variability in Electoral Behavior: Longitudinal Perspectives from Causal Modeling," *American Journal of Political Science*, 19 (February 1975) 15.

[23] Charles L. Clapp, *The Congressman: His Work as He Sees It* (Washington, D.C.: The Brookings Institution, 1963) pp. 372–76. Charles O. Jones, "The Role of the Campaign in Congressional Politics," in *The Electoral Process*, eds., M. Kent Jennings and L. Harmon Zeigler (Englewood Cliffs, N.J.: Prentice-Hall, Inc., 1966) p. 32.

[24] For example: *Report on Network News' Treatment of the 1972 Democratic Presidential Candidates* (Bloomington, Ind.: The Alternative Educational Foundation, Inc., 1972) pp. 91–92. Doris A. Graber, "Press Coverage and Voter Reaction in the 1968 Presidential Election," *Political Science Quarterly*, 89 (March 1974) 68–100; and Graber, "Personal Qualities in Presidential Images: The Contribution of the Press," *Midwest Journal of Political Science*, 16 (February 1972) 46–76.

[25] Maurice McCaffrey, *Advertising Wins Elections* (Minneapolis, Minn.: Gilbert Publishing Company, 1962) p. 100.

important as the impression that people make." [26] A candidate's ability to draw crowds impresses both those who are in the crowds and those who are not. In either case, people are given "a sense of enthusiasm or excitement, something recognizable, something understandable. Maybe there *is* some link between a candidate's ability to draw crowds and persuade them, and his ability to lead a country." [27]

If voters cannot realistically distinguish between candidates and issues, they have been advised not to try to make such a distinction in presidential campaigns. The political character of presidential candidates, as distinct from media personalities and images, is the best basis for judgment. Voters need criteria allowing them "to see the man whole—not as some abstract embodiment of civic virtue, some scorecard of issue stands, or some reflection of a faction, but as a human being." What a President will do, based on a knowledge of his character and prior responses to life's situations, is far more important information than his positions on issues.[28]

Abdication.   The second explanation may be more familiar. Voters are blamed for being too involved in their own affairs to be concerned with the great issues facing the nation. The problem with voters is not their inability to perceive issues separately from candidates and parties nor their incapacity to process information and use their minds. The problem is that they have failed to do what is expected of them. The *electorate has abdicated.*

Incompetence.   This third explanation carries a much more serious message. The *electorate* does not do what is expected of it because it is *incompetent and irrational.* In fact, the layman's opinions count for nothing any more. So-called Madison Avenue methods can promote an idea, a policy, a whole way of thinking. One of the most popular ways to win a political argument is to mobilize scientists, specialists, authorities on your side so as to overcome opposing views. The way to counteract this kind of attack is with another group of scientists, specialists, and authorities. These strategies have been used, for instance, in arguments over decriminalizing marijuana and the desirability of nuclear power plants. This means of settling conflicts reinforces contentions that public affairs have become too complex for the public to understand. All the layman can do is follow what appears to be the side with the weight of authority. Popular participation in decision-making can occur where the decisions are about simple matters. Otherwise, the public is a mass of political emotions which can only be measured and then

[26] Joseph Napolitan, "Zeroing in on the Voter," in *The Political Image Merchants*, eds., Ray Hiebert, Robert Jones, Ernest Lotito, and John Lorenz (Washington, D.C.: Acropolis Books Ltd., 1971) pp. 51–52.

[27] Jerry Bruno and Jeff Greenfield, *The Advance Man* (New York: William Morrow and Company, Inc., 1971) p. 136; italics in original.

[28] James David Barber, *The Presidential Character: Predicting Performance in the White House* (Englewood Cliffs, N.J.: Prentice-Hall, Inc., 1972) pp. 3–4; and Barber, "Strategies for Studying Politicians," *American Journal of Political Science*, 18 (May 1974) 443–67.

manipulated by emotional appeals. The logical end-result will be government by experts.[29]

The Rational Voter

Democratic theory gives preeminence to voters because it holds that people are discerning and rational. It is also a democratic belief that election campaigns help to differentiate between parties and their policies so that voters can understand the choices and their consequences. The fault, then, may lie with elections themselves. Voters do not choose what is discussed in campaigns nor does a campaign necessarily reflect their problems. Even if voters know what they want, they are not likely to have the information they need for an informed choice. To demonstrate they are rational, voters need rational presentations from candidates.[30] As the bare minimum of rationality in elections, voters want a responsive government, and parties want to hold offices. All the voters and parties have in common is the continuance of the political system.[31]

Democratic theory has not taken into account *candidates' images of voters*. Candidates presumably believe they are acting rationally and judge voters according to their responses to the campaigns the candidates conduct. From the evidence available, candidates believe issues make campaigns rational but do not necessarily believe voters behave rationally. Among winning legislative candidates there was a self-congratulatory interpretation that voters were issue- and candidate-oriented, but losing candidates complained that they could not overcome the obstacle of party identification in presenting their messages.[32]

The *rational voter* was finally flushed out after a laborious analysis of survey data from the 1930s through 1960. Party voters had views consistent with their parties, to the extent they perceived their parties' policies. Others related their expressed policy preferences to their vote. The electorate, it was concluded, behaved "about as rationally and responsibly as we should expect, given the clarity of the alternatives presented to it and the character of

[29] Harvey Wheeler, *The Politics of Revolution* (Berkeley: The Glendessary Press, 1971) pp. 140, 195. Henry W. Kariel, *The Decline of American Pluralism* (Stanford, Calif.: Stanford University Press, 1961) p. 182. Ralph E. Lapp, *The New Priesthood: The Scientific Elite and the Uses of Power* (New York: Harper & Row, 1965).

[30] Stanley Kelley, Jr., *Political Campaigning: Problems in Creating an Informed Electorate* (Washington, D.C.: The Brookings Institute, 1960) pp. 10–14, 16–22. Sidney Verba and Norman H. Nie, *Participation in America* (New York: Harper & Row, 1972) pp. 103–11.

[31] Downs, *An Economic Theory of Democracy*, p. 137.

[32] John W. Kingdon, *Candidates for Office: Beliefs and Strategies* (New York: Random House, 1968) pp. 22–31; and Kingdon, "Politicians' Beliefs about Voters," *The American Political Science Review*, 61 (March 1967) 137–45. Lewis A. Froman, Jr., "A Realistic Approach to Campaign Strategies and Tactics," in *The Electoral Process*, pp. 1–3.

the information available to it." [33] Once this counterattack was launched, the defense of voters quickly picked up momentum. Survey researchers inferred irrationality in voting from evidence of widespread ignorance of public affairs, especially from the large percentages of respondents who said they "don't know." The public should not be expected to be as well informed as those who conduct surveys. Respondents may be considered ignorant as a result of the choices offered them. What this finding proves is that what respondents find important is not always what students of politics find important.

The results of surveys and voting should be more carefully distinguished since election analyses show more public perception and coherence than individual answers given to interviewers. The deficiencies of individual voters in surveys may have been accepted as the aggregate characteristics of the whole electorate. If there is a crisis, it is in a theory of democracy which presupposes an unrealistic level of public performance on survey questions as though voters were students in a classroom.[34]

Not all survey research, by any means, shows voters to be irrational, manipulated, or unthinking. Respondents did demonstrate a reasonably complex decision process when they rated their preferred candidates differently on various criteria such as party, personal qualities, and issues.[35] Voting for Wallace in 1968, when issues stood by themselves without the cue of party identification, showed that voters could respond directly to issues when they were presented.[36]

The reassertion of the rational voter called into question the image of the purely candidate-oriented, or abdicating, or incompetent voter; but important limitations remained. *Rationality consists* of expressing approval or disapproval based on one's own self-interest as distinct from awareness of party differences or of matching a party vote with an issue preference. The electorate was shown to be made up of people who were subjective and

[33] V. O. Key, Jr., *The Responsible Electorate: Rationality in Presidential Voting 1936–1960* (New York: Vintage Books, a Division of Random House, 1966) p. 7, in general pp. 52–61. Also Theodore F. Macaluso, "Parameters of 'Rational' Voting: Vote Switching in the 1968 Election," *The Journal of Politics*, 37 (February 1975) 202–34. Kenneth Prewitt and Norman Nie, "Review Article: Election Studies of the S.R.C.," *British Journal of Political Science*, 1 (1971) 490–93.

[34] E. E. Schattschneider, *The Semisovereign People: A Realist's View of Democracy in America* (New York: Holt, Rinehart and Winston, 1960) pp. 134–36. Douglas Price, "Micro- and Macro-Politics: Notes on Research Strategy," in *Political Research and Political Theory*, ed., Oliver Garceau (Cambridge, Mass.: Harvard University Press, 1968) p. 120. John K. Wildgen, "The Detection of Critical Elections in the Absence of Two-Party Competition," *The Journal of Politics*, 36 (May 1974) 466. W. Lance Bennett, "The Growth of Knowledge in Mass Belief Studies: An Epistemological Critique," *American Journal of Political Science*, 21 (August 1977) 465–500.

[35] Michael J. Shapiro, "Rational Political Man: A Synthesis of Economic and Social-Psychological Perspectives," *The American Political Science Review*, 63 (December 1969) pp. 1106–19.

[36] Converse and others, "Continuity and Change in American Politics," *The American Political Science Review*, 63 (December 1969) 1095–99. The choice and wording of survey questions are also defended here.

retrospective, casting votes "directed primarily toward selfish ends." [37]
Moreover, *rationality has been defined* to cover any voting behavior or even
the failure to vote. The definition can be so broad as to make rationality
inherent. All behavior is rational to the extent it selects a more preferred
action over a less preferred action and, in this sense, becomes "close to
tautological." [38] Finally, there is the possibility that *rationality* in each individual election may add up, over a period of time, to *results* which the
electorate did not intend. Short-term rationality can conceivably become
long-term irrationality.

However, it should not be disturbing that rationality is linked to looking out for yourself. The whole party system is geared to the assumption
that people act in their own self-interest. Selfish concerns are not wholly
individual but are often expressions of interest group politics or, what is
sometimes called, issue publics. On the one hand, the effects of individual
irrationality in voting may be cancelled out in the total vote assuming that
group voting tends to reflect group interests and that individuals perceive
the norms of their own groups. [39]

On the other hand, as people become more directly involved in the
specific objectives of their own specializations, they are inclined to overlook
the general problems they share with those outside of their specialization.
In order to vote their broadly rational self-interests, voters must make some
decisions independently of their own issue publics. Although group interests are often accepted as expressions of rational objectives, all told, they
do not add up to a nationalized politics of issues in the classic democratic
sense.

The problem of *issue voting* is reminiscent of *coattail voting*. What
passes for either may really be *party* or *candidate voting*. If parties or candidates agree on an issue (at least do not differ), there can be no issue vote,
objectively speaking, even though a voter may think there is some kind of
difference. When we see a bear alone in the woods, are we afraid and run
or do we run and then become afraid? When we see an election, do we have
an issue preference and then a vote intention or do we have a vote intention
and then adopt an issue preference? Simply showing an increased correlation of issues with voting does not prove that the issues dictated the vote. [40]

Varying percentages of voters of different socioeconomic status do

[37] Michael Margolis, "From Confusion to Confusion: Issues and the American
Voter (1956–1972)," *The American Political Science Review*, 71 (March 1977) 368.
Downs, *An Economic Theory of Democracy*, p. 27. Peter B. Natchez and Irvin C.
Bupp, "Candidates, Issues, and Voters," in *Political Opinion and Behavior: Essays and
Studies*, 2nd ed., eds., Edward C. Dreyer and Walter A. Rosenbaum (Belmont, Calif.:
Duxbury Press, A Division of Wadsworth Publishing Company, Inc., 1970) pp. 433–35.

[38] William H. Riker and Peter C. Ordeshook, "A Theory of the Calculus of
Voting," *The American Political Science Review*, 62 (March 1968) 27.

[39] M. Brewster Smith, "Personality in Politics: A Conceptual Map, with Application to the Problem of Political Rationality," in *Political Research and Political Theory*,
ed., Oliver Garceau (Cambridge, Mass.: Harvard University Press, 1968) pp. 99–100.

[40] Nie and others, *The Changing American Voter*, p. 160.

tend to see party differences, but they do better when using issues of their own choosing. Yet, the proportion of voters accurately distinguishing party differences on at least one issue is no more than would be expected by chance, except for blacks' perceptions of racially relevant issues. Concern with specific issues helps to account for the direction of the vote. Those who have a stake in an issue are more likely to have an opinion, but they do not tend to perceive party differences more accurately. A person does not need political information to have an opinion on an issue of importance to his issue public.[41]

Each interpretation that issue voting is on the rise seemed to encounter resistance of one kind or another. Issue preferences are not being distinguished from candidate and party preferences. There are doubts about the significance of a specific issue in specific years or of any issues at any time. Furthermore, claims for issue voting are misleading because they fail to show respondents' intensity of opinion, knowledge of government policy, or actual awareness of party differences.[42] The Survey Research Center found presidential voting in 1972 to be issue-oriented although respondents' reactions to the candidates explained more variance in the vote than the issues. Then another debate ensued over the meaning of these findings.[43]

Despite conflicting evaluations and a seemingly endless variety of interpretations about the role of issues in elections, some evidence of a growing ideological division among American voters began to appear.

THE RISE OF IDEOLOGY

One of the objectives of survey research has been the ferreting out of ideology as the motivation in voting. Ideology is a system of belief involving a relatively high level of abstraction, complexity of perception, and con-

[41] William H. Form and Joan Huber, "Income, Race, and the Ideology of Political Efficacy," *The Journal of Politics*, 33 (August 1971) 670–71. David E. RePass, "Issue Salience and Party Choice," *The American Political Science Review*, 65 (June 1971) 389–400. Ruth A. Jones and E. Terrence Jones, "Issue Saliency, Opinion-Holding, and Party Preference," *The Western Political Quarterly*, 24 (September 1971) 501–9. Natchez and Bupp, "Candidates, Issues, and Voters," pp. 436–40.

[42] See articles, comments, rejoinders, *The American Political Science Review*, 66 (June 1972) 415–70. Benjamin I. Page and Richard A. Brody, "Policy Voting and the Electoral Process: The Vietnam War Issue," *The American Political Science Review*, (September 1972) 979–95. William R. Shaffer, "Partisan Loyalty and the Perceptions of Party, Candidates and Issues," *The Western Political Quarterly*, 25 (September 1972) 424–33. William R. Shaffer and David A. Caputo, "Political Continuity in Indiana Presidential Elections: An Analysis Based on the Key-Munger Paradigm," *Midwest Journal of Political Science*, 16 (November 1972) 700–11. Margolis, "From Confusion to Confusion," 34–38.

[43] Arthur H. Miller, Warren E. Miller, Alden S. Raine, and Thad A. Brown, "A Majority Party in Disarray: Policy Polarization in the 1972 Election," pp. 15, 22, 38, 67–69. Paper presented at 69th Annual Meeting, American Political Science Association, New Orleans, Louisiana, September 1973. Comments and Rejoinders, *The American Political Science Review*, 70 (September 1976) 779–849. Margolis, "From Confusion to Confusion," pp. 38–41.

sistency in relating a wide range of issues. One who is ideological has a great deal of information, which is structured in a coherent and integrated way. Political ideology means the capacity for maintaining such a belief system, as distinguished from the ideological orientations or beliefs themselves.[44]

Survey findings in the 1950s revealed an American electorate which seemed to be nonideological at its core with a thin ideological periphery. Ideology primarily characterized those with high socioeconomic status who were politically interested and informed. It was this elite which saw issues in liberal-conservative terms. Most respondents held individually inconsistent opinions. They also failed to perceive choices or respond to questions within the ideological framework of liberalism and conservatism. It was because of these findings that so much disagreement arose over the issue-orientation of voters. Granting that large numbers may be able to perceive self-interest in voting, there was only the most limited evidence of an ideological structure underlying the vote.

Growing Consistency on Issues

The growth of ideology to some extent comes down to the question of whether the picture of the American electorate in the 1950s is the same one as that immediately before and since. During the 1930s and 1940s, there was a basic division in the country on the size of the federal government and on welfare policies. During the 1950s, even this division became less apparent. Through these three decades, there appeared to be little connection in people's minds among the issues of civil rights, welfare, federal aid to education, and internationalism. For example, Democrats of lower socioeconomic status were liberal on domestic issues but tended to be conservative (that is, isolationist) on foreign issues.[45]

International problems became far more prominent in the 1950s, but they had a unifying, rather than a divisive, effect as illustrated by the fact that foreign policy became officially bipartisan. Actually, foreign policies did not affect many people directly because they were style issues rather than position issues—that is, they were not particularly controversial in their objectives. Racial issues came to the fore in the late 1950s but, initially, there was a weak relationship of either race or civil rights with economic issues, just as there continued to be a weak relationship between economic and

[44] George E. Marcus, David Tabb, and John L. Sullivan, "The Application of Individual Differences Scaling to the Measurement of Political Ideologies," *American Journal of Political Science*, 18 (May 1974) 405. Willard A. Mullins, "On the Concept of Ideology in Political Science," *The American Political Science Review*, 66 (June 1972) 498–510.

[45] Angus Campbell and others, *The American Voter*, pp. 197–98. Samuel J. Eldersveld, *Political Parties: A Behavioral Analysis* (Chicago: Rand McNally & Company, 1964) pp. 190–96. Richard F. Hamilton, *Class and Politics in the United States* (New York: John Wiley & Sons, 1972) pp. 87–95.

foreign policies. This appeared to be the general picture of the country during the 1950s when survey research found little evidence of ideology.

It was not until the late 1960s that the growth of ideology could be detected. Realization came slowly as one investigator after another noted that the ideological motivations, even of a minority, were having an influence upon American politics and that evidence of consistency of opinion on issues was growing. The proportion of respondents evaluating parties in ideological terms, generally, as well as associating them with particular issues, rose from 11 percent in 1956 to 22 percent in 1972.[46] It is noteworthy that a greater degree of ideology was being reported at the time another realignment was due on the thirty-two to forty-year cycle.

By confining the measurements to those respondents who voted, researchers probably overemphasized ideology. Nonvoters tend to be the least ideological. Therefore, voters with higher education and greater political information were given a weight out of proportion to their numbers in the whole samples. By equating ideology with respondents' ability to place themselves on a liberal-conservative scale, researchers probably underemphasized the extent of ideology.

Liberalism and conservativism have been accepted names for the opposing ideologies because elites, who are more articulate and more at home in discussing abstractions, use these words. Those possessing less education and information may not have much familiarity with the terms. For them, "liberal" and "conservative" either have little meaning or a meaning of their own. However, even if people do not understand the terms, they can be aware of and evaluate what government does or proposes to do. Their expressions of support or opposition can reflect a liberal or conservative ideology.

Elites are far more likely to give answers to domestic and foreign policy questions which are consistent along the entire liberal-conservative scale. *The public as a whole*, though less articulate and less abstract in its thinking, may use other dimensions than those of liberal-conservative and be more complex in its perceptions. Some of the nonelite may simultaneously be consistent economic liberals and consistent civil-rights conservatives. They may give answers to economic questions which, by themselves, seem inconsistent, yet may be perfectly consistent in the mind of the person giving the answers.[47] In any event, *consistency should not be confused with*

[46] Nie and others, *The Changing American Voter*, pp. 112, 179–85. John C. Pierce, "Party Identification and the Changing Role of Ideology in American Politics," *Midwest Journal of Political Science*, 14 (February 1970) 25–42. Norman H. Nie and Kristi Andersen, "Mass Belief Systems Revisited: Political Change and Attitude Structure," *The Journal of Politics*, 36 (August 1974) 540–91. Stephen Earl Bennett, "Consistency among the Public's Social Welfare Policy Attitudes in the 1960s," *American Journal of Political Science*, 17 (August 1973) 544–70.

[47] Marcus and others, "The Application of Individual Differences Scaling to the Measurement of Political Ideologies," pp. 406–8. James A. Stimson, "Belief Systems: Constraint, Complexity, and the 1972 Election," *American Journal of Political Science*,

motivation. The reasons for one person's holding an opinion may be different from another person's reasons, and the two can still be in general ideological agreement.

The rise of ideology becomes acceptable only if we ignore the formal elitist definition which is the ability to think abstractly, to perceive complexities, and to organize a wide range of issues into a coherent pattern. Instead, ideology is defined as responding to issues according to the judgments comprising one's own political universe. Individual self-interest, when congealed into a consistency of beliefs, is thus accepted as a growing liberal-conservative ideological split within the electorate. Consistency cannot be determined objectively because it is a personal process of integration, at whatever level of abstraction, for each individual man and woman.

The rise of ideology is also based on the discovery that more people are accepting the liberal-conservative continuum, in one or another set of terms. At the same time, they are reporting greater consistency in their opinions on domestic and foreign issues. This increase occurs among respondents on all educational levels, with those of lowest education showing a greater increase. Even though this consistency is achieved by associating answers to questions which have no logical connection, such as considering a dove on foreign policy and an advocate of welfare for blacks to be consistent, people are in fact, falling into this arbitrary classification.[48]

Continuing Limits on Consistency

It may be valid to tailor the definition of ideology to fit what people are saying. Furthermore, an increased consistency of attitudes may be something more than an arbitrary association of answers. Still, giving the benefit of the doubt in every case, it does not mean the whole electorate has suddenly been charged with a bolt of ideological energy. The rise of ideology seems impressive in comparative numbers over a period of approximately twenty years but no more than one-third of respondents in any sample have measured up to the easier standards for being classified as ideologues.

There is, in addition, a serious difficulty in the methodology used to measure ideology, unlike ticket-splitting and the rate of voting turnout, which are beyond dispute regardless of interpretations and methods of investigation.

Consistency in answering questions was found in one study to be greater for those who expressed fewer opinions. Actually, the major difference between 1956 and 1972 was not a large increase in the number of con-

19 (August 1975) 400–3, 406–10. Natchez and Bupp, "Candidates, Issues, and Voters," p. 435.

[48] Nie and others, *The Changing American Voter,* pp. 119–21, 129–39, 148–55. Stimson, "Belief Systems," pp. 411–13.

sistent answers but a growing tendency for answers to be either on the left or on the right and not to cross the center. This tendency was illustrated for respondents who expressed five opinions on issue questions. In 1956, their answers more likely fell into a pattern of four left and one right, or four right and one left. In 1972, the more likely pattern was four left and one center, or four right and one center. The percentage of those with no more than one inconsistent answer out of five was 29.6 percent in 1956 and 32.4 percent in 1972. On all sides, it is still agreed that there are limits upon issue consistency and no evidence of a well-defined philosophy among Americans.[49]

A far more serious *methodological problem* is the *wording of questions*. The rise of ideology has been found in various data over time, most particularly in the presidential-year surveys conducted by the Survey Research Center. Evidence of greater consistency on issues in Survey Research Center data appeared in 1964 when the wording of questions was changed. Undoubtedly the revised questions conveyed new meanings to many respondents. Wording is especially important for those with less education, so the new questions could help to account for their increased consistency on issues. In addition, respondents since 1964 have been offered two choices instead of one on some questions with the result that the number qualifying their answers or saying they were "not sure" declined. In 1956, respondents were asked if they had an "opinion" about the election but in 1964 were asked if they were "interested." The number filtered out by these questions varied when the two years were compared. Finally, the level of consistency would be expected to increase in 1964 because more respondents answered "don't know" and were thus screened out.[50]

No one can say how much the rise of ideology should be attributed to changes in attitudes and how much to changes in wording, at least in the case of Survey Research Center data. To the extent the method of measurement is responsible, the level of consistency in the 1950s must not have been as low as has been assumed. On balance, there has been some rise of ideology, but it may have risen from a level which was higher than it was thought to be.[51]

[49] Hugh L. LeBlanc and Mary Beth Merrin, "Mass Belief Systems Revisited," *The Journal of Politics*, 39 (November 1977) 1082–87. Nie and others, *The Changing American Voter*, pp. 135, 139.

[50] John L. Sullivan, James E. Piereson, and George E. Marcus, "Ideological Constraint in the Mass Public: A Methodological Critique and Some New Findings," *American Journal of Political Science*, 22 (May 1978) 239–44. George F. Bishop, Alfred J. Tuchfarber, and Robert W. Oldendick, "Change in the Structure of American Political Attitudes: The Nagging Question of Question Wording," *American Journal of Political Science*, pp. 253, 259–60, 265. George F. Bishop, Robert W. Oldendick, Alfred J. Tuchfarber, and Stephen E. Bennett, "The Changing Structure of Mass Belief Systems: Fact or Artifact?" *The Journal of Politics*, 40 (August 1978) 781–87.

[51] Sullivan and others, "Ideological Constraint in the Mass Public," pp. 238, 248. Bishop and others, "Change in the Structure of American Political Attitudes," pp. 264, 266.

Though subject to some question, the rise of ideology is supported by interpretations which do not rely upon the wording of specific survey questions but rather upon reactions among people as voters or as respondents.

IDEOLOGY AND ALIENATION

Struggles within and between the two major parties have shown increasing signs of ideological polarization, but the large numbers of Independents and ticket-splitters suggest that many people still see no reason to choose a party or vote a straight ticket. Although many are probably not motivated by ideology, those who feel their ideological interests are being ignored may suspect that the system has been closed or "rigged" in favor of moderation.[52]

The parties in Congress have been limited in their response to ideology. Ideological division in the legislature has been increasingly associated with sectionalism, which frustrates both parties and restricts presidential leadership. In the House of Representatives, the southern Democrats and eastern Republicans are moving further from the "center of gravity" of their respective parties. The prospects are that presidential support scores will continue to fall as party cohesion declines and sectional-ideological differences increase.[53] The reaction of the parties outside of the government is to be wary of responding to ideologies in writing platforms and making nominations. Not only is each party divided over how to respond, but the rise of ideology appears to be too limited to be taken much into account. If these calculations are wrong, if the parties have been ignoring a significant increase in ideology and confirming the public's sense of stalemate in government, the result could well be, not just a further withdrawal from parties, but a positive rejection of parties.

Position v. Style Issues

There is no question of increased alienation evidenced in distrust of parties and government. Is alienation largely a reaction by ignored and frustrated ideologues? Various bits of data may not answer the question fully but do suggest the answer is, at least, partly "yes."

If centrist policies are responsible for alienation, does the distrust arise

---

[52] Sundquist, *Dynamics of the Party System*, pp. 305–6. Theodore J. Lowi, "The Artificial Majority," *The Nation*, December 7, 1970, reprinted in *Readings in American Government 76/77* (Guilford, Ct.: The Dushkin Publishing Group, Inc., 1976) pp. 205–7.

[53] Barbara Deckard and John Stanley, "Party Decomposition and Region: The House of Representatives, 1945–1970," *The Western Political Quarterly*, 27 (June 1974) 249–64. Barbara Deckard Sinclair, "The Policy Consequences of Party Realignment—Social Welfare Legislation in the House of Representatives, 1933–1954," *American Journal of Political Science*, 22 (February 1978) 83–105.

over objectives (position issues) as a rejection of solutions offered to problems and a repudiation of moderation itself? Or, does distrust arise over methods of achieving objectives (style issues) as a result of governmental ineffectiveness in providing means for implementing solutions? It may be both unwarranted and premature to conclude that alienation arose from the inability to find *policy alternatives*. Most problems, such as energy, prosperity, inflation, do not involve disagreements on goals and are not polarizing. Alternatively, it is reasonable to conclude that the long-term growth of alienation is not the result of failure to find means to implement generally-accepted goals. It may be the result of failure to deal with polarizing issues, thus accounting for the distrust on both sides in such movements as civil rights and women's liberation.[54]

Despite changes in wording of Survey Research Center questions, the year 1956 was unusually low for ideological expressions, lower than 1952. The finding that one-third of the samples were consistent on issues was compared with findings using more stringent criteria where the same upward trend appeared after 1956, reaching 23 percent in 1968. From 1952 to 1960, ideological evaluation of presidential candidates by all respondents who could be classified as ideologues was very low. Then it quadrupled in percentage by 1964 and held at the same level through 1968 and 1972.[55] If nothing else, presidential candidates after 1960 were evaluated in ideological terms by one-third of those respondents who themselves expressed ideological attitudes.

There is some evidence that the rise of ideology occurred within a sequential order of political developments and became a cause of alienation. Interest in presidential elections rose from 1956 to 1960 and remained constant through 1968. Consistency on issues rose in Survey Research Center data in 1964, the same year negative evaluations of both parties also rose, without benefit of changes in the wording of questions. Evaluations hovered just below 30 percent of the samples in 1956 and 1960 but jumped to 36 percent in 1964, 42 percent in 1968, and 51 percent in 1972.[56] As disruptions and divisiveness increased throughout the 1960s, so did alienation. By 1972, interest had fallen to the 1956 level, but a larger proportion of the disinterested rejected politics rather than being merely apathetic. However, among those who were interested, consistency on issues increased.

Thus, the *growth of alienation paralleled the decline in party evaluations and identification*. So we can infer that there was a connection between the lack of party response to ideologies and the lack of response to parties. To the extent this was the relationship, there is substantiation for a genuine rise of ideology in the 1960s.

[54] Arthur H. Miller, "Political Issues and Trust in Government: 1964–1970," *The American Political Science Review*, 68 (September 1974) 951–72; *Ibid.*, 973–1001.
[55] Nie and others, *The Changing American Voter*, pp. 112–16.
[56] *Ibid.*, p. 58.

Conversely, ideology was not uniformly associated with alienation. Conservatives had generally been alienated since the 1950s, but it was the liberals who became the most distrustful of government after 1964. By 1972, however, liberals, conservatives, and centrists were all more distrustful of government and had weaker party attachments compared with the 1950s. To this extent, the causes of alienation were independent of position or style issues. Liberals were the exception. They apparently had come to feel more keenly the neglect of their ideology.[57]

In one instance, what came out as consensus in the 1960s could have been ideology in disguise. The Survey Research Center has always asked questions about specific reforms achieved through government that elicited a liberal or a conservative response. In 1964, the Survey Research Center added a new question asking if government had become too powerful. This general question did not separate liberals from conservatives. Both agreed that government was too powerful.[58] This area of apparent agreement would probably turn into polarization if liberals and conservatives explained what they objected to in big government.

Ideology, Alienation, and Realignment

Assuming that the events of the 1960s–1970s did not significantly increase the level of issue consistency, there could still have been an increase in alienation. At least, it seems reasonable that with a relatively low level of ideology, the public would become more distrustful if the government seemed unable to cope with problems. There is no way of knowing if alienation could have increased issue consistency.

What is important is the dual impact upon the party system of a *rise in ideology* and a massive *growth of alienation*. Without a higher level of ideology, why would there be such a noticeable decline in the evaluation of parties unless alienation was so comprehensive that it applied to every facet of public affairs? Why would alienation be so consuming without something comparable to ideology to fuel it?

Even if the ideological extremes were not uniformly the most alienated, ideologically oriented voters were among the most dissatisfied and distrustful. Perhaps these voters perceived a party difference despite the appearance of the parties being unresponsive. Voting has been found to be more relevant to ideology than mere party identification. In other words, those voting Democratic and Republican in presidential elections are, respectively, more liberal and conservative than those who merely profess a Democratic or Republican preference. In times of realignment, identification

---

[57] *Ibid.*, pp. 272–87.
[58] *Ibid.*, pp. 125–28.

would be expected to lag behind behavior, and behavior now may prove to be more indicative of the future.[59]

So far, the rise of ideology has produced no earth-shaking changes in the parties. If the growth of issue consistency should prove to be more than skin-deep within the body of the electorate, it has the potential to transform the parties. The party system might shift from what has been called "a consensus of error" in adhering to varying degrees of liberal philosophy, into a realigned system where one party conserves values and one party is innovative.[60]

The possibilities for realignment based on this kind of ideological division is the question to be considered in Chapter 10.

[59] *Ibid.*, pp. 107-8, 169-73, 295-303. Margolis, "From Confusion to Confusion," pp. 41-42. Everett C. Ladd and Charles D. Hadley, "Party Definition and Party Differentiation," *Public Opinion Quarterly*, 37 (Spring 1973) 21-34.

[60] Allan C. Brownfield, "The Irrelevance of American Politics," *The Yale Review*, 60 (Autumn 1970) 8, 11, 13.

10

Ideologies and New Coalitions

The prospects for continuity of the party system through another realignment are not particularly bright. Heretofore, ideological differences have periodically created a "triggering event" which, in turn, acted as a political "detonator." [1] Giving the strongest interpretation to the present evidence of a rising ideology, it promises, at best, to be a slow-burning fuse and, even then, the relative strength of the new party coalitions can only be surmised. Just the same, there have been enough developments to permit a forecast of the kind of ideological divisions which can materialize.

THE SHAPE OF NEW PARTY COALITIONS

The two major parties did not come through the 1960s–1970s completely unscathed. Both of them felt the forces of change, but the pressures bore more heavily upon the dominant Democratic party. Black migration to northern cities had already disturbed the New Deal urban coalition. A growing hostility between blacks, on one side, and middle- and lower-class whites on the other polarized two principal groups which had sustained the Democrats at the polls. Simultaneously, the new politics of the counterculture threatened the solidarity of the left, for divisions among the liberals led to their being identified as "old" and "new." This combination of the Civil Rights Revolution and new politics seemed for a time to be capable of shattering the Democratic party as were the Whigs in the 1850s.

An Emerging Cultural Conflict

Unlike the provocations of the 1930s, which had divided social classes, those of the 1960s aroused opposing cultural responses. The pressures had economic significance in the emphasis upon poverty and demands for equalitarianism, but social welfare issues became entangled with discontents over

---

[1] Walter Dean Burnham, *Critical Elections and the Mainsprings of American Politics* (New York: W. W. Norton and Company, 1970) p. 170.

taxation and inflation. The outlines of the emerging political forces could have been forecast, but some of the groups were unfamiliar in the roles of antagonists.

There were the upper middle-class intellectuals, the new liberals of the counterculture, who sensed no threats to themselves in policies like welfare costs and affirmative action. They strongly supported giving priorities to the plight of blacks and to the urban crisis. The *new liberals* transformed liberalism from a concern for individual opportunities to concern for equal treatment of the poor and racial minorities.[2] New liberals were active in the anti-Vietnam protests, and their attacks upon foreign policy widened to an indictment of America, its institutions, and its social structure. As they attacked the Military-Industrial Complex, they were likewise described by a member of Congress as the Educational-Poverty-Industrial Complex.[3]

Opposition to the *counterculture* included those who believed they had a stake in the existing system and continued to support such traditional institutions as the family, the neighborhood, and the church. These were people concerned with law-and-order who were more inclined toward patriotism and belief in the nation's heritage. Where the policies of the Democratic party had been accepted because they taxed the few for the benefit of the many, the affluence of the 1950s spread the tax burden much more widely. By the 1960s–1970s, much of the middle class, whether specifically opposed to the counterculture or not, were protesting that the government was taxing the many for the benefit of the few.

Liberals, as a whole, had strongly supported the labor policies of the Democratic party, but the new liberals began noting that labor was no longer liberal, and they turned to positions in universities and government in preference to employment by labor unions.[4] When workers' protests countered anti-Vietnam demonstrations, the new liberals began denouncing workers with the epithet "hard hats."

Eric Hoffer, the San Francisco longshoreman-philosopher, doubted that anyone could have "foreseen that affluence would radicalize the upper rich and the lowest poor and nudge them toward an alliance against those in the middle." [5] George Meany, president of the AFL-CIO, struck out against the "moneyed interests," the "so-called limousine liberals," whom he ac-

[2] Charles R. Adrian and Charles Press, *American Politics Reappraised: The Enchantment of Camelot Dispelled* (New York: McGraw-Hill Book Company, 1974) pp. 50, 60–71.

[3] Edith Green of Oregon, quoted in Kevin P. Phillips, *Mediacracy: American Parties and Politics in the Communications Age* (Garden City, N.Y.: Doubleday & Company, Inc., 1975) p. 17.

[4] Nathan Glazer and Daniel Patrick Moynihan, *Beyond the Melting Pot*, 2nd ed. (Cambridge, Mass.: The M.I.T. Press, 1970) p. xxxiv.

[5] Eric Hoffer, "Whose Country Is America?" *The New York Times*, November 22, 1970, reprinted in *Readings in American Government 72/73* (Guilford, Ct.: The Dushkin Publishing Group, Inc., 1972) p. 32.

cused of trying to elect their candidate and seize control of the Steelworkers Union.[6]

New liberals were attacked as a minority who were trying to force their values upon the country by controlling the school system, the media, and the courts. Walter Lippman, an old liberal, saw new-liberal policies as a resurgence of the belief in the essential goodness and perfectability of human beings and attacked this philosophy as an attempt to tax the public to do things it is impossible to do.[7]

Equality and status were subtly intermixed in people's attitudes and responses. Some who opposed the equalitarianism they saw in the counter-culture were betraying their own sense of status insecurity. The discrepancy between achieved status and ascribed status explains some of the affinity of the rising economic elite for lower socioeconomic groups. That is, there can be an inconsistency between the status a person has achieved through high income and the status accorded him by others, for example, because of low ethnic status. High income and low ascribed status were associated with a preference for liberal ideology and the Democratic party, and this preference was greatest for those in the highest economic group who were status inconsistent. Class differences did not account for differences in party identification nearly as well as status inconsistencies.[8]

Democratic Party Divided

The Democratic party began to display a symptom common to American party coalitions, "reciprocal hostility," which appears when the disaffection of one faction has the effect of strengthening the attachment of another faction.[9] The struggle for control of the party was no longer between the familiar northern liberals and southern conservatives. It became an outright ideological antagonism complicated by a division within the liberal faction itself, for example, the fight between Robert Kennedy and Eugene McCarthy for the presidential nomination in 1968.[10]

A liberal-conservative choice became increasingly untenable because Democratic conservatives, although not as numerous as Democratic liberals, had grown in number. The rise of ideology had a significantly different

[6] *St. Louis Globe-Democrat*, January 12, 1977.

[7] Walter Lippman interview with his biographer, Ronald Steel, in *Ibid.*, April 8, 1973, p. 6F.

[8] David R. Segal and David Knoke, "Class Inconsistency, Status Inconsistency, and Political Partisanship in America," *The Journal of Politics*, 33 (November 1971) 941–54.

[9] Samuel Lubell, *The Future of American Politics* (New York: Harper & Brothers, 1952) pp. 211–14.

[10] Daniel J. Elazar, *American Federalism: A View from the States*, 2nd ed. (New York: Thomas Y. Crowell Company, 1972) pp. 137–39. Lanny J. Davis, *The Emerging Democratic Majority* (New York: Stein and Day, 1974) pp. 33–34.

effect upon the two parties. As the center of the Democratic party shrank, both conservatives and liberals increased, indicative of the larger and more heterogeneous nature of the party. As the center of the Republican party shrank, the proportion of conservatives increased. The Republican party, being smaller, was more ideologically unified and therefore easier to represent.[11]

In 1968, Wallace waged a campaign against intellectuals, calling them, among other things, "pointy heads." He received 13.5 percent of the total presidential vote, but 15 percent of manual workers said they supported him. In Pennsylvania, the Wallace vote among blue-collar workers increased with the number of nonwhites in a community.[12] An interesting historical parallel had occurred among native-born workers in Pittsburgh in the years before the Civil War when immigrant workers moved into the city. The native workers, too poor to move away and thus compelled to remain and compete with foreign Catholics, were most likely to vote for nativist candidates.[13]

At the Democratic national convention in 1972, the AFL-CIO, satisfied only with the bread-and-butter provisions of the platform, was dissatisfied with McGovern and refused to endorse him after his nomination.[14] The national Republican vote that year increased 17.4 percent over 1968, but the Republican increase among manual workers was 22 percent, noncollege 21 percent, high school graduates 23 percent and college-educated respondents only 9 percent. The increase for whites was 21 percent but for blacks 7 percent.[15]

Issue and ideological differences among Democrats in 1972 were greater than the difference between all Democrats and all Republicans. According to the normal vote analysis, liberal Democrats voted more heavily than expected for McGovern, and conservative Democrats voted more heavily than expected for Nixon. Blacks made up 20 percent of the McGovern vote and 2 percent of the Nixon vote. A cultural orientation index, constructed to show various degrees of polarization by educational

[11] Norman H. Nie, Sidney Verba, and John R. Petrocik, *The Changing American Voter* (Cambridge, Mass.: Harvard University Press, 1976) pp. 198–99, 209. Samuel J. Eldersveld, *Political Parties: A Behavioral Analysis* (Chicago: Rand McNally & Company, 1964) pp. 191–94.

[12] Everett Carll Ladd, Jr. and Seymour Martin Lipset, *Academics, Politics, and the 1972 Election* (Washington, D.C.: American Enterprise Institute for Public Policy Research, 1973) p. 13, citing Gallup Poll data. Walter Dean Burnham and John Sprague, "Additive and Multiplicative Models of the Voting Universe: The Case of Pennsylvania: 1960–1968," *The American Political Science Review*, 64 (June 1970) 472.

[13] Michael Fitzgibbon Holt, *Forging a Majority: The Formation of the Republican Party in Pittsburgh, 1848–1860* (New Haven, Ct.: Yale University Press, 1969) pp. 150–51.

[14] Denis G. Sullivan, Jeffrey L. Pressman, Benjamin I. Page, and John J. Lyons, *The Politics of Representation: The Democratic Convention 1972* (New York: St. Martin's Press, 1974) pp. 95–96.

[15] Ladd and Lipset, *Academics, Politics, and the 1972 Election*, p. 72.

level, by age, and by race, revealed that Democrats and Independents were the most internally divided groups. The total sample, and whites as a group, were "pro-establishment" but blacks, those with college degrees, and those under thirty years of age were "pro-counterculture." [16]

Generational Change and Cultural Politics

New generations appear to be so oriented toward change that they have been compared with new immigrants. They see old liberal policies as mere props for the status quo and look upon the traditional welfare state as a concern for blue-collar whites in order to manipulate them to vote for the Democratic party. These new voters are distinguished from previous generations by longer periods of schooling, and by prosperity, which they consider to be their rightful heritage.[17]

However, these are not descriptions of all people entering the electorate since the 1960s. *Generational change* largely accounted for the decline in the relationship between social class and presidential voting—that is, increased Democratic support among middle-class whites and decreased Democratic support among working-class whites. The expected youth explosion for McGovern in 1972 was only 55 percent of a small turnout among those 18 to 20 years of age and 49 percent of a somewhat larger turnout among those aged 21 to 24. The gap in cultural values between students and workers of the same age was much greater than the generation gap.[18]

Education, in Survey Research Center 1970 and 1972 national data, was a much better indicator of attitudes on public policy among whites than income, occupation, or age. All blacks, irrespective of generation or education, and young white college graduates were most likely to favor government aid to minorities. They also supported proposals to attack poverty as the solution to urban unrest and were sympathetic toward campus disturbances. There was a generational difference only among highly educated whites. Otherwise, differences were found within the same generations between those of high and low educational levels, and these differences were greater among young whites than among older whites. White college graduates, born in 1940 and after, who favored government aid to minorities and

[16] Arthur H. Miller, Warren E. Miller, Alden S. Raine, and Thad A. Brown, "A Majority Party in Disarray: Policy Polarization in the 1972 Election," pp. 11–12, 22, 77, 61. Paper presented at 69th Annual Meeting, American Political Science Association, New Orleans, Louisiana, September 1973.

[17] Frederick G. Dutton, *Changing Sources of Power: American Politics in the 1970s* (New York: McGraw-Hill Book Company, 1971) pp. 27–33, 60–62.

[18] Paul R. Abramson, *Generational Change in American Politics* (Lexington, Mass.: Lexington Books, 1975) pp. 15–49; and Abramson, "Generational Change in American Electoral Behavior," *The American Political Science Review*, 68 (March 1974) 93–105. Miller and others, "A Majority Party in Disarray," pp. 85–86. Davis, *The Emerging Democratic Majority*, p. 117.

sympathized with campus disturbances, were most likely to be Democrats and to vote for McGovern in 1972. They also differed from both the white population as a whole and from most other white Democrats. This reinforced the division within the Democratic party and suggested that realignment could take place through the process of generational change.[19]

A Tenable Realignment?

The reality of an emerging cultural division capable of being organized into two party coalitions depends upon the potential of ideology to sustain them. Heretofore, realignments have resulted from clashing ideologies, but these were soon toned down as the party system entered its stable phase of the equilibrium cycle. If the hostilities between the *counterculture* and *traditional culture* become the ideological basis for a realignment, there is no prospect for an accommodation permitting a return to consensus. Either one side or the other must abandon much of its zeal. Otherwise, the two sides would exist in a state of hostility. In this case, they would break the continuity of the party system with realignment instead of maintaining the system with realignment.

As dubious as this prospect seems, it is not entirely outside the realm of possibility. There was evidence between 1964 and 1974 that party influence among white voters was magnified by a hostile attitude toward the other party. Respondents were more likely to support their own party's presidential candidate if they had an unfavorable evaluation of the other party. They were more likely to defect from their own party if they had a favorable evaluation of the other party. Irrespective of their evaluations of Republicans, blacks voted Democratic.[20] There was nothing in these data to suggest that hostility arose from ideological or cultural sources. However, if hostility should be reinforced by these sources, it could become so intense that it would be apparent long before its documentation through survey research.

Because of its implications for realignment, the potential motivating force of ideology deserves closer attention.

THE DIMENSIONS OF IDEOLOGY

Liberalism and conservatism, defined as support of or opposition to the use of government resources to accomplish social objectives, were not seriously

---

[19] Abramson, *Generational Change in American Politics*, Chapters 5, 6.

[20] Michael A. Maggiotto and James E. Piereson, "Partisan Identification and Electoral Choice: The Hostility Hypothesis," *American Journal of Political Science*, 21 (November 1977) 745–68.

polarizing before the 1960s–1970s. Respondents were found to be cautious about abstract philosophical ideas but overwhelmingly in favor of specific federal government programs such as aid to education and providing jobs. Large majorities also favored government doing something about unemployment. Yet, 79 percent believed there should be more reliance on individual initiative and less on government welfare programs. In addition, 76 percent agreed that an able-bodied person could find a job and earn a living, a view shared by 70 percent of those with incomes under $5000 a year and by 60 percent of blacks.[21] These apparent contradictions were actually a measure of an ambivalence between the abstract and the concrete.

Abstract v. Concrete

To demonstrate this distinction, two spectrums were constructed: The *ideological spectrum* consisted of responses to general questions regarding the use of federal government powers and the *operational spectrum* for responses to questions about specific government policies. Of the total sample, 23 percent were liberal on the operational spectrum and conservative on the ideological spectrum. Slightly more than one-fourth of the self-identified liberals were liberal on the ideological spectrum, but 81 percent were liberal on the operational one. Self-identified conservatives responded about as expected on the ideological spectrum, where 70 percent were conservative, but only 29 percent of them were conservative on the operational spectrum. When the factor of party identification was added, Republicans were distributed fairly evenly on the operational spectrum but were overwhelmingly conservative on the ideological spectrum. The Democrats were strongly liberal on operational spectrum and well distributed on the ideological one. Independents in each case fell between Republicans and Democrats but were operationally liberal and ideologically conservative.[22]

The Renaissance of Conservatism?

Following the rise of ideology in the 1960s–1970s, moderate responses to survey questions began to decline. The proportion of respondents with a centrist attitude on issues fell from 41 percent in 1956 to 27 percent in 1973. The Gallup Poll reported that respondents who said they were conservatives had increased significantly over the years: 1953—32 percent; 1970—39 percent; 1978—52 percent. In one Gallup sample, 43 percent said they were, to

[21] Lloyd A. Free and Hadley Cantril, *The Political Beliefs of Americans* (New York: Simon and Schuster, 1968) pp. 1–40.

[22] *Ibid.*, pp. 47, 48, 137, 138.

some degree, right of center compared with 30 percent, to some degree, left of center; the 10 percent who said they were middle-of-the-road were outnumbered by the 17 percent with no opinion.[23]

This movement to the right in the polls was reflected in congressional voting and was explained as a popular conclusion that government undertakings were futile because actions appeared to be ineffective or ill designed. If liberal policies had been correct initially there would not be such a host of problems now. Moreover, there was evidence of new *reactions against permissiveness*, consistent with a revival of *conservative values*. Finally, conservatism was a reflection of disillusionment with the decline of American power abroad, particularly as a hangover from the Vietnam adventure.[24]

It still was not clear, when people said they were conservative, that they meant what they were supposed to mean. In the context of the rise of ideology, did the growth of conservatives signify a conscious preference for individual responsibility and a rejection of the liberal doctrine of attacking problems through collective government action? Or, were people saying they would like more benefits but, upon realizing they would have to pay for them, were willing to do without them?

The belief in self-reliance, now considered conservative, continues to act as a restraint upon demands for government help. Yet, Americans are still liberal on bread-and-butter issues and conservative when it comes to ideological labels. We can accept, simultaneously, conservative rhetoric and the politics of liberalism. The coexistence of different ideological dimensions may support the observation that Americans conserve principles which are liberal and even radical.[25] The change signified by the move to the right may mean that many no longer want to express liberal principles in liberal terms.

Since ideological ambivalence was shown to depend upon questions being abstract or concrete, it is reasonable to suppose that the percentage of liberals and conservatives would vary with the form of concrete questions themselves. The high level of liberal answers to some Survey Research Center questions in 1956 is attributed to an unintentional bias in framing the questions because the word "agree" proved to be positive for respondents and, therefore, influenced the answers. In 1956, "agree" was the liberal answer. In the 1964 Survey Research Center questionnaire, "agree" was the

[23] Nie and others, *The Changing American Voter*, pp. 42–43. Newspaper reports of Gallup poll data, 1978.

[24] *U.S. News & World Report*, January 23, 1978, pp. 24–25 and January 30, 1978, pp. 29–31.

[25] Paul M. Sniderman and Richard A. Brody, "Coping: The Ethic of Self-Reliance," *American Journal of Political Science*, 21 (August 1977) 500–521. Louis Hartz, *The Liberal Tradition in America* (New York: Harcourt, Brace and World, Inc., 1955) pp. 58–59. Alan P. Grimes, "Conservative Revolution and Liberal Rhetoric: The Declaration of Independence," *The Journal of Politics*, 38 (August 1976) 1–19.

conservative answer, and the percentage of conservative responses increased significantly.[26]

The wording of questions does not have to depend upon the word "agree" to elicit contrary responses. If a question regarding national health insurance were put in terms of a remote and benevolent government— "Should government help people with their doctor and hospital bills?"—an outpouring of liberal answers would be expected. If the question carried a reminder that with a carrot comes a stick—"Should there be a program of compulsory socialized medicine?"—conservative answers should predominate.

That some evidence of ideology is really the result of how questions are put to people reduces the prospects of extreme confrontations. At the same time, interpretations of answers to questions can be misleading even if there is no methodological question involved.

Consistency of Culture and Economics

The polarization resulting from the counterculture was superimposed upon a preexisting liberal-conservative division measured on an economic scale. Both the rise of ideology and the growth of conservatism are predicated upon consistency in culture and economics together, as well as upon either one of them alone. Although the move to the right has received a great deal of attention in the 1970s, it appears that the left has been more consistent on the two issues.

When the new liberals of the counterculture attacked old-liberal positions, they were not taking a conservative economic position. On the contrary, they pushed for even greater government control and preeminence in environmental, consumer, and business regulation. Liberalism on the economic scale really became irrelevant to them, for their commitment to *collectivism* seemed to extend completely across the board in every aspect of living, except for government investigative activities in national security. Likewise, consistency should require a cultural conservative to be an opponent of government expansion into social welfare and an opponent of government interference in individual personal decisions.

The increase in the number of self-identified conservatives, however, was primarily on the cultural scale. Many of them opposed the counterculture and looked upon the militant poor as beneficiaries of new liberal policies paid for with the taxes of wage-earners. These cultural conservatives have been attacked as dangerous reactionaries, but as a group they have been found to be liberal on government regulation of the economy, govern-

---

[26] John L. Sullivan, James E. Piereson, and George E. Marcus, "Ideological Constraint in the Mass Public: A Methodological Critique and Some New Findings," *American Journal of Political Science*, 22 (May 1978) 244–47.

ment aid to education, and national health care.[27] The public's position on the economic scale, born of insecurity in an impersonal and interdependent society, seems to be as liberal as it ever was. Americans are still concerned with the effect of economic policies on their well being and their status. When economic questions predominate, economic voting coalitions tend to form. When economic issues recede, cultural coalitions tend to form.

Only spasmodic evidence encouraged expectations of realignment based on a liberal-conservative cultural division because new cultural conservatives continued to be perceived as old economic liberals. Therefore, it has been argued that the Democratic party can remain dominant if only the proper strategies are developed to make such policies as racial quotas palatable. Democratic supremacy can be sustained if big government is associated with specific benefits instead of a centralized power structure and if the party changes its image even to the extent of dropping the word "liberal."[28] (One wonders if Jimmy Carter had access to similar advice.) This is a well-conceived party strategy because economic divisions have been related to party identification, but cultural divisions have not. By keeping the two divisions separate on two dimensions, the political potential of ideology can be minimized.

The difficulty in thinking of *economics and culture* as being consistent with each other and, therefore, on one dimension, is the result of a long conditioning process. It has been drummed into us that to be liberal is to favor social security, unemployment compensation, veteran benefits, agricultural supports, and so on. Conversely, to be conservative is to oppose such government policies. To think in this way completely confuses the political significance of proposed changes. On the one hand, it makes conservatives the stand-patters who oppose change and, on the other, makes liberals those who want no change in social-welfare legislation. This confusion can be illustrated in two different issue areas.

Distribution of Government Benefits. One of the principal means traditionally used to create consent or diminish controversy has been the distribution of government benefits, whether by an outright expenditure, the conferring of a legal right or a title to government property, or a policy to pacify contending groups. The usual result was some degree of satisfaction whether people's objective was materialistic and practical or abstract and altruistic. In either case, government policies had something for everyone either by what was done or how it was articulated.

---

[27] James F. Ward, "Toward a Sixth Party System? Partisanship and Political Development," *The Western Political Quarterly*, 26 (September 1973) 403–5. Donald I. Warren, *The Radical Center* (Notre Dame, Ind.: University of Notre Dame Press, 1976). Stephen Earl Bennett and Alfred J. Tuchfarber, "The Social-Structural Sources of Cleavages on Law and Order Policies," *American Journal of Political Science*, 19 (August 1975) 419–38.

[28] John G. Stewart, *One Last Change: The Democratic Party, 1974–76* (New York: Praeger Publishers, 1974) pp. 96–105, 112–13, 149. Also Davis, *The Emerging Democratic Majority*, pp. 222–41.

Problems can no longer be solved so easily by appropriation bills. An ideological division cannot basically be resolved by simply spending more money. To make matters worse, many controversies no longer pose a choice between government action or inaction. Both liberals and conservatives want government decisions on a range of issues, such as abortion, welfare, and national defense. The problem is that they want diametrically opposite decisions.[29]

Conservation of Benefits. Conservatives are consistent on culture and economics if they want to conserve traditional cultural values and to conserve their vested property rights, including those granted to them by government. To threaten these property rights is not a conservative but a radical confiscation comparable to expropriating one's home or farm. It is conservative for people to want to save or protect what they look upon as theirs: their human relations in family, neighborhood, and country as well as the property they have acquired. Social security benefits and a salary from a private company are indistinguishable as property for the person who sees them both as what has been rightfully earned.

Ideological consistency on the two dimensions is easier to demonstrate analytically than to organize for political party realignment. In general, people do not make such a direct association between their basic rights and a political party. Some conservatives who urge an ideological realignment have maintained that a conservative party can build a coalition on one dimension for those who have something to conserve both economically and culturally because basically, their interests are compatible.[30] Other conservatives fail to see the compatibility. They are not convinced that a conservative leadership would be any more acceptable than a liberal leadership to the blue-collar and lower middle class, once associated with George Wallace whether they voted for him or not.[31]

If *cultural and economic beliefs are ideologically consistent,* two new party coalitions can be organized, granted a strong enough desire, enough hard work—and enough ideologues. If ideology is visualized as a distribution along one continuum, the conception of Anthony Downs, pointed out in Chapter 9, becomes more plausible. Of course, a single dimension representing a unified ideology is not the Downs' continuum which is loaded at the center by voters with weak or ambiguous positions on issues.

There are at least three problems that arise in trying to create these new coalitions. *First,* a continuum of many ideologically consistent and polarized voters may require each party to campaign in its own issue sphere and not cross into enemy territory—to appeal from each extreme toward a theoretical center that can probably be located only in the findings of survey

---

[29] Nie and others, *The Changing American Voter,* pp. 106–9.

[30] William A. Rusher, *The Making of the New Majority Party* (New York: Sheed and Ward, Inc., 1975).

[31] Chilton Williamson, Jr., "Country and Western Marxism: To the Nashville Station," *National Review,* June 9, 1978, pp. 711–16.

research. This undertaking seems unprecedented and would be delicate work, indeed. *Second*, as matters now stand, there is no reason to believe that clear-cut ideological appeals can overcome strong party identification or the attraction to incumbents. The *third* and clinching point is that the number of ideologues is still much too small to warrant ideological parties on the national level, much less on the state and local levels.

Practicality with a Semblance of Ideology?

What has been taken as evidence of heightened ideology, especially a growth of conservatism, may well be a new awareness of the effects and implications of government growth. Such a reevaluation need not create widespread ideological polarization but can conceivably lead to a new political division combining ideology for a relatively few, and pragmatic self-interest for most. The growing agitation over taxing and spending, cuts two ways and can create opposing coalitions of people who differ both in their immediate advantages and in their conceptions of proper public policies.

There is already a coalition committed to tax and spend for both expanded and new government programs. Here are found a preponderance of labor union leaders, a large number of blacks, many bureaucrats and planners, probably a large portion of welfare recipients, and private research organizations dependent upon both government subsidies and expansionist policies. There are also industrial corporations that have become dependent upon government or accustomed to protective regulations.

There is no more than an outline of the limited-government coalition, so the groups composing it can only be tentatively and generally identified. The coalition would rely upon the growing proportion of the electorate that has been to college, is white collar, and is threatened by taxes and inflation. People who tend to question government-as-usual would anticipate benefits from those reforms which restrict the growth of bureaucracy and control the expenditure of public funds. Their conception of acceptable government programs would be tempered by the realization that resources are limited, just as government performance is limited. These potential supporters feel a greater personal confidence and competence and demand the opportunity to have control over the spending of more of their own money. They are in a position to see in a new light, and thus reject, that part of liberal philosophy which holds that government should perform primarily for the benefit of the poor and minorities.

A political division involving two such coalitions would not be predominantly ideological, for it would involve more style issues than position issues. Both sides would agree on the need for welfare, for instance, but would differ on standards for eligibility and methods of administration. The definition, not the existence, of poverty has long been a source of controversy: whether to count only cash income or to include noncash government benefits as well, such as food stamps and Medicaid. Although this kind of political division seems possible during a period of greater awareness and dissatisfaction with the levels of taxes and inflation, the coalitions could dissolve if public attention should shift to a new set of concerns.

THE TENUOUSNESS OF IDEOLOGY

After all the build-up that something extraordinary was to happen in the 1970s, the era of confrontations seemed to have passed, and national politics proceeded in its more conventional style. Carter's narrow presidential victory in 1976 was attributed to the sharply reduced defection rate among Democrats combined with the defection rate among Republicans.[32] The victory also featured a strange ideological contradiction. Carter projected a conservative image with his "born again" Christian theme and his agrarian roots while campaigning on typical liberal issues such as "soak-the-rich" tax reforms, national health insurance, and reduced defense spending.

To rely upon sustained ideological voting is dubious at best. Ideologues have different degrees of intensity of opinion on various issues and they also make personal evaluations of candidates just as nonideological voters do. Otherwise, why, in 1972, would 42 percent of New Liberals have voted for Nixon and 7 percent of the Silent Minority have voted for McGovern? [33]

Expressions of ideology often are misleading in their implications, for ideology can also be a stance or a mood that is not predictive of behavior. A voter, angry from ideological frustration, can just as well vote for an incumbent who has recognized the frustration and made concessions to it without sharing the ideology itself. Some liberal Democratic leaders who had constantly taxed and spent, suddenly became solicitous of the taxpayers in the face of evidence of a tax rebellion. They began campaigning as champions of frugal government while bragging about their record of cutting taxes and appropriations. Consequently, the Democrats benefited more from this conservative mood than the Republicans did. Perhaps we will yet vindicate the Jeffersonian belief that government can be satisfactorily responsive without any change in government officials.

Polarity and Coexistence

Political polarization has become so commonplace that we search for new ways to express it. This is, no doubt, one reason for the revival of the word

---

[32] Warren E. Miller and Teresa E. Levitin, *Leadership and Change: Presidential Elections from 1952 to 1976* (Cambridge, Mass.: Winthrop Publishers, Inc., 1976) pp. 203–11, 228–30.

[33] *Ibid.*, p. 151.

"populism." When it first came into political usage in the 1890s, *populism* was a name for the *agrarian revolt* in the South and West that was created, to some extent, by farmers' perception of their inability to deal with the power centers of government and industry.[34]

Populism was used so loosely in the 1970s, that it has no distinctive meaning beyond *unrest and dissatisfaction.* When the word is used to designate those who see themselves at the periphery of power, it seems to have engulfed the nation, as alienated groups have become polarized from one another. In 1972, populism was applied both to the coalition that supported McGovern and to the coalition supporting Wallace. McGovern followers saw entrenched traditionalists at the center of power. Wallace followers saw the counterculture as the established power.[35]

When polarized groups are equally alienated, the politics of polarization becomes much less extreme and both sides have demonstrated this by coexisting within the present party system. Blacks are often considered one of the most alienated groups. Yet, some of their leaders have expressed unhappiness that monolithic support from blacks permits Democrats to take them for granted. The Reverend Jesse Jackson became notably bipartisan. "Neither party is worthy of blind loyalty and religious veneration. Both are merely means to one end: economic advancement." [36] Playing both sides of the political street is the classic operation of group politics, not polarized confrontation.

The Center Still Wins

Democrats and Republicans, when they govern, may appear to be beleaguered helmsmen who have learned to remain passive while steering a vessel through the howling winds and lashing seas of a monstrous storm. These difficulties may be insignificant compared with the confusion and dissensions they would risk by ideological appeals when party identifiers are both liberals and conservatives. What concessions should be made to ideologies when voters continue to reward the appearance of moderation and punish the appearance of "extremism" at the polls?

In an experiment conducted in 1973, *centrist candidates* won against noncentrist candidates because a candidate on one extreme gained from that extreme, lost from the other extreme, but failed to offset these losses by

[34] There have been many interpretations of populism. See *The Populists in Historical Perspective*, ed., Raymond J. Cunningham (Lexington, Mass.: D. C. Heath and Company, 1968). Also Michael Paul Rogin, *The Intellectuals and McCarthy: The Radical Spector* (Cambridge, Mass.: M.I.T. Press, 1967) pp. 172–80.

[35] Adrian and Press, *American Politics Reappraised*, pp. 67–68. Philip E. Converse, Warren E. Miller, Jerrold G. Rusk, and Arthur C. Wolfe, "Continuity and Change in American Politics: Parties and Issues in the 1968 Election," *The American Political Science Review*, 63 (December 1969) 1100–1.

[36] Quoted in *U.S. News & World Report*, April 10, 1978, p. 65.

gains from the center. The effect of two centrist candidates opposing each other was to increase party and candidate orientation.[37] The experiment confirms experience. As long as voters are not attracted to extremist candidates, and the link between distrust of government and political behavior appears weak, the "mainstream" political leaders can hold to their course and continue to talk about inspiring trust and administering government more efficiently.[38] They can fortify themselves with the knowledge that "Promoting an idea, however partisan in implications, is different from promoting a party." [39] A "convulsive epoch," we are told, lies ahead of us.[40] There were also convulsions at the turn of the twentieth century, but the parties managed to absorb the changes with a minimum amount of change themselves.

The Political Center and Big Government

There must be a connection between voters' preference for the political center and the fact that dissatisfaction with government has not led to any reduction in the size of government. Because we usually associate big government with the federal government, we have insisted upon invigorating the governments closest to us with outpourings of federal money. The result is that we now have big government both in Washington, D.C. and close to us.

Incentives for government expansion seem irresistible when the costs are diffused through a broad-based tax system and the benefits are concentrated. To withdraw a benefit and make a corresponding tax cut results in a far greater loss to the beneficiaries than the gain to the taxpayers. If the benefits are also tax exempt, the beneficiaries reap a whirlwind profit. Groups have every incentive to push for new and bigger benefits, and coalitions supporting new government undertakings are more politically attractive than coalitions offering the alternative of tax reduction. It is certainly not news that government, as the public sector, has grown much faster in the twentieth century than the private sector.[41]

Conceivably, the policies of tax and spend can be controlled by tying them together in the public's mind. Large majorities in both houses of Congress in 1978 adopted a proposal to reduce taxes each year if Congress

[37] Nie and others, *The Changing American Voter*, pp. 315–16, 334–48.

[38] James D. Wright, *The Dissent of the Governed* (New York: Academic Press, 1976) pp. 199–200.

[39] Richard Rose, *The Problem of Party Government* (New York: The Free Press, 1975) p. 74.

[40] Dutton, *Changing Sources of Power*, p. 24.

[41] Allan H. Meltzer, *Why Government Grows*, International Institute for Economic Research (Ottawa, Ill.: Green Hill Publishers, Inc., 1976). James L. Clayton, "The Fiscal Limits of the Warfare-Welfare State: Defense and Welfare Spending in the United States since 1900," *The Western Political Quarterly*, 29 (September 1976) 364–83.

would keep spending within specified limits. If Congress failed to observe these limits, taxes would not be reduced. Thus, taxpayers would have a vested interest in holding down spending. This proposal was finally abandoned at the insistence of the Carter Administration but, even if adopted, it may prove to be of limited effectiveness.

Centrist politics may be thought of as being on dead-center, without much movement in any direction. This belief is only possible if we pay attention to forms and structure and fail to see what actually happens. The fact is that centrist politics are associated with gradual, incremental increases in government services and regulations so that, as the center wins, so does big government. This situation is more easily understood by recognizing that the center is not a fixed point, or even a point at all, but a shifting concept.

THE SHIFTING CENTER

Moderation and extremism are relative terms. What has been accepted is likely to appear moderate or at least unexceptional. What is proposed may appear extreme, depending upon the way the proposal is presented as well as upon its substance. What makes for a moderate, centrist party system at one time could have been denounced fifty years previously as a bundle of dangerous tendencies. In little more than a decade, the political center shifted as the extremes moderated to produce a two-way accommodation.

A Decline in Cultural Polarity?

Beginning with its 1970 national survey, the Survey Research Center asked respondents four questions to measure attitudes toward: the values of the counterculture, violent protest, law and order, and agents of law and order (the police and the military).[42] Those who favored *new-politics* positions on all four questions were designated the "New Liberals" and those who *rejected new politics* on all four, the "Silent Minority." These two polarized groups, who constituted one-third of the total sample, differed sharply on candidates but represented nearly equal numbers of Democrats and Republicans. Two-thirds of the sample occupied three other positions: pro-counterculture on three questions, anti-counterculture on three questions, and the center which was either indifferent or evenly divided on the four questions. Table 10.1 shows the shift to counterculture positions in the space of two years.

[42] The following data are taken from Miller and Levitin, *Leadership and Change*, Chapters 3–5 and pp. 191–92, 211–14.

TABLE 10.1 Trend in Cultural Polarization, 1970 and 1972.*

	Pro-Counterculture		Center	Anti-Counterculture	
	4 questions	3 questions	evenly divided	3 questions	4 questions
1970	14%	21%	25%	23%	17%
1972	25	24	27	17	7

* Data taken from Warren E. Miller and Teresa E. Levitan, *Leadership and Change* (Cambridge, Mass.: Winthrop Publishers, Inc., 1976) p. 86.

The precipitous decrease in the *Silent Minority* and a comparable increase in *New Liberals* gives the superficial appearance of a virtual collapse of the defenders of traditional values. However, there were special factors involved which help to explain the changes in percentages. The Silent Minority suffered from a lack of leadership, for most political leaders by 1972 either posed as New Liberals or temporized with the counterculture. Also, by 1972, the campuses had cooled off and urban riots had ceased. The counterculture, by becoming more familiar, may have appeared more acceptable, and to some extent, it had been eclipsed by economic issues. The shift toward the new politics had occurred among whites, not blacks, and was partly accounted for by both the 18 and 19 year-old voters and by Independent leaners in party identification. The least politically involved moved away from the Silent Minority while the most involved moved toward the New Liberals.

The two polarized groups, however, maintained their identity in 1976 and were more strongly related to the presidential vote than such factors as age, income, and religion. It would be premature to conclude that the cleavages of the 1960s–1970s will never reappear. The decline of the Silent Minority may prove to be no more than temporary, and they may reassert themselves again if there are new cultural provocations.[43]

Moderation of New Politics

The counterculture was initially characterized by a headstrong insistence upon having its own way. They expected a sinful nation to turn to them as saviors and accept their simplistic morality as eternal verities. Only the faithful, who scorned compromise and conciliation, were entitled to lead.

With the coming of political reality, especially the election returns in the 1972 presidential race, the counterculture began to change its ways.

[43] Glenn Abney, "Book Review," *The Journal of Politics*, 39 (August 1977) 830–32.

Some realized that they were powerless if they did not win elections, so they entered party politics and began to bargain.[44] They ran for office by soft-pedaling abortions and marijuana, while concentrating on problems of constituent interests and on the need to restore trust in government. Undoubtedly, they were sobered once they were elected and discovered the limitations imposed by the responsibilities of office.

Accommodation and moderation does not mean that the more things change, the more they are the same. New-liberal moderation occurs at a point some distance to the left of the old political center. Even without confrontations and demands shouted into television cameras, there are potentially explosive substantive conflicts such as the growing resistance to taxes or the opposing requirements of an economic growth society and an environmentalist no-growth society.

The rippling effects of *generational change* may prove to be truly momentous. One does not have to attend college to appreciate free and easy mores pertaining to sex, attitudes toward work, and standards of success. It seems reasonable that the liberal elements within the younger age groups, as within older groups, would have a more powerful effect upon the future of American politics. They are more likely to exert leadership than the much larger and more conservative groups which lack the incentive to become political activists.[45] This distinction between the relatively few influentials and the relatively many uninfluentials may help to account for the continued liberal direction of government policies while more and more respondents in surveys say they are conservatives.

No matter how imbued liberals and conservatives become with their ideologies, it is unlikely they will advance very far without an energizing leadership. The negative principle of avoiding extremism does not necessarily preclude a candidate who masks extremism by projecting an acceptable image. To a great extent, negative perceptions of candidates like Goldwater and McGovern were due to their opponents portraying them as extremists and incompetents. The opposition may be less successful if an extremist candidate should prove to be fuzzy enough on the issues to appear to be moderate.[46] This, after all, is what centrists candidates always appear to be doing.

WHAT PARTY SYSTEM?

Lacking the gift of clairvoyance, there can be no certainty about the future of the party system. Expectations of a realignment like those in the 1850s, the 1890s, and the 1930s, have not been borne out, but they may be yet.

---

[44] Davis, *The Emerging Democratic Majority*, pp. 33, 256–57.
[45] Dutton, *Changing Sources of Power*, pp. 44–54.
[46] Nie and others, *The Changing American Voter*, pp. 339–44.

Alternatively, if the Democratic party should be left as the sole surviving party, there is the precedent of the 1820s–1830s, when the party system started all over again from under the umbrella of one party. Among other alternatives, dissatisfactions with the present parties may lead them to greater ideological differences or may encourage other parties which could have a continuing role in the political system.[47] We can be sure there are various possibilities while being doubtful about any one of them.

Responsible Parties

Even a moderate rise in ideology should have strengthened the prospects for more responsible parties, a proposal made by a committee of the American Political Science Association in 1950 for making the parties more meaningful.

By the committee's definition, responsible parties mean more distinctive party differences. Party members would develop policy positions through popular participation and use centralized party machinery to enforce these positions upon the party in the government. Thus, when a party wins an election, it can be held responsible for implementing its program. The result would be a reorganization of the political system in order to create party government. There are strong implications in these proposals that a program coordinated at both ends of Pennsylvania Avenue would, in effect, replace the constitutional system of checks and balances.[48]

However, these proposed reforms were not entirely an aimless striking out into the unknown. As early as the 1840s, the votes of Democrats and Whigs in Congress reflected different party positions on national questions until the intrusion of sectional issues divided each party against itself.[49] There was party voting in Congress at the turn of the twentieth century, but it was undercut by both the withdrawal from parties and the reformers.

It is doubtful that centralized, disciplined parties could have developed anyway because private groups attacked party voting in Congress for the defeat of their bills. It seemed to be generally accepted that more

---

[47] Gerald Kent Hikel, *Beyond the Polls: Political Ideology and Its Correlates* (Lexington, Mass.: D. C. Heath and Company, Lexington Books, 1973) p. 90.

[48] *Toward a More Responsible Two-Party System: A Report of the Committee on Political Parties*, American Political Science Association (New York: Rinehart & Company, Inc., 1950). Other proposals of the same nature: Stephen K. Bailey, *The Condition of Our National Political Parties* (New York: The Fund for the Republic, 1959). James MacGregor Burns, *The Deadlock of Democracy* (Englewood Cliffs, N.J.: Prentice-Hall, Inc., 1963). Charles M. Hardin, "Emergent Defects in the American Constitutional System," in *Political Parties, U.S.A.*, ed., Robert A. Goldwin (Chicago: Rand McNally & Company, 1964) pp. 84–101. Gerald M. Pomper, "Toward a More Responsible Two-Party System? What, Again?" *The Journal of Politics*, 33 (November 1971) 916–40.

[49] Joel H. Silbey, *The Shrine of Party* (Pittsburgh, Pa.: University of Pittsburgh Press, 1967) Chapters 7–8.

effective government action would be achieved through groups allied with party factions rather than through united parties. Disciplined parties were portrayed as standing between people and government and thus usurping the people's authority. This opposition from special interests was reinforced by the argument that effective party government would threaten constitutional safeguards against the exercise of power.[50]

These and other proposals for responsible parties have not been well received even in academic circles. It has been pointed out that, among other weaknesses, the proposals not only failed to take account of the actual world of party politics but also failed either to clarify or to justify the objectives being sought.[51]

The rise of ideology should have encouraged reforms along the lines of the doctrine of responsible parties. The Democrats did reform their presidential-nomination processes, but such proposals as a system of dues to identify Democrats at caucuses and conventions came to nothing, and it remains to be seen how far other reforms will go. There are factions in each party which would emphasize party differences by representing greater ideological purity enforced by party sanctions, and no one can say positively that they will not eventually prevail. In the main, however, ideologues have blamed the parties for not being responsive rather than undertaking as a group a complete reform of the way parties operate and respond.

Attempts to save the party system by sharpening party differences tend to deny that winning is an end in itself, a reversal of the whole rationale of the party system. Party leaders have generally contented themselves with general understandings, knowing that when people try to define what it is they agree about, they may only create greater discord.[52] If both parties are seeking the public interest, how can they be in fundamental disagreement? How can one party adopt a popular position and keep the other party from adopting it? Under the circumstances, we have to settle for a more mundane

[50] David J. Rothman, *Politics and Power* (Cambridge, Mass.: Harvard University Press, 1966) pp. 256–60. Also Jerome M. Clubb and Howard W. Allen, "Party Loyalty in the Progressive Years: The Senate, 1909–1915," *The Journal of Politics*, 29 (August 1967) 567–84; and note 58, Chapter 8, above.

[51] Evron M. Kirkpatrick, "Toward a More Responsible Two-Party System: Political Science, Policy Science, or Pseudo-Science?" *The American Political Science Review*, 65 (December 1971) 965–90. Nelson W. Polsby and Aaron Wildavsky, *Presidential Elections: Strategies of American Electoral Politics*, 4th ed. (New York: Charles Scribner's Sons, 1976) pp. 208–13. Julius Turner, "Responsible Parties: A Dissent from the Floor," *The American Political Science Review*, 45 (March 1951) 143–52. Austin Ranney, "Toward a More Responsible Two-Party System: A Commentary," *The American Political Science Review*, 45 (June 1951) 488–99. J. Roland Pennock, "Responsiveness, Responsibility and Majority Rule," *The American Political Science Review*, 46 (September 1952) 790–807. Edward C. Banfield, "In Defense of the American Party System," in *Political Parties, U.S.A.*, ed., Robert A. Goldwin (Chicago: Rand McNally & Company, 1964) pp. 21–39. William Goodman, "How Much Political Party Centralization Do We Want?" *The Journal of Politics*, 13 (November 1951) 536–61.

[52] Daniel J. Boorstin, *The Genius of American Politics* (Chicago: The University of Chicago Press, 1953) p. 169.

definition of responsibility such as consistency between what a party does or says at different times so that when it formulates new programs, it does not repudiate positions taken in the past.[53]

The doctrine of responsible parties does more than collide with the brick wall of political reality. It reminds us of the limitations upon parties even in realignments, when the insistence upon responsiveness was not a demand for central organs and official pronouncements, but a demand for adjustments; not party membership by cards and dues, but by voting.

A New Party System?

One prescription for saving the party system goes beyond mere reforms of party structure and clearer party differences. It has been contended that realignments, despite their appearance of bringing changes, accomplished little. They were really periodic attempts to bring up to date a political system that was inherently out of date. The attempts failed because they were under the control of the middle class. Now, the cyclical process, from maintaining to realigning, and back to maintaining elections, no longer works because the parties have become so irrelevant to so many people that the system itself is dying. It can only be saved by a new kind of realignment that will once and for all bring the unresponsive political system into line with the dynamic social and economic system. The party system can only become meaningful if it is responsive to Americans of lower economic status who will then begin to vote in larger numbers. America can only become a "developed" and "modernized" country if our party system becomes more like those of Western Europe.[54]

Understandably, this interpretation has drawn fire. It seems more nearly a call for massive reshaping, rather than realignment, for revolution, rather than evolution. Through realignments, parties have demonstrated their ability to do what was required by absorbing stresses and strains without making war upon American values. American parties do not have to become something they have never been in order to be modern. There is more evidence that parties in other countries are emulating their American counterparts than there is evidence that American parties need to emulate them. The projected end-of-parties is a matter of interpretation of data, and

[53] Anthony Downs, *An Economic Theory of Democracy* (New York: Harper & Row Publishers, 1957) p. 105. For other meanings, Austin Ranney, *The Doctrine of Responsible Party Government: Its Origins and Present State* (Urbana: University of Illinois Press, 1962). Pennock, "Responsiveness, Responsibility and Majority Rule," pp. 796–97.

[54] This thesis has been presented in the writings of Walter Dean Burnham. For example: "The Changing Shape of the American Political Universe," *The American Political Science Review*, 59 (March 1965) 7–28. "The End of American Party Politics," *Trans-Action*, VII (New Brunswick, N.J.: TRANS-Action, Inc., 1969) 12–23. "Revitalization and Decay: Looking Toward the Third Century of American Electoral Politics," *The Journal of Politics*, 38 (August 1976) especially 146–52.

it also defines parties exclusively as voting behavior, ignoring the institutional party organization that is not suffering a decline.[55]

The Pressures on the Party System

Allowing for a margin of error in our understanding of what is going on about us, we apparently are witnessing, not just the decomposition of a dominant party coalition, but a *decomposition of the electorate*. The growing emphasis upon private social and recreational activities may signify a disenchantment with all large amorphous groups. It may be a mistake to attach too much significance to the subjective meaning of voting behavior. Many voters may not mean much of anything at all. The results of mass voting responses can be significant over time without conscious awareness on the part of voters. When ticket-splitters revived Republican competition in presidential elections, were they voting their reactions to candidates and campaigns, or were they intending to introduce historical change?

We still cannot be sure if the political scene is a calm before a storm that will reinvigorate the party system. In fact, we cannot be sure how calm it really is, or what the propensities are, of subsurface tensions to produce a storm. We do know that the party system has lost a great deal of ground as the structure through which conflicts are resolved or minimized. The extent and diversity of government became too overpowering to be managed exclusively through parties. Changes in political forces required realignment when parties were the principal organizations for political mobilization. Now, party leaders are forced to share this responsibility with elites outside of the parties. If the party system is just one structure for dealing with conflicts, there is less need for realignment, and concern for continuity of the party system becomes a concern for its survival.

Attempts to revive parties with rationalizations or prescribed conduct are about as effective as the alternative reaction, the crocodile-tear syndrome, expressing pity over the coming demise of parties. It would be more useful to accept parties as we find them and go on from there. We may need to reexamine long-held judgments about the party system. For example, uneven party competition may not have been a measure of the party system's failure to develop, but the only way the system could survive.[56] So far, the institutional party is still intact because party organization has been able to perpetuate itself. If the party as an institution should end, we would be reduced to the minimum definition of party, noted in Chapter 1, the party name itself.

[55] Ward, "Toward a Sixth Party System?" pp. 385–413, especially 407–8, 411–12. Also Leon D. Epstein, *Political Parties in Western Democracies* (New York: Frederick A. Praeger, 1967) p. 356.

[56] Joseph A. Schlesinger, "The Structure of Competition for Office in the American States," *Behavioral Science*, 5 (1960) 208.

If we can only make progress when "we begin to use the political parties as they are meant to be used," [57] the outlook is indeed bleak because there never has been general agreement on how parties were meant to be used. When parties arose in the eighteenth century, they were attacked for encouraging conflicts and threatening national unity. Now, they are attacked for trying to maintain harmony and create an illusion of consensus.[58] Parties are not irrelevant to issues but even if they were, they would still be relevant to elections. What other kind of system would work so well for such a diverse and independent-minded people?

Parties have long been criticized for satisfying people's self-interests, illustrated in the use of patronage, but now parties seem neither to serve personal selfish purposes, nor to satisfy general interests. Is it possible for people to retain a close attachment to parties if they differ only over principles, divorced from individual incentives for political involvement?

If, nearly 200 hundred years after the appearance of the first party system, it all should end, it will probably be neither at some dramatic Armageddon, nor in a spontaneous uprising tantamount to a coup d'état. One can guess that parties will more likely fall victims to an irrelevance born of tedium. If we do not live by bread alone, neither does our political life consist solely of solemn considerations of the pressing issues of the day. Parties will not survive if we do not believe in them, and it is easier to believe when we find excitement, along with food for thought. As Samuel Lubell so gratuitously put it, leaving out journalists and pollsters among other occupations, "All voting is an emotional experience for ditch diggers and professors alike." [59]

[57] David S. Broder, *The Party's Over* (New York: Harper and Row, 1972) p. xvi.

[58] Richard Hofstadter, *The Idea of a Party System* (Berkeley, Ca.: University of California Press, 1969) pp. 270–71.

[59] Samuel Lubell, *The Revolt of the Moderates* (New York: Harper and Brothers, 1956) p. 90.

11

Politics Beyond the Party System

When the last book is written on the party system in America, it may well be concluded that the New Deal was the great landmark in time, the reference point for relating all other events, the B.C. and the A.D. of the party system. The impact of economic and social changes, taken in conjunction with the challenges noted in Section II, has changed the whole political terrain of America, and nothing will ever be the same or even remotely similar again.

The progressive decline of the party system may seem rapid but, after nearly a century of decline, "the parties still have a long life remaining to them if their speed of demise remains constant."[1] Without presuming to prophecy what will happen and when, it is reasonable to ask what America would be like without parties, for the party system has become an intimate part of the American constitutional system. Of course, if we consider all of the cosmic possibilities in the light years ahead, one nation's party system becomes so infinitesimal that it hardly leaves an imprint on the sands of time. In case we should find ourselves living in outer space, it seems highly unlikely we would find a need for the Democratic and Republican parties although we cannot be positive. Some people must have concluded long ago that the parties were already out of this world.

Living in the present and not in the future makes it reasonable to ask what political life would be like without parties. The best way to proceed is by asking what practical use parties still have. At least if we know what the benefits of the party system are, we will have some idea of what we would be giving up if we adopt a different system.

WHAT PARTIES DO

The only way to be sure what results can be assigned to parties is to live the last two centuries all over again without them and compare the results.

---

[1] Jerrold G. Rusk and Herbert F. Weisberg, "Perceptions of Presidential Candidates: Implications for Electoral Change," *Midwest Journal of Political Science*, 16 (August 1972) 407.

In the absence of such an experiment, it is difficult to be sure that parties are responsible for the results we associate with them. There are a few results which seem properly attributable to the party system.

Nation Building

That political parties made a significant contribution in the creation of the United States is an insight more apparent to scholars than to the general public. It is easy to see parties as sources of contention and divisiveness but difficult to appreciate them as integrating mechanisms. Parties may have intensified conflicts by organizing them, but parties also became the means for the orderly settlement of conflicts and, in the process, helped to keep the nation together.[2] It was sectionalism, not parties, which threatened America in the decade immediately before the Civil War. In fact, the two major parties held the sections together, even when other institutions capitulated under the pressures, because party loyalty proved to be stronger than sectional loyalty.[3] When sectional loyalty finally overwhelmed the parties, there was no remaining force capable of preventing the dissolution of the Union.

The nation-building role may be more apparent in the past than in the present. Parties have little corrective effect upon current divisive tendencies although if there were another threat of secession, the party system might again be an effective counteractant. Perhaps parties have been more integrative than one would suspect, for making accommodations to dissent is itself part of unifying. To the extent that decentralization can be a means toward this accommodation, parties have contributed both directly, in their own decentralization, and indirectly by their responsibility for some governmental decentralization.[4]

---

[2] Paul Goodman. "The First American Party System," in *The American Party Systems: Stages of Political Development*, eds., William Nisbet Chambers and Walter Dean Burnham (New York: Oxford University Press, 1967) p. 64. William Nisbet Chambers, *Political Parties in a New Nation: The American Experience, 1776–1809* (New York: Oxford University Press, 1963) pp. 202–5; and Chambers, "Parties and Nation-Building in America," in *Political Parties and Political Development*, eds., Joseph LaPalombara and Myron Weiner (Princeton, N.J.: Princeton University Press, 1966) pp. 79–106.

[3] Michael Wallace, "Changing Concepts of Party in the United States: New York, 1815–1828," *American Historical Review*, 74 (December 1968) 453–91. This argument was made by Martin Van Buren in the 1820s, Robert V. Remini, *Martin Van Buren and the Making of the Democratic Party* (New York: Columbia University Press, 1959) pp. 131–32.

[4] Morton Grodzins, "American Political Parties and the American System," in *American Politics: Research and Readings*, eds., Stephen V. Monsma and Jack R. Van Der Slik (New York: Holt, Rinehart and Winston, Inc., 1970) pp. 588–93; and Grodzins, "Party and Government in the United States," in *Political Parties, U.S.A.*, ed., Robert A. Goldwin (Chicago: Rand McNally & Company, 1964) pp. 102–32. Daniel J. Elazar, *American Federalism: A View from the States*, 2nd ed. (New York: Thomas Y. Crowell Company, 1972) pp. 158–70.

Political Stability

If the nation-building value of parties is obscure to many, the claim that party identification has a stabilizing effect in public affairs would have been difficult to miss.

Without party identification, it is said, there is the danger that people will flounder about, responding to whims and extraneous currents of political pressures. Nonvoters, in 1952 and 1956, who were weak partisans, less involved with politics, and more susceptible to media stimuli, were also more responsive to bandwagon influences. They reported massive shifts in their preference for Eisenhower, especially after he won. While strong party identification acts as a brake on hasty action during crises, weak party identification may make one more susceptible to demagogues. Young voters in the North, who had not yet developed a strong party identification in 1968, were more likely to vote for Wallace.[5] There are some difficulties with this claim for political stability.

Other Protections Against Extremism. Support for extremism has been virtually nil since 1968, but the intensity of partisanship has declined. There may be other protections against extremism such as the complexity of society and an electorate not highly polarized by issues.[6]

The Effect of Incumbency. Incumbency, like party identification, also has a stabilizing effect. Respondents with greater political interest and information were more likely to switch parties in presidential elections between 1952 and 1972. Those least concerned and involved were more likely to cast a party vote when no incumbent was running in 1952, 1960, and 1968, but to vote for the incumbent in 1956, 1964, and 1972.[7] This kind of stability has nothing to do with protection against extremists nor is it the kind which would be commended or advocated.

Party Identification; Stabilizer or Crutch. The stabilizing effect of party identification may, in reality, be akin to a crutch. In an experiment using candidates without party names, extremist candidates proved to be less attractive to Independents than to Democrats and Republicans. Some identifiers apparently needed the party cue to bolster their judgments. In the ab-

[5] Angus Campbell, Philip E. Converse, Warren E. Miller, and Donald E. Stokes, *The American Voter* (New York: John Wiley & Sons, Inc., 1960) pp. 110–15, 365–68. Norman H. Nie, Sidney Verba, and John R. Petrocik, *The Changing American Voter* (Cambridge, Mass.: Harvard University Press, 1976) pp. 41–42. Herbert B. Asher, *Presidential Elections and American Politics: Voters, Candidates, and Campaigns since 1952* (Homewood, Ill.: The Dorsey Press, 1976) pp. 51–52.

[6] Otto A. Davis, Melvin J. Hinich and Peter C. Ordeshook, "An Expository Development of a Mathematic Model of the Electoral Process," *The American Political Science Review*, 64 (June 1970) 440.

[7] Johannes T. Pedersen, "Political Involvement and Partisan Change in Presidential Elections," *American Journal of Political Science*, 22 (February 1978) 18–30.

sence of party designation of candidates, Democrats of lower socioeconomic status were most attracted to demagogues.[8]

Whether it be protection against extremists or the encouragement of party voting, party identification seems to have a stabilizing influence, but more so, perhaps, for apoliticals and for those who acquired no alternate sources for evaluation in the course of their political socialization. Party identification serves individuals by "bringing a somewhat fictitious order out of the apparent chaos of the political universe."[9] Even more informed and interested voters, who make personal judgments, benefit from this service but for party identifiers as a whole, it becomes a matter of interpretation how much of a price they pay.

From one point of view, parties obstruct democracy by making the voting decision too easy. It is possible that voters would still vote the same way on the basis of their own analysis as they do when they vote their party identification, but they should not be relieved of the necessity for doing their own thinking by relying upon party labels.

From the point of view of the party system, voters have access to information but under the best of circumstances, they need a guide through the maze of public affairs. Party identification is a rational guide for this purpose, for the party cue is far less likely to create distortions or misperceptions than a partyless system. The organizational framework of a party system provides a continuity and an efficient means for evaluating new information. Despite misperceptions and even emotional party commitments, voting party identification can be a rational means for achieving objectives and is certainly consistent with democracy.[10]

Superiority of Parties over Factions

Those who favor a party system can be expected to find it has advantages, but even when investigators have the same standards for judgment, they do not always find the party system distinctly superior. In states with varying degrees of party competition, voters in two-party states have the advantage of party cues both in trying to influence public affairs and in making sense out of them.[11] But these advantages of parties may more easily be detected

[8] Dean Jaros and Gene L. Mason, "Party Choice and Support for Demagogues: An Experimental Examination," *The American Political Science Review*, 63 (March 1969) 100–110.

[9] Charles Sellers, "The Equilibrium Cycle in Two-Party Politics," in *Electoral Change and Stability in American Political History*, eds., Jerome M. Clubb and Howard W. Allen (New York: The Free Press, 1971) p. 163.

[10] David Knoke, *Change and Continuity in American Politics: The Social Bases of Political Parties* (Baltimore, Md.: The Johns Hopkins University Press, 1976) pp. 4–10. John D. May, *Sources of Competitive Disequilibrium between Competing Political Parties* (Morristown, N.J.: General Learning Press, 1973) p. 4. Chapter 9, above.

[11] Glen T. Broach, "A Comparative Dimensional Analysis of Partisan and Urban-Rural Voting in State Legislatures," *The Journal of Politics*, 34 (August 1972) 905–21.

on a state level than on local levels. After examining three North Carolina counties—one with party competition, one with two factions, and one with several factions—it was concluded that party competition may make a contribution to democratic decision-making but there was no assurance that it would.[12]

Little serious attention has been given to a factional system, as distinct from a party system, even though both are organized competition in politics.[13] Inasmuch as factions are thought of as subdivisions of a party, one-party factional politics has most frequently been used to demonstrate that the party system has beneficial consequences.

There is no question that one-party domination in an individual state debilitates both parties. The years of Republican domination in California continued to have its effects upon the party system in the state even after the revival of the Democratic party.[14] However, it was state politics during the era of the Solid South that was constantly cited to show the negative effects of a one-party system. Quite aside from these effects, the causes of fragmentation within southern Democratic parties is also a matter of interest.

The late V. O. Key, Jr. concluded that differences in the degree of Democratic party disunity in southern states depended upon the degree of strength of the Republican party. Where there was no Republican party, except in name, the Democrats were likely to become atomized into several factions, for example, Alabama and Mississippi. Each factional leader had his own personal following, referred to as his "friends and neighbors." But in those states where the Republican party was strong enough to win a state election if the Democrats failed to maintain some semblance of unity, for example, Tennessee and Virginia, the Democratic party was prone to divide into just two factions which could pull together in a general election.[15]

Key's explanation appeared in the late 1940s and since then the Republican party has increased in strength in every one of the southern states. Yet, the patterns of southern factionalism have not changed much. The number of factions in the Democratic party seems to be better explained now by the individual states' laws governing the direct primary. Where there is only one primary and the highest candidate is automatically nominated, the Democratic party has two factions competing in the primary. Where the law requires a runoff primary if no candidate receives a majority

[12] Edwin H. Rhyne, "Political Parties and Decision Making in Three Southern Counties," *The American Political Science Review*, 52 (December 1958) 1091–1107.

[13] Frank P. Belloni and Dennis C. Beller, "The Study of Party Factions as Competitive Political Organizations," *The Western Political Quarterly*, 29 (December 1976) especially 548–49.

[14] Stanley D. Hopper, "Fragmentation of the California Republican Party in the One-Party Era, 1893–1932," *The Western Political Quarterly*, 28 (June 1975) 372–86.

[15] V. O. Key, Jr., *Southern Politics in State and Nation* (New York: Alfred A. Knopf, Inc., 1949) Chapters 2–14.

of the vote in a primary, the Democratic party still has more than two factions.[16]

Next, the question can be asked if two factions can be adequate substitutes for two parties so that the negative effects of a one-party system can be overcome.

Two factions competed in Louisiana during the years the Democratic party was divided between the Long faction and the anti-Long faction. In the direct primary, each faction presented its own slate of candidates much like two party tickets, and the polarization between them offered voters a choice on state policies. As formal as this competition was, it was still pronounced inferior to a two-party system. *First*, various parish (county) organizations decided in each election which faction to support, depriving the factions of a permanent local base. In a party system there is a permanent base, for Republican organizations will not suddenly decide to support the Democratic ticket or vice-versa. *Second*, there was no factional identification among voters comparable to party identification. For all of its formality, voters were confused by the lack of factional names and by political leaders freely moving from faction to faction.[17]

Bifactionalism, or two factions, is conceded to be preferable to multifactionalism, or several factions, but both tend to be leaderless and issueless. With either of them, selecting candidates is much more a random choice than choosing between the two parties. It is worth noting that, after the long experience with the party system, parties are found to be superior to party factions just as the early party system in the nineteenth century has been considered superior to preparty factions, as pointed out in Chapter 1.

The Restraint and Insulation of Parties

The case for the party system rests upon its contributions to nation building, political stability, and calibre of government. These three are not meant to be all-inclusive, but they do allow us to make judgments about the values of political parties in important areas of national life. Even if other areas were added, we would still be likely to conclude that the benefits of parties are not as clear-cut as we would like and that the party system does not fulfill all expectations.

Winston Churchill once said that democracy was the worst form of

[16] Bradley C. Canon, "Factionalism in the South: A Test of Theory and a Revisitation of V. O. Key," *American Journal of Political Science*, 22 (November 1978) 833-48. Even after the Republican party was established in Florida, the Democrats were still found to be splintered although their divisions were more along ideological lines than personal followings. Margaret Thompson Echols and Austin Ranney, "The Impact of Interparty Competition Reconsidered: The Case of Florida," *The Journal of Politics*, 38 (February 1976) 142-52.

[17] Allan P. Sindler, "Bifactional Rivalry as an Alternative to Two-Party Competition in Louisiana," *The American Political Science Review*, 49 (June 1955) 641-62.

government except when compared with all of the other forms. Perhaps the party system is also the worst except when compared with all other political systems. Realistically, we must settle for something less than our conceptions of perfection. Yet, a system can hardly be accepted if its negative features outweigh its positive ones. But making this determination becomes something more than a balancing act between two sides of a scale. Positive and negative results cannot simply be separated and then compared, for some are more important than others and each is subject to interpretations and qualifications. At the end, how do we evaluate the final result?

One explanation offered for the success of American institutions is "the amazing poverty and inarticulateness of our theorizing about politics." In a nation where we have believed we had a perfect theory in political life, we have produced less theory than any other country.[18] The party system may be a victim of our lack of theorizing because there is no philosophical niche especially reserved for it. Like a commercial product, the party system must continue to survive the test of pragmatic evaluations in order to justify its existence.

Thus, we return to the question raised at the beginning of this book: the interrelation between democracy and the party system. Democracy is necessary for parties, but are parties necessary for democracy? Because of their close association, it seems that if one dies, the other dies. Now, however, there is an entirely different question to be raised, that is, are parties being destroyed by the new roles expected of leaders? Democracy seems to have become a search for candidates who can appear to communicate to us one-by-one, coupled with a desire—or even a demand—that candidates should at least arouse us if not thrill us.

The party system is an institution and, like other institutions, imposes restraints upon the way power is sought by those who are politically ambitious. The parties are a means for discouraging personalized factions and for limiting the opportunities of demagogues. If candidates must appeal to voters as representatives of parties, then their personal ambitions are submerged to the extent they are dependent upon parties.[19] The party system offers a safer course in public affairs in that it is less likely to arouse individual expectations but more likely to provide dependability. Lack of theorizing about politics may have supported American institutions in the past but is not supporting them now. The breakdown of the party system is part of the turning against institutions as such, starting with the institution of government itself.

Just as the institutionalized party system can be a restraint upon leaders, so it also has an insulating effect, by making it easier to do some things

[18] Daniel J. Boorstin, *The Genius of American Politics* (Chicago: The University of Chicago Press, 1953) pp. 3, 8.

[19] James W. Ceasar, "Political Parties and Presidential Ambition," *The Journal of Politics*, 40 (August 1978) 712-25, 727.

than others. It offers opportunities and restricts opportunities, and on this ground its effects upon democracy have to be judged. The party system in a democracy can be seen as though it were a fulcrum between elites and the public. It insulates the public from the excesses both of narrowly based elitist groups, and of those popular opinions that are like a "sandheap given quick and passing shape by whatever winds may be blowing." [20]

In the remainder of this chapter, we will look at some examples of responsiveness without political parties and at participation in the political process.

RESPONSIVENESS WITHOUT PARTIES

Governments are, by nature, oligarchic, but political parties made a significant change in the origins and performance of governing elites. In the absence of parties, elites were chosen from, and were representative of, an aristocracy, as they were in colonial America. Parties arose from wider political participation, so elites in a party system are recruited from, and are representative of, the public. This distinction led to the contention that a dictatorship with a single party is more representative than a partyless dictatorship, such as a military junta.[21]

It does not follow that elites drawn from the general public are invariably more responsive than elites drawn from an aristocracy. Nor is a one-party regime necessarily more benevolent than a regime without parties. Nevertheless, a party system with popular election of elites would be expected to be less conservative, in the sense of propping up a status quo that benefits only a select segment of the population.

To test this evaluation of party systems is difficult because there is so little basis for valid comparisons. To draw inferences for one society from the experiences of some other society fails to take into account a multitude of other differences between the societies themselves. What America would be like without parties cannot necessarily be gauged from other countries that have no parties. The best course is to compare the effects of parties in the United States with partyless political systems that are also in the United States.

Looking for governments without real party influence, we can begin with the President of the United States, as strange as that may seem; then take account of experience with the nonpartisan system in local governments throughout the country and its extension in the power of privately organized elitist groups.

[20] Robert Nisbet, "Public Opinion versus Popular Opinion," *The Public Interest*, No. 41 (Fall 1975) 168.

[21] Maurice Duverger, *Political Parties: Their Organization and Activity in the Modern State*, 2nd ed. (New York: John Wiley & Sons, Inc., 1959) pp. 425–26.

The Presidency

In view of the tremendous accumulation of data about presidents, our inquiry here is limited solely and briefly to presidential relationships with their political parties and the consequences of parties being largely banished from the White House.

During the twentieth century, presidents became the focal point for the nation and, therefore, the symbol of their respective parties. The national program of a party is the program of its President. The President defines the party's coalition even though many members of the party do not accept the program. Presidents still symbolize their parties but in a personal rather than an institutional manner. In the parliamentary system, there is collegial responsibility for government policy in cabinet decisions. In the American presidential system, a President makes decisions and, alone, is officially responsible for them. This isolation of the President puts him at the center of an ongoing realignment of sorts as voters respond by voting for him or against him.[22]

Because the President's power is personalized, this office has become centralized through the development of an integrated decision structure in the White House. In contrast, the congressional decision-making structure is fragmented. The presidential office is also what Americans have made it, for we have formed the habit of turning to the President for action in solving problems and even for inspirational leadership. This has been a general reaction irrespective of status differences. Americans leaders in every walk of life, when asked who is the most influential person in the country, have consistently and overwhelmingly chosen the President, even giving 63 percent of their first-place votes to Nixon in the year of his resignation.[23]

To fulfill the roles, both self-imposed and expected of them, presidents have tried to create the illusion that they are above controversies and are acting as nonpartisan leaders of all the people. There is no way a President can keep aloof from the unceasing conflicts and clashes because these can only be settled by a presidential decision.

This transformation of American government and politics is evidence of the decline of political parties. Presidents have already replaced parties as the cues for some voters in nonpresidential voting. They may, in time, become the perceptual screen for evaluating the whole range of elections. To maintain their nonpartisan image, presidents have disassociated themselves, in the public eye, from their parties except during their own election campaigns or when they sensed they were in political trouble. An example of this sort of response was Jimmy Carter paying public tribute to the Chicago

---

[22] Carl D. Tubbesing, "Predicting the Present: Realigning Elections & Redistributive Policies," *Polity*, 7 (Summer 1975) 502.

[23] "Leadership Survey," *U.S. News & World Report*, April 22, 1974, p. 30. Subsequent surveys published during April each year.

Democratic organization in 1978. The Federal Elections Campaign Act of 1974, by severing any financial connection between presidential candidates and their party's national committees, makes the presidential office appear to be even more aloof from the party.

As presidents have outgrown their parties, the weakness of parties, in turn, has contributed to presidential difficulties. Parties are no longer the screening device in presidential selection. Qualities of leadership are more generally determined by performance in primaries and polls, not by the judgment of political associates who are in a position to know the candidates and assess their competence. As an extension of "direct democracy," presidents have become "popular leaders." In this process the constitutional character of the presidential office has been greatly changed at the same time that parties can no longer provide a cushioning effect within the constitutional system. Consequently, presidents have to face the rigors of being miracle workers all by themselves.[24]

The nonpartisan aura of the presidency must be popular, considering how carefully presidents have cultivated it. To the extent it has contributed to unrealistic expectations of presidential performance and has given a king-like image to chief executives, it has contributed to weakness, not strength, in evaluating government performance. Presidents now prefer to surround themselves with advisors who lack party and even political experience. The irony is that the unpopularity of party politics as such has been damaging to democracy. Members of the White House staff, as the nation learned the hard way in the Watergate affair, isolate presidents both physically and politically, in order to protect them. The dissimilar ordeals of Vietnam and Watergate had a common element in that both Johnson and Nixon had cut themselves off from the kind of political advice which stresses what will win and lose votes. If presidents received political, as well as specialized and technical, advice on problems, they would remain in the political realm where good judgment is a product of differences of interpretations from people knowledgeable in politics. Relying upon men and women with practical political understanding not only helps to protect presidents from disastrous decisions, but also benefits the public because party politics "is always too divided to govern us too harshly." [25]

Nonpartisanism

The nonpartisan system of local elections was neither accidental nor unpremeditated. It was a purposeful intention to be free of the party system. The case for nonpartisanism was built upon the need for a rational, as opposed to

[24] Ceasar, "Political Parties and Presidential Ambition," 739. Also interviews with Richard E. Neustadt and Seymour Martin Lipset, *U.S. News & World Report*, June 26, 1978, pp. 29, 30.

[25] Henry Fairlie, "The Unpolitical Presidency," condensation from *Harper's Magazine*, December, 1977, reprinted *The Miami Herald*, December 4, 1977, p. 7E.

a political, approach to local problems. These problems required expertise in planning and administration, supported by an informed and interested body of citizens. Although some advocates foresaw active public participation, their principal objective was to get rid of political parties. Therefore, the characteristically low voting rate in nonpartisan cities has not been their major concern.[26]

The institutional effect of nonpartisanism itself is difficult to assess because of the separate influences of at-large and district elections to city councils. There is evidence that partisan and district elections are more likely to integrate political and social structures, for example, by facilitating group representation in neighborhoods. At-large nonpartisan city elections tend to reduce the working-class vote, to encourage ethnic bloc-voting, and to emphasize trivial personal characteristics of candidates. When the institutional effects are mixed, it is hypothesized that nonpartisanism combined with district election is likely to result in higher turnout. In addition, there is less bias in favor of those of upper socioeconomic status, the minority political party, and ethnic groups. Partisan and at-large elections are likely to favor the majority party and groups affiliated with it rather than neighborhood groups. The one thing nonpartisan elections do accomplish is increase the political influence of the press because candidates are dependent upon it for publicity.[27]

A further difficulty in assessing nonpartisanism is that it has sometimes proved to be more of a name than a political reality. Having no party names on the ballot constitutes a nonpartisan election, but candidates may already be associated with a party or make sure voters know their party affiliation. In some nonpartisan elections, lists of party candidates are distributed to voters as though the election were partisan. The fact remains that the minority political party may have a greater opportunity to elect its candidates. A considerable amount of discussion has revolved around the contention that the dropping of party names from the ballot has helped more Republicans to be elected. Whatever the degree of party voting in nonpartisan elections, they still are not the same as partisan elections.[28]

[26] Statement of Richard Childs, a prominent leader in the nonpartisan movement, cited in Robert R. Alford and Eugene C. Lee, "Voting Turnout in American Cities," *The American Political Science Review*, 62 (September 1968) 810.

[27] James H. Svara, "Unwrapping Institutional Packages in Urban Government: The Combination of Election Institutions in American Cities," *The Journal of Politics*, 39 (February 1977) 166–75. Robert L. Lineberry and Edmund P. Fowler, "Reformism and Public Policies in American Cities," *The American Political Science Review*, 61 (September 1967) 701–16. Also Albert K. Karnig, " 'Private-Regarding' Policy, Civil Rights Groups and the Mediating Impact of Municipal Reforms," *American Journal of Political Science*, 19 (February 1975) 91–106. Fred I. Greenstein, *The American Party System and the American People*, 2nd ed. (Englewood Cliffs, N.J.: Prentice-Hall, Inc., 1970) pp. 67–70. Gerald Pomper, "Ethnic and Group Voting in Nonpartisan Municipal Elections," *Public Opinion Quarterly*, 30 (Spring 1966) 77–97.

[28] Willis D. Hawley, *Nonpartisan Elections and the Case for Party Politics* (New York: John Wiley & Sons, 1973) pp. 22–25. Oliver P. Williams and Charles R. Adrian, "The Insulation of Local Politics under the Nonpartisan Ballot," *The American Political Science Review*, 53 (December 1959) 1062–63.

The effects of nonpartisan election upon the behavior of officials have likewise appeared mixed. Delegates elected as nonpartisans to the Maryland constitutional convention voted in a random fashion without the guidance of party or other reference group, in contrast with convention delegates in New York who were elected as partisans.[29] Party membership of Illinois delegates was not "blacked-out," so to speak, by their nonpartisan election to that state's constitutional convention. Cleavages between known Republicans and known Democrats proved to be the best of several variables in accounting for divisions on the roll calls.[30]

It was assumed that local elections, without the distraction of parties, can be decided on issues and performance. One of the classic nonpartisan slogans, "there is no Democratic or Republican way to pave a street," is correct in the sense that local issues revolve around services and development instead of matters of high policy. The standard retort to the slogan is that politics, whether partisan or not, may determine whose street is paved. If personal and group interests are not taken into account in a political process, there will indeed be issues at the next election whether it be partisan or nonpartisan.

Nonpartisanism was a local application of the Progressives' concept for restoring harmony in a neutral state administered by experts, but many people refused to be bound by neutral decisions even at the risk of appearing to be opposed to efficiency. The homogeneity of American society envisioned by Progressives became a politics of organized interests, an end result Progressives specifically did not intend and did not want.[31] The irrepressible group pressures in politics then demonstrated the advantages of the party system. In large systems, without the reference point and the collegiality of party to provide some standard for identifying norms, the result can either approach chaos or reflect the formation of a new factional division on each issue.

The relative merits of partisan and nonpartisan elections in cities may come to an uncertain verdict. The verdict is on firmer ground when government is more clearly a contest between the organized and the unorganized.

The Nonpartisanism of Organized Groups

If we let our imaginations run free in conceiving of government without political parties, we can soon find ourselves contemplating the group basis of

---

[29] Wayne R. Swanson, Jay S. Goodman, Elmer E. Cornwell, Jr., "Voting Behavior in a Nonpartisan Legislative Setting," *The Western Political Quarterly*, 25 (March 1972) 39–50. Also Susan Welch with assistance of Eric H. Carlson, "The Impact of Party on Voting Behavior in a Nonpartisan Legislature," *The American Political Science Review*, 67 (September 1973) 854–67.

[30] Jack R. Van Der Slik and others, "Patterns of Partisanship in a Nonpartisan Representational Setting: The Illinois Constitutional Convention," *American Journal of Political Science*, 18 (February 1974) 95–116.

[31] Michael Paul Rogin, *The Intellectuals and McCarthy: The Radical Specter* (Cambridge, Mass.: M.I.T. Press, 1967) pp. 192–203.

politics. From the multiple group pressures of the present, it would be possible to foresee a multiparty system where many groups would run candidates and bargain over their relative rewards in holding offices and choosing policies after each election. The major trouble with these mental gymnastics would appear sooner or later. Interest group political parties would be too narrowly based and could not appeal, even to a sizeable minority, without some comprehensive view of government. If one of these parties should finally subordinate its concern for its own special interests in order to win more votes, it would be pulled further and further until eventually, it would begin to resemble the major parties we know. By this route, we return to the insulation of the party system against elites representing organized interests.

There are millions of Americans outside of the interest group system. For them, and even for the millions more who are members in name only, groups are no substitute for political parties. Consequently, parties are linked, however tenuously, to far more people than are organized groups, and party leaders must keep in mind the interests of the unorganized as well as the organized. It is not necessary to "prove" that parties benefit the "have-nots" as opposed to the "haves." [32] What commends parties to a democratic society is their capabilities for giving expression to a wide range of interests.

The insulation of the party system is not fool-proof, but it offers people a choice between two broadly based elites without having to trust either one of them completely. As they were in the eighteenth century, parties are still a device for counteracting the power of the relatively few on behalf of the many. Those whose power lies only in their numbers find public opinion inarticulate until leaders give it expression.[33]

There have, of course, been some changes. The insulation of parties has become less effective because organizations of private interests have grown stronger.

Elites, the Government, and Parties

The essence of the popular democratic creed in America has been the virtue of the people. Thomas Jefferson was one of the foremost spokesmen of this

[32] Eric M. Uslaner, "Comparative State Policy Formation, Interparty Competition, and Malapportionment: A New Look at 'V. O. Key's Hypotheses,'" *The Journal of Politics*, 40 (May 1978) 409–22. Also Chapter 8, above.

[33] Walter Dean Burnham, *Critical Elections and the Mainsprings of American Politics* (New York: W. W. Norton and Company, 1970) p. 133. Chambers, *Political Parties in a New Nation*, pp. 100–101. Thomas A. Flinn and Frederick M. Wirt, "Local Party Leaders: Groups of Like Minded Men," *Midwest Journal of Political Science*, 9 (February 1965) 97. George E. Lavau, "Political Pressures by Interest Groups in France," in *Interest Groups on Four Continents*, International Political Science Association, ed., Henry W. Ehrmann (Pittsburgh, Pa.: University of Pittsburgh Press, 1958) p. 62. Michael T. Hayes, "The Semi-Sovereign Pressure Groups: A Critique of Current Theory and an Alternative Typology," *The Journal of Politics*, 40 (February 1978) 134–61, especially 159–61.

creed as he championed the cause of the great unorganized against the elites of an aristocratic society. Elites in America long ago ceased to represent a "natural" aristocracy, but the duality of the few as opposed to the many is still a basis for interpretation and evaluation. Expressions of the Jeffersonian philosophy continue to appear. If American democracy contains the seeds of its own destruction, it will not be attributed to the "self-corruption of the masses," but to the destructive powers of the "best people." [34] To a great extent, however, perspectives have changed.

Just as political parties led to a new kind of governing elite, so did democracy permit people to rise in all fields of activity and attain leadership without having been "born to the purple." As leaders emerged through their own abilities, ambitions, and sense of competitiveness, the duality of public and elites became blurred. Political activists have made effective use of public relations and communication systems in molding public opinion. By adopting democratic styles and expressing popular values in seeking their objectives, some elites are seen as representing a consensus rather than the distinctive minority attitudes of an upper class.

The course of public affairs has been characterized by the growth of authority of public officials, and the latitude of their discretion has widened as institutional restraints, like political parties, have declined. What distinguishes the network of interest group activists is that specific issues and individuals come and go, but group interests remain constant. The potential advantages for private interests can be enormous when high public esteem reinforces their relationships with government decision-makers. Actually, there is much interchange between private and public elites as private citizens move into government administrative offices and back to private life. On matters of great importance private groups can, in effect, set the government agenda itself even before official policy-makers begin dealing with problems through the governmental process. [35]

Some survey-research data bolster the influence of the elites even further. These findings indicate that elites are more supportive of democratic principles than the mass public in their greater tolerance for individual liberties and minority rights. It has even become commonplace to observe that elites, rather than the public at large, are committed to democratic values. [36] A principal explanation for these findings has been the socialization process

[34] V. O. Key, Jr., "Public Opinion and the Decay of Democracy," *Virginia Quarterly Review,* 37 (Autumn 1961) 494.

[35] Thomas R. Dye, "Oligarchic Tendencies in National Policy-Making: The Role of the Private Policy-Planning Organizations," *The Journal of Politics,* 40 (May 1978) 329, in general 309–31.

[36] Thomas R. Dye and Harmon Zeigler, *The Irony of Democracy: An Uncommon Introduction to American Politics,* 2nd ed. (Belmont, Ca.: Duxbury Press, a Division of Wadsworth Publishing Company, Inc., 1972) p. 20. Samuel A. Stouffer *Communism, Conformity, and Civil Liberties* (New York: Doubleday and Company, Inc., 1955). Herbert McClosky, "Consensus and Ideology in American Politics," *The American Political Science Review,* 58 (June 1964) 361–82.

of elites. One instance of disagreement on this point arose from a methodological dispute over the handling of data.[37] Still, the findings are subject to qualifications; for example, the well educated are more likely than the poorly educated to support equality in the abstract but are not much more likely to support concrete government action to promote equality.[38]

Fortified with evidence of their greater devotion to democracy, elites have reversed the Jeffersonian philosophy when they express their fears of uncontrolled majorities. They emphasize that the large public has to be watched closely and controlled because of its tendencies to accept repressive measures and its susceptibility to demagogic appeals. Guidance by elites is necessary to preserve democratic stability, which has become the stability of elitist values.[39]

The fear of majorities has been especially evident since the 1960s when movements were started to use popularly-elected national conventions for proposing amendments to the United States Constitution. This method, it has been emphasized, could even be used to make changes in the Bill of Rights. Its opponents argue that it should be rejected in favor of congressional proposals of amendments where elites have a greater voice in determining the kinds of reforms to be submitted to the states for approval.

If the prestige and influence of the elitist group networks are often a match for the power of government itself, the insulation offered by the party system seems, not just inadequate, but nonexistent. Yet, the parties are channels for organizing controversies even if parties, as such, initially hold aloof from popular challenges to elites such as demonstrations of dissatisfaction with mounting taxes. Candidates for office, elected officials, and party platforms can publicize dissent over the protective role of elites in public affairs. Political parties have been outlets for challenges to the elitist role of the Supreme Court in substituting the judicial process for the political processes of legislatures and referenda. Otherwise, the very substantial public issue of judges expressing their own policy preferences in the guise of constitutional principles has largely remained a remote, if not esoteric, controversy among students of constitutional law.[40]

[37] Robert W. Jackman, "Political Elites, Mass Publics, and Support for Democratic Principles," *The Journal of Politics*, 34 (August 1972) 753–73. David R. Johnson, Louis St. Peter, and J. Allen Williams, Jr., "Comments on Jackman's 'Political Elites, Mass Publics, and Support for Democratic Principles,'" and Jackman, "Much Ado about Nothing," *The Journal of Politics*, 39 (February 1977) 176–92.

[38] Mary R. Jackman, "General and Applied Tolerance: Does Education Increase Commitment to Racial Integration?" *American Journal of Political Science*, 22 (May 1978) 302–24.

[39] James D. Wright, *The Dissent of the Governed* (New York: Academic Press, 1976) pp. 15–34. The desirability of elite influence in a consensual and stable society has been a theme in the writings of political specialists as well as among public leaders; for example, Gabriel A. Almond and Sidney Verba, *The Civic Culture: Political Attitudes and Democracy in Five Nations* (Boston: Little, Brown and Co., 1965).

[40] For example: Wallace Mendelson, "Mr. Justice Douglas and Government by the Judiciary," *The Journal of Politics*, 38 (November 1976) 918–37. Sheldon Goldman,

PARTIES AND PARTICIPATION

Despite their general acceptance of a guardian democracy by elites, Americans continue to respond to the Jeffersonian concept of participatory democracy reinforced by the themes of the Progressive Movement. One recurring attitude is that public affairs is a contest between good and evil and should be undertaken, among other reasons, to purge sin from society.[41] Many fictional presentations which draw a strict line between good and bad political leaders reinforce political morality. News reporting often implies there is only one correct way to govern, and the same message is often conveyed throughout the educational system.

It is equally characteristic that the enthusiasm with which we greet reforms soon turns to disillusionment because their implementation does not measure up to our expectations. Anticipating that one change will correct one evil, we soon find other evils popping up around us. Attacks upon making nominations through the party organization led to the direct primary which multiplied the evils associated with campaigning. In order to tame the power of government, we attack an instrument through which power is exercised rather than the wielding of power itself. In order to limit political party power, we magnified the personalities and roles of elected government officials.

One of the most troublesome problems in reconciling experience with expectation is the discrepancy between our official doctrine and our actual performance in political participation.

The Limits of Participation

It is bedrock doctrine that voting is basic to a healthy democracy. As the state of our political well-being has become a quantitative measure of the voting rate, it has become necessary to plead with voters to exercise their franchise. People know they can express themselves through the ballot box if they see some reason to do so. If they have a particularly strong party attachment, they do not have to be reminded to vote. Otherwise, voting may be considered too much effort for too little reward.

It is sometimes alleged that the party system itself is responsible for

---

"In Defense of Justice: Some Thoughts on Reading Professor Mendelson's 'Mr. Justice Douglas and Government by the Judiciary,'" *The Journal of Politics*, 39 (February 1977) 148–58; and Mendelson, "A Response to Professor Goldman, *The Journal of Politics*, 39 (February 1977) 159–65. Raoul Berger, *Government by Judiciary: The Transformation of the Fourteenth Amendment* (Cambridge, Mass.: Harvard University Press, 1977). Ward E. Y. Elliott, *The Rise of Guardian Democracy: The Supreme Court's Role in Voting Rights Disputes, 1945–1969* (Cambridge, Mass.: Harvard University Press, 1974).

[41] Seymour M. Lipset, "The Paradox of American Politics," *The Public Interest*, No. 41 (Fall 1975) 142–47.

the low voting rate by excluding the inactive voters, especially the poor and the blacks. The implication is that there is a purposeful intent within the system to keep these people from voting through legal or other barriers.[42] In this sense, of course, the allegation is now wrong, although it was certainly true for many blacks in the South until the 1960s. It is correct that the party system has created a stability by the very fact that things go on much the same no matter who is elected. Unless one is strongly oriented toward a candidate or a party, the party system itself fails to provide a motive for many people to vote, especially those under age 35.

Being able to play the numbers game in voting turnout is a symptom of a society that appears to be politically relaxed. The dire warnings of not voting, under the circumstances, confuse means and ends. Only if we were prevented from holding elections would freedom be threatened, but there is certainly no evidence that elections have become an endangered species. On the contrary, the American political system appears to be election-ridden. We sometimes have two or three elections in one year, counting special referenda on local questions or on amendments to state constitutions. We insist upon electing officials in preference to their being appointed even if we are losing interest in voting. The total number of elected officials in the United States is now about one per 400 people in the total population.

The fact is that, despite urging people to vote, and the strong beliefs in the values of elections, voting turnout continues to decline. Removal of legal restrictions have not helped much; for the easier it has become to vote, the smaller the proportion of the potential vote that is cast. About the only voting requirements remaining are age, residence, registration, and citizenship. Age and residence are now reduced to minimum levels. Registration is a restriction, but changing registration laws is not the answer to the problem of nonvoting. There has been a decline in turnout among *registered* voters, especially in states that adopted postcard registration, New York, New Jersey, and Pennsylvania, although there has been a slight increase where voters can register on election day. Even enfranchising all aliens would not raise the voting rate appreciably.

If elections should become crucial because of ideological polarization or because of threats to groups' well-being, presumably turnout would increase. If the purpose of an election is to make government officials legitimate, irrespective of who wins, then the size of the vote is really unimportant. Only if we can return to the gods of our fathers and believe in political parties again, is the voting rate likely to soar.

The peripheral political interests of many Americans neither threaten the system nor are they threatened by it. In fact, since they are not threatened, Americans can afford to keep politics as a peripheral interest. Voluntary nonvoting, consequently, has been found to be evidence of consensus,

---

[42] Gerald M. Pomper, "Toward a More Responsible Two-Party System? What, Again?" *The Journal of Politics*, 33 (November 1971) 919.

if not of satisfaction. A high voting rate has been associated with high tensions and even with democratic breakdown. Democracy does not require everyone to vote, for there are as many modes of citizenship and varieties of political interests as there is diversity of tastes in music, sports, and literature.[43]

The relatively low importance attached to parties and elections may help to account for the extent of participation across a range of activities. If participation is defined only as voting, it is comparatively low in the United States. If it is defined more broadly, it is comparatively high. In one major investigation, respondents divided approximately in half in their patterns of participation. Among the lower half, 22 percent were found to be completely inactive, 21 percent voted regularly but did nothing else, and 4 percent contacted officials on particular problems of their own but were otherwise inactive. In the upper half, 20 percent contacted officials on broad social issues and voted fairly regularly, 15 percent were very active in political campaigns, and 11 percent were completely active in every way.[44]

In ranking the forms of participation, voting falls toward the bottom. It requires relatively little information and motivation. It is also weakly related to other forms of participation and conveys comparatively little information about citizen preferences.[45]

Broader definitions of participation make it easier to understand that there are limits to what is desirable or even possible for an election to settle. Only rarely has there been a tragic case like slavery which would not respond to political processes and had to be settled by the Civil War. Some policies, like constitutional rights, are considered too crucial to be determined at the polls. Private interests of all kinds are submitted to executives, legislators, or judges but not to the voters, and questions of high national policy like war and peace are not settled by referenda. In some areas, like economic policies, the public may be as competent at forecasting as elites, but elections, by their nature, are considered occasions to pass judgments on what has been done. Elections are not expected to set a specific course to be followed in the future.[46]

---

[43] Seymour Martin Lipset, *Political Man: The Social Bases of Politics* (Garden City, N.Y.: Anchor Books, Doubleday & Company, Inc., 1960) Chapter 6. Herbert McClosky, "Consensus and Ideology in American Politics," p. 374, 376, 377. Eugene Burdick, "The 'Citizen' of Democratic Theory and the 'Voter,'" in *American Voting Behavior*, eds., Eugene Burdick and Arthur J. Brodbeck (New York: The Free Press, 1959) pp. 144–48. Lester W. Milbrath and M. L. Goel, *Political Participation: How and Why Do People Get Involved in Politics?* 2nd ed. (Chicago: Rand McNally College Publishing Company, 1977) 146–47, 153.

[44] Sidney Verba and Norman H. Nie, *Participation in America* (New York: Harper & Row, 1972) pp. 25–29.

[45] *Ibid.*, p. 333. Milbrath and Goel, *Political Participation* pp. 12–13.

[46] Walter Dean Burnham, "Rejoinder," *The American Political Science Review*, 68 (September 1974) 1057. V. O. Key, Jr., *The Responsible Electorate: Rationality in Presidential Voting 1936–1960* (New York: Vintage Books, a Division of Random House, 1966) p. 61.

That voting, by itself, offers little protection from a real threat has been illustrated anew by the attempts to politicize nonpolitical institutions and groups and to make their every activity a part of public controversy over public issues. The act of politicizing requires other forms of participation than casting an anonymous vote in the privacy of a voting booth. Intimidation by confrontation is not a threat to the unorganized from the organized so much as a threat to the nonactivists from the activists. Those who fail to become activists and make counter-demands run the risk of political annihilation. If it becomes impossible either to escape or withdraw from the politicized society, those who do not have a cause will have to find one.[47]

Alienation and Participation

Nonvoting cannot be attributed entirely to the passive consent of the apathetic. There are also those who are alienated. The difference is between those who do not vote because it does not matter and those who refuse to vote because there are no acceptable choices available.[48]

Alienation, however, is a complex phenomenon to define.[49] It results, to some extent, from the inherent limitations of elections in settling problems. If it were manifested solely as a refusal to vote, it would merit less attention. Lack of trust in government reflects a feeling of inability to control or even understand public events but not necessarily because of failure to participate. Some people apparently assume that if they participate in a decision-making process, the decision should meet with their approval. Alienation, therefore, includes the frustration and disillusionment which result when participation does not produce the expected results. As the public became more involved, it also became more alienated.[50]

Even if government does what one wants, trust can decline if the decision-making process is seen as deceptive or corrupt. Hawks on Vietnam

[47] David C. Schwartz, *Political Alienation and Political Behavior* (Chicago: Aldine Publishing Company, 1973) pp. 238–40, 242.

[48] Gerald Garvey, "The Theory of Party Equilibrium," *The American Political Science Review*, 60 (March 1966) 29–38.

[49] Sidney Kraus and Dennis Davis, *The Effects of Mass Communication on Political Behavior* (University Park, Pa.: Pennsylvania State University Press, 1976) pp. 181–89.

[50] Nie and others, *The Changing American Voter*, pp. 279–80. Verba and Nie, *Participation in America*, p. 40. Schwartz, *Political Alienation and Political Behavior*, p. 228. Jack Dennis, "Support for the Institution of Elections by the Mass Public," *The American Political Science Review*, 64 (September 1970) 833. Martin D. Abravanel and Ronald J. Busch, "Political Competence, Political Trust, and the Action Orientation of University Students," *The Journal of Politics*, 37 (February 1975) 78. Richard L. Cole, "Citizen Participation in Municipal Politics," *American Journal of Political Science*, 19 (November 1975) 778. James M. Elden and David R. Schweitzer, "New Third Party Radicalism: The Case of the California Peace and Freedom Party," *The Western Political Quarterly*, 24 (December 1971) 761–74.

were upset about escalation of the war when the government denied there was any escalation.[51] Those who are trustful and have a sense of efficacy appear to participate more in acceptable ways such as discussion, voting, and campaigning. The efficacious-mistrustful may participate more in unacceptable ways, such as riots and street protests.[52]

People in the upper socioeconomic status are likely to look upon alienation as a loss of values. However, there is no sense of loss when alienation, particularly in the sense of being powerless, is part of socialization. The alienated are a diverse lot in age and in ideology as well as in the sources and intensity of their feelings. These diversities help to explain why "extremist" candidates have not been more successful in mobilizing the alienated.[53]

If neither the usual party candidates nor "extremists" can increase the vote, the solution for alienation would seem to be a new kind of participatory, or "citizen," party composed of people who now have the time to involve themselves in the new issues and are willing to be led by a new cadre. Accordingly, the rules applied in the 1972 Democratic convention were looked upon as a promising beginning.[54] Unquestionably some new citizens became active, but the overall turnout still continued to decline. So far, anyway, this does not appear to be the solution to the problem of non-voting. Furthermore, greater participation by a new elite of committed, militant activists leads to the type of irrationality which "undermines liberal democratic consensus" and eventually calls for a reevaluation of the relative importance of stability and participation.[55]

The efforts to stimulate more participation for the sake of more participation may encourage political movements which can capture people's imagination by giving them something to believe in. A politics of "movements" rather than a politics of political parties may even become commonplace. The phenomena of the Goldwater, Wallace, and McGovern movements, instead of being exceptions, may become more typical. These phenomena are both highly emotional and candidate-oriented. They create what can be called a constituency but the supporters, as noted in the case of Robert Kennedy in 1968, can have an unpolitical, moblike relationship with their candidate. The throngs who turn up all along the campaign trail exist

---

[51] Wright, *The Dissent of the Governed*, p. 194.

[52] John Fraser, "The Mistrustful-Efficacious Hypothesis and Political Participation," *The Journal of Politics*, 32 (May 1970) 444–49. Brett W. Hawkins, Vincent L. Marando, and George A. Tayler, "Efficacy, Mistrust, and Political Participation: Findings from Additional Data and Indicators," *The Journal of Politics*, 33 (November 1971) 1130–36.

[53] Wright, *The Dissent of the Governed*, Chapter 9.

[54] John W. Saloma III and Frederick H. Sontag, *Parties: The Real Opportunity for Effective Citizen Politics* (New York: Alfred A. Knopf, 1972) Chapter 1.

[55] Lester G. Seligman, *Recruiting Political Elites* (New York: General Learning Press, 1971) p. 9. Peter Y. Medding, "'Elitist' Democracy: An Unsuccessful Critique of a Misunderstood Theory," *The Journal of Politics*, 31 (August 1969) 654.

on a politics of ethereal expectations and have no political leverage when their candidates are elected because they have no leader to speak for them. The wildly enthusiastic supporters must wait until evidence of their renewed alienation requires another performance to bolster their morale.[56]

The Unreality of Majorities

The two-party system may inadvertently have created a serious misconception. Candidates are elected by a majority because there are only two candidates. A majority can be looked upon mistakenly as conferring a mandate because it has a being of its own. No one who has examined the shifting tides in elections is likely to draw this conclusion. Even without survey data, voters make clear that there are separate majorities in each election and on each issue, not the same majority all the time.

A majority in an election is a concurrent majority in composition. Its verdict is an expression of a composite judgment on individuals' personal well-being and on governmental performance. If a majority could be constructed which was in agreement on all issues, it would have to be restrained before it posed a threat to popular government.[57]

No matter the intensity and extent of participation, it does not lead to a "natural" majority. As appealing as the thought may be, there is no majority "some place out there" impelled by altruism and consisting of "persons each moving in an individual orbit, adrift from parties and other structures, and yet capable of exercising power if only every man had one vote." [58] Majorities are constructed out of minorities and perpetuated as coalitions, and in this activity the parties have become experts.

The difficulty is not solely a misunderstanding of what a majority is or can be. Some activists, realizing these limitations, have abandoned any attempt to form a majority. As elections are seen as opportunities to influence the course of public policy for self-protection or advancement, parties are no longer valued as "insulators" to contain conflicts. They are expected to be "live conductors." [59] An excess of participation by minority activists overloads the system with demands. A democratic system needs some restraint, or apathy, for everyone cannot be involved all the time.[60]

---

[56] Henry Fairlie, *The Kennedy Promise: The Politics of Expectation* (New York: Doubleday and Company, Inc., 1973) pp. 356–57.

[57] F. H. Giddings, "The Nature and Conduct of Political Majorities," *Political Science Quarterly*, 7 (March 1892) 118, 131.

[58] Alexander M. Bickel, *Reform and Continuity: The Electoral College, The Convention and the Party System* (New York: Harper Torchbook, 1971) p. 2.

[59] Samuel Lubell, *The Hidden Crisis in American Politics* (New York: W. W. Norton and Company, Inc., 1971) pp. 42–43, 65. John E. Jackson, "Issues, Party Choices, and Presidential Votes," *American Journal of Political Science*, 19 (May 1975) 184.

[60] Aaron Wildavsky, "Government and the People," in *Watergate and the American Political Process*, ed., Ronald E. Pynn (New York: Praeger Publishers, 1975)

There has always been a theoretical choice between government by parties as opposed to government by individuals and groups. There seems to be a persistent belief that, somehow, everyone—"the people"—can run the whole show solely in their own collective interests. It is felt that the people can nominate the candidates, decide the issues, and supervise the operations; that then they can truly be able to make the proper judgments at election time.

There are too many candidates, too many elections, and too many issues (local, state, national, international) for even the party cadre, volunteers, or any one elite to do all of these things. Nevertheless, the people when they are not working, going on vacation, watching television, or gossiping *are* supposed to do these things. There will always be a cadre, an elite, whether of parties or of something else. The people can only pass judgment on what has been done and read the political tea leaves in forecasting if they judged rightly.

As it is unlikely that all of the activists will be satisfied and that everyone will be motivated to participate, we can at least hope that we will not escape from a lasting regime of ordered conflict, no matter which regime we choose.

pp. 22–39. Samuel P. Huntington, "The Democratic Distemper," *The Public Interest,* No. 41 (Fall 1975) 36–37.

Glossary

Activists-purists. The term applies to those who are active in political party work but are committed to advance their own particular cause or ideology. Since their loyalty is to the purity of their beliefs, they are generally not inclined to compromise in order to achieve party harmony and unity.

Caucus. This is one of the oldest terms in American politics, going back to colonial times. It has come to mean, literally, a meeting. All members of the same political party in a legislative body hold a caucus to decide party policies and strategy. In the presidential nomination process, a caucus is a meeting held on the local level to select delegates to the state convention and/or to select delegates to the national convention.

Classification of Presidential Elections. Maintaining, deviating, and realigning. (Table 7.1).

Coalition. The sum total of the various groups that make up the regular body of electoral support of each major political party.

Competitive Disequilibrium. A feature of two-party competition wherein one party had majority support and the other was in the minority.

Consensus. The existence of a wide area of agreement (at least a low level of disagreement) within a society about the fundamentals of its political and social systems.

Deferential Politics. The system of aristocratic politics in America before the Revolutionary War when those of higher status held public offices because they were considered to have special qualifications for governing.

Disconnections in Voting. This situation results from ticket-splitting, where there is little party connection in the outcome of elections; a Republican wins one office, a Democrat, another office.

Drop-off Vote. The difference between the total vote cast for presidential candidates and for all candidates for the House of Representatives at midterm elections.

Faction. Before political parties, a faction was a group supporting a candidate for public office. Thereafter, the word designated a segment of a political party, separately identified because of its position on issues and/or its support of a particular party leader.

General-ticket System. Candidates who are elected by the voters of an entire state as distinguished from candidates who are elected from districts or counties within states. Presidential electors are chosen on a general-ticket system in the states but, in order to save space, most states do not print the names of presidential electors on the ballot.

Gerrymander. Drawing the lines of legislative or congressional districts in a state in order to favor one political party by distributing its voting strength so as to give it a majority in as many districts as possible and to give the other party a majority in as few districts as possible.

Independent "Leaners." Those respondents in surveys who say they are Independents but lean toward one party or the other.

Issue Publics. A group of people concerned with an issue is an issue public. There are many such groups and, taking them all together, they constitute issue publics.

Liturgicals. During the nineteenth century, those voters identified by membership in certain Christian denominations (e.g., German Lutheran and Roman Catholic) who tended to oppose government regulations, particularly in morals, and who tended to be Democrats. Opposed to Pietists.

Majority. A number of votes in an election that is more than half of all of the votes cast. (See Plurality.)

Pietists. During the nineteenth century, those voters identified by membership in certain Christian denominations (e.g., Episcopal and one branch of Presbyterians) who tended to favor government regulations, particularly in morals, and who tended to be Whigs and, later, Republicans. Opposed to liturgicals.

Plurality. The number of votes received by a candidate in an election that is more than any other candidate received but is less than a majority. (See Majority.)

Position Issues. Those issues where the controversy occurs between groups of people who differ in the objectives they want to achieve, as opposed to style issues. (See Style Issues.)

Roll-off Vote. The practice of some people to vote only for candidates for the highest offices. The vote cast for each office, going down the ballot, therefore, declines or rolls off.

Style Issues. Those issues where the controversy is not over different objectives but different methods or means for achieving an objective, as opposed to position issues. (See Position Issues.)

Unit Vote. A system of voting by groups, as in national conventions, where a whole state's vote is cast the way the majority of the state's delegates vote. Unit voting is no longer permitted in either party's national conventions. However, states cast a unit vote in presidential elections because the party receiving the majority or plurality of the popular vote in a state elects all of its presidential electors.

Volatility in Voting. Unstable and unpredictable voting, particularly in presidential elections, but often in voting for other offices such as governors and United States senators.

AUTHOR INDEX

SUBJECT INDEX